T0303040

FEAR

OF A
MUSLIM
PLANET

FEAR
OF A
MUSLIM
PLANET

GLOBAL ISLAMOPHOBIA IN
THE NEW WORLD ORDER

ARSALAN IFTIKHAR

Skyhorse Publishing

Skyhorse Publishing books may be purchased in bulk at special discounts for sales promotion, corporate gifts, fund-raising, or educational purposes. Special editions can also be created to specifications. For details, contact the Special Sales Department, Skyhorse Publishing, 307 West 36th Street, 11th Floor, New York, NY 10018 or info@skyhorsepublishing.com.

Skyhorse® and Skyhorse Publishing® are registered trademarks of Skyhorse Publishing, Inc.®, a Delaware corporation.

Visit our website at www.skyhorsepublishing.com.

10 9 8 7 6 5 4 3 2 1

Library of Congress Cataloging-in-Publication Data is available on file.

Cover design by 5mediadesign

Print ISBN: 978-1-5107-6187-2
Ebook ISBN: 978-1-5107-6363-0

Printed in the United States of America

Contents

Contents

To My Amma & My Ummah . . .

Acknowledgments

Bismillah—the first word of the Holy Quran and this trisyllabic Arabic phrase which means "In the Name of God"—is how two billion Muslims seek Divine blessings for all of our life's projects. Similarly, my favorite Malcolm X quote of all time is "All praise is due to Allah . . . Only the mistakes are mine," which also perfectly explains how I feel about my life's work.

At the personal level, I would first like to thank my wonderful family (my wife, Noreen, my mother, Warda, my father, Tariq, my sister, Savera, and my brother, Altamash) for their love and support throughout our lives.

On the editorial side, I would like to thank Skyhorse Publishing—especially Tony Lyons, Mark Gompertz, and Caroline Russomanno—for publishing my last two books. I would also like to thank Scott Kenemore and Farzana Gardee for their contributions and Mr. Zak Elyazgi from Daze Studios for his artistic consultations for TheMuslimPlanet.com

Finally, I absolutely must acknowledge every single one of the fifty-one individual victims of the March 2019

Christchurch, New Zealand, mosque massacre. While writing about their fifty-one life stories throughout this book, I literally sobbed numerous times while commemorating their legacies for posterity's sake and I hope to meet all fifty-one of them in heaven one day, *inshallah* (God willing).

Introduction

Somehow, I have to remind myself that it isn't personal.

This is the strange but unavoidable conclusion that looms back at me through the lens whenever I try to examine the fear and mistrust the world's 1.7 billion Muslims arouse in so many populations today.

People are afraid of Muslims. Of that, they are absolutely *certain*. They will tell you this quite directly. They are convinced that Muslims are worth fearing for very good reasons, and that everyone else should be afraid of them too.

But *which* Muslims? Why? Why *them* and not others?

Here, the respondent hesitates and wavers (even though their resolve does not).

A remarkable thing has occurred in the past few decades. People have realized that to be afraid of Muslims, they do not have to be afraid of a specific person, ideology, or even a specific thing. It is enough for them to declare that Muslims—as a whole—are not to be trusted. Are to be feared. Specific examples are not necessary. Facts just get in the way.

It is not personal; it is a generalized fear. It is enough to simply be afraid.

You can get a sense of this phenomenon just by looking at anti-Muslim attitudes in my own country, the United States. (I'm a person very driven by data, and you're going to see me cite statistics to back up my positions throughout this book . . .)

For instance, according to a study by the Pew Research Center, over half of all Americans (62 percent) agree with the statement "Islam is not a part of mainstream society," and nearly half agree that "There is a natural conflict between Islam and democracy."[1] A further 25 percent of respondents go even further, saying they agree that a majority of US Muslims "are anti-American." (The percentage of respondents agreeing with these statements rises dramatically when you look at sub-groups like white Evangelicals, Republicans, and Americans with only a high school degree or less.)

And when President Donald Trump's "Muslim Travel Ban" went into effect in 2017, a Politico-Morning Consult poll[2] found that 60 percent of Americans said they either "strongly supported" or "somewhat supported" the Muslim ban.

That's a majority of the nation.

Simply put, Americans are afraid of Muslims.

They fear them. They mistrust them. They agree that—as a people—Muslims are a scary bunch.

But *who*, precisely, is so terrifying?

Here, Americans have a tougher time. It is much easier to be clear about who they *don't* mean.

They don't, of course, mean Dave Chappelle, the funniest man alive. They don't mean Muhammad Ali, the greatest athlete of all time. They don't mean the legions of Muslim musicians whose creative work they enjoy so deeply—from Snoop Dogg to Ice Cube, from Art Blakey to DJ Khaled.

They don't mean all the lifesaving physicians who are Muslims. Over 5 percent of America's doctors are now Muslim, and that number grows year after year. From celebrity MDs like Dr. Mehmet Oz to the hardworking doctors at their local community health centers during the 2020 COVID-19 coronavirus pandemic, Muslim healthcare providers from coast to coast are busy curing Americans' cancers, their acne breakouts, and everything in between. But Americans don't mean *these* Muslims.

Neither do Americans mean trusted media personalities like Fareed Zakaria or Oscar-winning actors like Mahershala Ali. They don't mean trendy fashion icons like supermodels Iman or Bella Hadid.

And they don't mean the Muslim job creators who have founded and/or helmed such all-American brands as Edible Arrangements, Ethan Allen, and the NFL's Jacksonville Jaguars—just to name a few.

Most certainly, they do not mean the thousands of Muslims currently serving in America's armed forces. They do not mean the Muslim veterans who have fought and died in all major American conflicts back to the Civil War—and possibly before. (Soldiers named "Yusuf ben Ali" and "Bampett Muhamed" fought in the Continental Army during the Revolutionary War. Record of their religions does not exist, but it now seems likely to historians and scholars that they were followers of Islam.)

Which leaves us, again, with the question:

Who *do* they mean?

Rather than a specific person who has committed (or is likely to commit) a specific act, Americans seem to fear Muslims as a group because they present a dangerous *potentiality*.

There is a pervading sense that if left unchecked and unregulated, Muslims will do . . . something. We don't know what it is, but we're certain that it's bad. Something we don't want. Something definitely un-American.

Yet despite our certainty, we're unable to articulate the master plan . . . or at least unable to agree upon it. According to those casting the aspersions, Muslims desire to destroy America, to take over America, or to impose the strictest form of theocracy on America. (This last one seems to strike a particular chord; at least seven US states have passed laws or ballot measures forbidding sharia law. Ironically, these measures have generally been introduced in sparsely-populated states with the smallest overall populations of Muslim residents, but that's beside the point.)

Though it may certainly reveal a comical lack of worldliness on the parts of those who possess and propagate it, I do not wish to make this nonspecific fear of Muslims seem laughable. Because the impact it has on real people is anything but funny.

Despite being only about 1.1 percent of the US population, Muslims have been the victims of anywhere from 18–25 percent of the hate crimes committed in the United States since 2016, according to estimates by the FBI.[3] And that figure may be inaccurately low since many Muslims are not comfortable reporting such crimes. There is also reason to suspect that the 17 percent increase in hate crimes targeting Sikhs since Donald Trump's election in 2016 may have resulted in part from perpetrators who thought they were attacking Muslims instead.[4]

On a macro level, this fear is disconcerting because of how easily it can be weaponized for political gain. In the 2016 presidential election in the United States, we saw a veritable "race to the bottom" when it came to positioning Muslims as a dangerous enemy of the state. Candidates seemed in a hurry to outdo one another when it came to who could vilify Muslims the most. These political candidates often spoke of Islam as though it were indistinguishable from terror groups like ISIS. (Can you imagine if a political candidate were to speak of mainstream Christians as though they were indistinguishable from the Ku Klux Klan [KKK]?) And, most alarmingly, this time it worked. American politicians rode a nonspecific fear of something Muslims might potentially do into elected office—including the highest office in the land!

Over in Europe, a refugee crisis created by the Syrian Civil War—a complicated conflagration with many nations invested in the outcome—has resulted in increased xenophobia across the EU. European far-right-wing candidates have been ushered into office on their political pledge that Muslim refugees will not be assisted and will not be allowed to remain and integrate into their respective European societies.

Even in places like India, right-wing politicians are consolidating their political power by using hateful rhetoric to dehumanize Muslims.

This is a problem because it impacts us all. This is a problem because it is not a new story; it is an old story. It is an old lie that has been deployed since time immemorial for these same purposes.

In the past, the targets have been Jews, the Irish, the Chinese, Roma (pejoratively referred to as "gypsies"), LGBTQ people. . . . The list goes on and on. Each time it has been expedient for a scapegoat or a nonspecific "threat" to be found, morally bankrupt politicians and race-baiters have been happy to do so.

To defeat the anti-Muslim hate that threatens freedom across the globe, a first step is to understand that it is not new. It is old. It has been here since time immemorial. We know from antiquity the biblical concept of "scapegoats" and how this sort of hate has been used across time to further the ends of a few at the expense of the freedoms of the many.

But merely knowing what is happening is not enough. We have to understand *why* and *how* this is unfolding if we are to have any hope of stemming the global tide of hate and fear that now threaten Muslims . . . and which holds the potential to threaten every kind of person around the world, given time.

For me, this is personal because I am a proud Muslim. But it is also not personal, because anyone can be impacted by hate and fear. Anyone's demographic can come under fire from bigots, or be used by unscrupulous zealots to further their political purposes.

This book is my story, but it is also the story of how all of us must awaken to this threat before it is too late.

Too late for Muslims, and too late for us all.

1

"Open Your Eyes!"

In March 2019, Daoud Nabi was a seventy-one-year-old grandfather of nine living in Christchurch, New Zealand. An engineer by profession, he had escaped war in his native Afghanistan over forty years before, moving his family to New Zealand so they could have a safer life and pursue better opportunities. Upon his arrival in the Kiwi nation, Mr. Nabi had immediately immersed himself in his adopted homeland's language and culture. He also founded a mosque and became president of an ethnic Afghan civic association, with an eye to helping other Muslims who were likewise new arrivals. He assisted Muslim immigrants with basics like finding housing, and helped them acculturate more broadly into their new community.

"He used to make everyone feel at home," his son Omar told Al Jazeera News.

"Hello, brother. Welcome!" were the seventy-one-year-old Muslim grandfather's last words.

He spoke them—on March 15, 2019, at about 1:40 in the afternoon—to a twenty-eight-year-old white supremacist who entered the Christchurch, New Zealand mosque armed with military-style semi-automatic weapons.

Unbeknownst to the worshippers that day, the interloper's hideous plan was to live-stream a deadly anti-Muslim rampage on Facebook Live for the entire world to see.[5] And that was exactly what he did.

When the dust had finally settled on that fateful day in Christchurch—a day that still resonates for Muslim communities around the world—the white supremacist had brutally murdered fifty-one innocent Muslim worshippers in one of the worst cases of Islamophobic terrorism in modern times. (It was the worst terrorist attack ever in New Zealand's history.)

The twenty-eight-year-old terrorist—whom I choose not to name—had legally purchased online at least four semi-automatic weapons used in the attack.

While live-streaming a mass murder of this type was unprecedented, the terrorist predictably had authored a manifesto which he posted online. It was a seventy-four-page rant against Muslims, immigration, and multiculturalism.

The title of the manifesto was "The Great Replacement"; it is a document obsessed with the idea that non-white Muslim people will one day "replace" white people in countries like New Zealand by becoming a larger percentage of the population. (The words "birth rate" and "fertility" occur repeatedly throughout the document.)

But more broadly, it is a document driven by a fear of change. The author disliked that modernity has made it easier for people to travel to new countries and/or to adopt new homelands. The author seemed to pine for a "black and white" world of yore, in which people of a certain race and religion all lived in one country and never traveled or moved. The author was obsessed with the idea that non-white immigrants to New Zealand were having more children than white New Zealanders, and slowly creating demographic change.

Yet after lodging this general complaint, the author seemed unable to say exactly why it was a complaint at all.

Why would it be a bad thing if the number of Muslims in New Zealand increased slightly?

The white supremacist had no answer.

Why is it bad when Muslim people go to live in Christian-majority countries, but not when Christians go to live in Muslim-majority countries? (Consider all the British expats in Dubai, for example.)

Again, there was no answer.

Throughout the terrorist's manuscript, the *things that Muslims are going to do* are left unwritten, but the author is certain that they're very bad.

Chillingly, the white supremacist's racist manifesto also said that he deliberately chose his targets—a mosque and an Islamic center—simply because they were the most visible symbols of Islam in the area. The worshippers had committed no particular crime or infraction in his view, other than being Muslim in a country where Muslims are not the majority. To the terrorist's way of thinking, that was enough to warrant their murders.

It wasn't personal.

It's worth noting that "The Great Replacement" was also peppered with racist jokes and references to right-wing internet message boards like 8chan. It made references to the Crusades and the Barbary Pirate War—invoking conflicts involving Muslims that are both centuries old and long-settled—just as posts and memes on those message boards often do. Not coincidentally, one of the "heroes" of many 8channers is an infamous

Norwegian anti-Muslim terrorist named Anders Breivik, who murdered seventy-seven people in 2011 in Norway's worst terrorist attack ever. In the Christchurch terrorist's manuscript, he credits Breivik as an inspiration for his own mass killing spree.

The two men shared eerie similarities in many ways.

Almost a decade before the 2019 New Zealand mosque massacre, anti-Muslim terrorist Anders Breivik carried out an attack in Oslo, Norway. Breivik had targeted a multicultural-themed summer camp for teenagers, and many of his seventy-seven victims, hideously, were children.

In court, Breivik proudly admitted to the attacks and said they were his personal response to Norway's welcoming, multicultural embrace of Muslim immigrants. According to the *New York Times*, Breivik's own 1,500-page fascist manifesto was deeply influenced by right-wing extremists who had preceded him in promoting hate, violence, and Islamophobia (as well as—bizarrely—copying multiple passages from the Unabomber's manifesto word-for-word).[6] Breivik denounced Norway's politicians for failing to defend the country from multiculturalism and Muslim immigration. He cited American right-wing anti-Muslim activist Robert Spencer at least sixty-three times within his manifesto. Breivik also quoted from other prominent white supremacists who shared his racist worldview that Muslim immigrants posed a danger to Western societies.

But again, that danger was never expounded upon or articulated. More Muslims in Norway would be bad because . . . it would be bad. A government that encouraged multiculturalism was bad because . . . it was just bad.

Most of the people killed by Breivik had done nothing to offend him personally. Many of the victims were young white Scandinavian teenagers who were simply attending a camp celebrating multiculturalism.

Once again, it was not personal. These victims were not leaders who had enacted a policy Breivik disliked. They were not Muslims who had committed a crime or transgression. They were literally children at a summer camp. But for Breivik, that didn't matter. Once again, it wasn't personal.

Like the Christchurch terrorist, Breivik described himself as a righteous crusader on a mission to save white Christian European societies from the rising tide of brown Muslim immigration. Also like the shooter in Christchurch, Breivik made pop culture references and attempted to associate mainstream cultural touchstones with his agenda of murder and terror; for example, he suggested that the video game *Call of Duty: Modern Warfare* 2—which is enjoyed by millions of peaceful gamers—was "part of my training-simulation" and ideal for target practice before mass shootings.[7]

The links between the Christchurch killer and Breivik are many layers deep. One directly cites the other, yes. You cannot get much more direct than that. But both evil men also parroted the same anti-Muslim memes and talking points. Both attempted to make pop culture references that would connect with young people as part of their approach. One suggested that video game first-person shooters were a good way to warm up for a mass killing and the other live-streamed his massacre in the first person.

Both men were unable to say with any specificity why it was a bad thing that immigration to their country by Muslims (and others) was happening.

And for both men, it did not matter that their victims had done nothing personally. In the eyes of their killers, the simple fact of their Muslim existence had made them "fair game."

***

The second victim of the 2019 New Zealand mosque massacre was a seventy-eight-year-old black Muslim man named Abdukadir Elmi. A native of Somalia and the patriarch of his family, he was lovingly referred to as "Sheikh" by many people in the Christchurch Muslim community. Elmi had come to New Zealand ten years previously.

"This is devastating," his son told the *Washington Post* after the terrorist massacre. "My father survived through civil war in Somalia. I never thought this kind of stuff would happen to him in New Zealand."[8]

Sadly, however, that kind of stuff was happening in plenty of places that were not war-torn countries. And it was happening to Muslims of African origin just like Elmi.

In January 2017, Quebec City, Quebec witnessed its own brutal act of weaponized Islamophobia when a twenty-something Trump-supporting white supremacist named Alexandre Bissonnette casually walked into a mosque during evening prayers and opened fire, killing six innocent Muslims (whose names were Ibrahima Barry, Mamadou Tanou Barry, Khaled Belkacemi, Abdelkrim Hassane, Azzeddine Soufiane, and Aboubaker Thabti) as they prayed together with nearly fifty other worshippers that fateful evening in Canada.

Though he could not vote in American elections, Bissonnette was a huge fan of Donald Trump, proudly posting selfies on social media while wearing a red *Make America Great Again* hat. After the mosque massacre, Quebec City police found that Bissonnette had spent hours on the internet having searched for Donald Trump a grand total of 819 times on Twitter, Google, YouTube, and Facebook shortly before his murderous act. But millions of fans of Donald Trump do not shoot up mosques. Why was Bissonnette different?

Bissonnette had previously stated that he was totally against immigration, because he thought that brown-skinned immigrants would take over neighborhoods, hurt the economy, and increase unemployment for white people. (Actual economists, of course, agree that immigration grows a country's economy and tends to create jobs.) After his arrest, Bissonnette eventually revealed to police that he'd finally "snapped" when Canadian Prime Minister Justin Trudeau implied in a tweet that Canada would accept Muslim refugees who were turned away by Donald Trump's Muslim travel bans. The *Washington Post* did further digging and reported that Bissonnette was obsessed with the Twitter accounts of other prominent right-wing personalities, including FOX News hosts Tucker Carlson and Laura Ingraham, former Ku Klux Klan leader David Duke, Alex Jones of *Infowars*, American conspiracy theorist Mike Cernovich, white supremacist Richard Spencer, and even Donald Trump's senior White House adviser Kellyanne Conway. Bissonnette also enjoyed the Twitter account of right-wing provocateur Ben Shapiro—the belligerent editor-in-chief of the conservative news site the *Daily Wire*—checking Shapiro's social media feed at least ninety-three times in the month leading up to his massacre.[9] Bissonnette had found media personalities who would confirm his existing beliefs. Who would assure him that, yes, this feeling in his gut was correct. Immigrants and Muslims did pose a perilous threat. Of some sort. The pundits and personalities Bissonnette enjoyed did not openly advocate the murder of Muslims, but it is hard to imagine that their attitude—that Muslim immigrants present a gravely serious problem that literally threatens the soul of the nation—would do anything to dissuade him.

The terror attacks that would quickly culminate in Christchurch did not only target Muslims. This is because in the mythological narrative of the murderous and hate-filled, any minority group can be implicated when it suits the purposes of white supremacists. A mass murderer can reconcile striking at a different group as a "roundabout way" of striking at Muslims.

In October 2018, the Tree of Life synagogue in Pittsburgh, Pennsylvania was devastated when a white supremacist brutally executed eleven innocent Jewish congregants in a horrible act of anti-Semitic terrorism. It was the single deadliest attack exclusively targeting Jews ever to happen in the United States and the shooter later told police that he was inspired to commit these murders because Donald Trump was not doing enough to stop immigration. Yet millions of Americans take a hard line on immigration but do not shoot up synagogues.

This shooter had bought into the deeper and age-old conspiracy theory (often used as a recruiting tool by anti-Semites) suggesting that whatever racial or ethnic group a bigot dislikes, they ought to *also* dislike Jews because Jewish people are somehow "behind" things that they don't like. To them, Jewish politicians are behind pushing policies that allowed minority groups to immigrate. Jewish business owners are behind profiting from doing business with minorities. That movie you saw where a white person and a non-white person kissed? It was probably written by a Jew, or directed by a Jew, or greenlit by a Jewish studio head in Hollywood.

This particular strain of anti-Semitism (suggesting Jews are "behind" trends in immigration policy and culture) is widely promulgated on white supremacist internet message boards like 8chan that serve as the nexus of so many white supremacist mass murderers today.

When it comes to the Tree of Life shooter, once again, the deeper truth was in his unhinged racist manifesto.

"Open your Eyes!" the shooter had posted on social media in a disjointed anti-Semitic and Islamophobic rant.[10] "It's the filthy EVIL jews Bringing the Filthy EVIL Muslims into the Country!!"

A white supremacist set out to hate Muslims, but—convinced by online histrionics and internet memes that Jews were pushing for Muslim immigration—shot up a synagogue in Pittsburgh. It did not matter that these Jews had done nothing personally to push any kind of agenda. For the shooter, it was enough that they were Jews, and they were nearby.

And less than a year later, in April 2019, the Jewish community in Poway, California was attacked by a nineteen-year-old white supremacist who opened fire with a semi-automatic rifle inside the Chabad of Poway synagogue. A sixty-year-old congregant named Lori Gilbert-Kaye was killed as she tried to protect her rabbi, who thankfully survived the shooting.

After the California synagogue shooting, the parents of the nineteen-year-old white supremacist stated that they were "shocked and deeply saddened" by the terrible attack. "But our sadness pales in comparison to the grief and anguish our son has caused for so many innocent people. [Our son] has killed and injured the faithful who were gathered in a sacred place on a sacred day. To our great shame, he is now part of the history of evil that has been perpetrated on Jewish people for centuries."[11]

I think this statement by the killer's parents is interesting because—while it may have been written from a place of genuine concern—it also reduces people to anonymous, impersonal groups. Jews have been killed for centuries, and now our son has killed some more of them. The statement by the parents does not explore why their son chose to kill *these* Jews. In a way, I think this is problematic because it gives rise to the sense that a bad person killing some Jews (or some Muslims, or some LGBTQ people) sometimes "just happens." But it doesn't just happen, as a closer examination of this case made clear.

It was, in fact, like all the others.

Like many of the aforementioned white supremacist terrorists, the Poway shooter posted his own racist manifesto online to 8chan as well. Just that should have been enough, but there was more. The manifesto described the anti-Muslim Christchurch shooter as his primary inspiration, at one point stating quite directly about the New Zealand terrorist: "He showed me that it could be done."

And it's not just adjacent groups. Sometimes adjacent people end up targeted.

Professor Brian Levin from the Center for the Study of Hate & Extremism has conducted exhaustive studies of the rise in hate crimes since Donald Trump's election. He often points to the high-profile murder of two brave Good Samaritans on a Portland, Oregon city train in May 2017. The Samaritans were simply trying to help shield two young women who were facing anti-Muslim racist slurs from a thirty-five-year-old white supremacist who was already known to local police.[12] And for this, two Good Samaritans were brutally stabbed to death in front of horrified Portland commuters.

Earlier that same year, a mosque in Victoria, Texas was burned to the ground by an alleged anti-Muslim bigot[13] in a fire that impacted the whole community. Just a few months before that, several members of a right-wing extremist group calling themselves "The Crusaders" had plotted a "bloodbath" at a residential housing complex serving black Somali Muslim immigrants in Garden City, Kansas before police foiled their plot.[14] Had it been carried out, the attack would have almost certainly killed and injured many non-Muslims as well. (What sin would these non-Muslims have committed in the eyes of the killers?

Probably none at all; they would have simply been acceptable collateral damage to the white supremacists.)

And it's not just North America and New Zealand either. In addition to famous bake-offs inside pristine lily-white tents, the Western colonial mothership of Great Britain has also seen its fair share of weaponized hatred attacks targeting Muslims. In England, a thirty-nine-year-old man named David Moffatt was sentenced by a British court in August 2017 for threatening to blow up an Islamic bookshop in London—in an attack that would have almost certainly hurt non-Muslims too—and publicly stated that his motivation was to "kill all the Muslims." (Parroting a talking point from right-wing Internet websites, when police officers finally confronted Moffatt, he bizarrely replied during his arrest: "I'm not anti-Muslim . . . I'm Catholic!")[15]

Another British case involved another middle-aged white man named Darren Osborne who was found guilty of murder in 2018 and sentenced to forty-three years in prison after he deliberately plowed a rental van into innocent Muslim worshippers outside a London mosque (which killed one person and left many bystanders, of several backgrounds, injured). A witness told the court that when Osborne was being subdued by members of the mosque, he said: "I've done my job; you can kill me now." As several men wrestled Osborne to the ground, a loud voice shouted to the growing crowd: "No one touch him! No one! No one!" That voice came from Mohammed Mahmoud— the mosque's imam—who was later dubbed the "Hero Imam" by British media for urging his fellow Muslims to show restraint until the London police arrived.[16]

As these cases show, "attacks on Muslims" aren't always attacks on Muslims. Though they may stem from anti-Muslim hatred, they can easily touch people from other communities. The killers draw from the same well of hate, and employ the same perverse logic: If something is done in the service of fighting Muslims and what they represent, then any act, against anyone, is permissible.

***

The third victim of the 2019 New Zealand massacre was a seventy-seven-year-old man named Muse Nur Awale. A resident of Christchurch for over thirty years, Awale was a beloved Sunday school teacher for the children at the mosque. Since he and his wife did not have any children of their own, those who knew him best told mourners afterward that Awale considered all of the mosque youngsters as his own children.

***

When it comes to crimes motivated by hatred for a particular group, there is a phenomenon called the "wrong address problem" which Professor Vijay Prashad explained to me during a joint TV interview on Al-Jazeera English after the August 2012 massacre at a Sikh gurdwara (temple) in Oak Creek, Wisconsin which killed seven Sikh worshippers. The "wrong address problem" occurs when the actual victims of a terrorist hate crime appear to be—but are not—the intended targets. After the September 11, 2001 attacks, the vast majority of post-9/11 bias-motivated hate crimes in the Western world ostensibly targeted Muslims, but also impacted the larger Arab and South Asian communities as a whole. (Anyone else who could be mistaken for a Muslim might be, and often was targeted.)

As sadly evidenced by the 2012 Oak Creek Sikh temple massacre, there is no doubt that the Indian Sikh community across America has faced the disproportionate brunt of the "wrong address" problem since 9/11. It does not help things that the America media (and movies and TV shows) often does not distinguish between the different sorts of people who live in the Middle East and South Asia. The distinctions are never teased-apart for audiences. For far too many Americans, it is still the case that people who appear "like that" are somehow "Muslim," even if they might belong to a hundred other diverse religious or ethnic groups.

Since many observant Sikh men keep a turban (known as a "*dastār*" or "pagri") and unshorn hair—which often manifests itself into a long beard—after 9/11 many Americans wrongly conflated Sikhs with Muslims because of this "turban-and-beard" stereotype look. To highlight the sheer human stupidity of bias-motivated hate crimes today, I should note that the first victims of post-9/11 hate crime murders in the United States were not even Muslim.

Only four days after 9/11, Mr. Balbir Singh Sodhi—a forty-nine-year-old Indian Sikh-American businessman—was brutally shot and killed at an Arizona gas station in the first "wrong address" murder after the attacks. The prosecuting attorney in the case told reporters that Mr. Sodhi had been killed for no other apparent reason than that he was dark-skinned, and wore a turban. The murderer simply "thought he was a Muslim."

On the same day as the Sodhi murder, a forty-eight-year-old Egyptian Orthodox Coptic Christian man named Adel Karas was viciously murdered outside his suburban Los Angeles import shop.

And that same day in Texas, both the FBI and local police investigated the murder of Waqar Hasan, a store owner who was found shot to death outside his grocery store in suburban Dallas in another post-9/11 hate crime murder.[17]

All told, in the days after 9/11, there was a surge of bias-motivated hate crime attacks on all sorts of houses of worship—including Muslim mosques, but also Hindu temples, Sikh gurdwaras, and Jewish synagogues. I believe that many of these attackers were not even "targeting Muslims" after a point. Instead, white supremacists were simply seeking to lash out at whatever convenient people they could find that looked different from them.

Whether these sorts of hate crime attacks had anything to do with "getting revenge for 9/11" has continued to be murky in the intervening years between 2001 and the upsurge in anti-immigrant feeling that accompanied the last few US presidential elections.

In April 2014, a white neo-Nazi attacked a Jewish community center in Kansas City, Missouri. According to CNN, the neo-Nazi shooter had made no secret of his anti-Semitic views[18] and he had even written letters to newspapers inviting people to white supremacist meetings at his own home. Furthermore, this shooter also bizarrely believed that Jews were somehow "behind" the immigration of Middle Eastern people more largely to the United States.

Because of how America's culture, its laws, and its regulations regarding weapons are oriented, there is reason to believe that these sorts of crimes of mistaken identity will have the potential to threaten us all. Americans who wish to commit white supremacist hate crimes have the motive, yes, but they also have the means and the opportunity . . .

It is not possible to write honestly and openly about the threat that anti-Muslim terrorists pose in the United States, without writing about the status of the gun as a religious artifact in our culture.

After mass shootings in places like Australia and New Zealand, these countries have enacted meaningful gun legislation. The United States has not.

Whether or not it bears any relationship to reality, many Americans feel that they are living in a world of "Cowboy settlers" who need to be armed to the teeth in order to survive in a harsh and forbidding land. Never mind that this harsh, forbidding land is now mostly filled with paved roads, strip malls, and Starbucks coffee shops on virtually every corner! Still, the mythology seems to run that since the white settlers who colonized America carried guns, guns must be an integral component of our success. That if guns were regulated in the United States, the country would cease to be successful or special. The gun is seen as part of the sacred "special sauce" that has allowed American culture to be so dominant. This has led to strikingly lax gun laws in most of the country. There are still gun shows where firearms may be bought and sold without a criminal background check. Laws against people who are mentally ill or addicted to drugs purchasing guns are almost never enforced.

However, it is not the 1700s or even the 1800s. If the "gun show loophole" were closed tomorrow—or if people purchasing guns were required to take a urine test to screen for illegal drugs—America would still have the largest economy in the world. It would still have most of the top-ranked colleges and universities in the world. It would still be the center of art and commerce that it is today.

Yet those with vested, moneyed interests in preserving the status quo have fought tooth-and-nail to ensure that even small, common-sense adjustments to our gun laws are never made. Propaganda is used to frighten sportsmen into thinking that if assault rifles are regulated, it will be only a matter of time before hunting rifles are taken from law-abiding citizens.

Certain moneyed interests—like the National Rifle Association (NRA) and handgun manufacturers—have seen fit to stoke this "gun mania" to further their own interests and to position firearms as sacred objects (that are the sole reason why the United States has become a wealthy and powerful country). Not only have these interests advocated against gun control generally, but they have also sought to position Muslims specifically as agents of anti-gun advocacy.

In the years since 2016, we have seen coordinated nationwide efforts by networks of armed protestors to associate Muslims with gun control. They had the audacity to publicly advertise their gatherings on Facebook, which culminated in nearly twenty armed protests outside mosques across the United States which were supposed to be done simultaneously. These protests were euphemistically called the "Global Rally for Humanity," but a child could see these were nothing more than anti-Muslim bullies who had decided that intimidating Muslims would further their own interests.

In an article that I wrote for *The Atlantic*, I featured one of the organizers of these armed demonstrations—a former US Marine and "Oath Keeper" named Jon Ritzheimer. In the past, he had proudly sold "FUCK ISLAM" T-shirts directly outside of mosques, and had once bizarrely threatened to arrest a female Democratic senator for treason because of her support for a nuclear weapons treaty with Iran.[19]

Men like Ritzheimer represent an omnipresent effort to scapegoat Muslims for anything they perceive as society's ills. These kind of polemicists are not new and it is only coincidental that they now seek to scapegoat Muslims. From their twisted way of thinking, they can impugn any minority group that seems to get in the way of what they perceive as their rights—which are, of course, constantly seen to be in grave peril. (When, in fact, every statistic shows that gun ownership in the United States is not imperiled, and only continued to rise between 2008 and 2016. As Barack Obama once observed, if Republican rhetoric were true, and Democrats truly wanted to "take your guns away" then Democrats are doing a really terrible job of it!)

It is unfortunate that the world needs to have boogey-men. For Muslims, it is doubly unfortunate that entities like the NRA and their adjacent right-wing political organizations have decided that today they are these boogeymen. It is apparently easy to convince the indoctrinated that Muslims want to take away guns, even though no real evidence for this position exists. Whether someone has been a Muslim for only a short time, or whatever political party they may personally be associated with, it is not a "tough sell" to convince people that Muslims are the enemy.

***

The fourth victim of the 2019 New Zealand mosque massacre was a seventy-year-old man named Hussein Moustafa. He was a native of Egypt who had served as the secretary general of the Muslim Association of Canterbury and had earned a master's degree in the United States at the Thunderbird School of Management at Arizona State University. After the Christchurch massacre, police found Mr. Moustafa's body in his favorite corner of the Al Noor mosque where he had been gunned down.

"He loved the mosque," his daughter-in-law remembered.[20] "He was always a welcoming face there."

Unfortunately, the Christchurch mosque shooter *did* become inspirational fodder for other white supremacist terrorists around the world. In El Paso, Texas, a young white supremacist brutally murdered over twenty people inside a crowded Walmart near the US-Mexico border in August 2019 out of a hatred of Hispanics and Latinos. The shooter's decision to use violence drew on the kind of conspiracy theories that had been disseminated by the mosque shooter in New Zealand.

"In general, I support the Christchurch shooter and his manifesto. This attack is a response to the Hispanic invasion of Texas," the El Paso shooter wrote in his own racist screed.

An August 2019 *New York Times* report identified the Christchurch mosque shooter as a rallying cry for white supremacists around the world, noting that the El Paso shooter's manifesto drew "direct inspiration from the mass murder of Muslims at two mosques in New Zealand" even though he personally targeted Latinos in his act of mass murder inside the Walmart superstore in southern Texas that day.[21] The El Paso shooter echoed the Christchurch shooter's argument that acts of disruptive violence were necessary, because otherwise white people would be "replaced."

The New Zealand shooter's online manifesto was copious and diverse in its strange, hate-filled content. However, one particularly virulent and virus-like idea it promoted was a debunked white supremacist conspiracy theory called the "Great Replacement." It is generally agreed to have been first propagated by a French writer named Renaud Camus who argued that elites in Europe are working behind-the-scenes to replace white Europeans with brown-skinned Muslim immigrants from the Middle East and North Africa.

The *New York Times* noted in a September 2019 article that before he became a major ideological grandfather for modern white supremacists with his conspiratorial "Great Replacement" conspiracy theory, Renaud Camus was mainly known by other

French novelists as a "pioneering writer of gay literature" who wrote pornographic novels while living comfortably in his four-teenth-century castle in the south of France.[22]

In addition to demonizing Muslims, Renaud Camus has also bizarrely warned of white Europeans being replaced by "black Africans"[23] and once publicly whined about there being too many Jewish people on French public radio explaining Francophone culture to pure lily-white European Christians like him.[24] One of the most confounding and upsetting aspects of Renaud Camus and his white supremacist "Great Replacement" theory is that it seems like a sort of Grand Unification theory of hate that can implicate any person for any reason (or for any action they have taken). Because it can never be proven—because it is insane, false, and theoretical—it also cannot be disproven, which seems to be enough for the adherents who are dedicated to believing in it no matter what the facts before them show.

Though despicable, it is important to understand how the Great Replacement theory is applied by racists and bigots today. In doing so, we can see how and why Muslims are always impli-cated (no matter what they actually do).

The Great Replacement involves a particularly cynical worldview, holding that all the world's diverse races and/or ethnic groups—whites, blacks, Jews, Muslims, Asians, Latinos, etc.—are in constant competition for wealth and power, and to see that their culture is the dominant one. It is a kind of global game of "King of the Hill." At the moment, the top of the hill is occupied by non-Jewish whites. (Conspiracy theorists who believe in the Great Replacement believe that everything of value that humanity has accomplished is—more or less—because of non-Jewish whites. Were the established hierarchy to be upset—and a different king installed atop the hill—chaos would reign and all of our progress and good work would come undone.)

Believers in the Great Replacement theory hold that minority groups know that they cannot numerically supplant or defeat the majority white society, so their goal is to dilute or weaken it by advocating for as much immigration from non-white groups as possible. Thus, anyone who takes anything less than the hardest possible line on immigration can be accused of working to further the Great Replacement conspiracy theory.

The simple truth is that advances in technology and transportation are making the globe increasingly diverse simply because travel is now easier and more affordable than ever before. Hundreds of years ago nations tended to be more homogenous—not out of a racist sense of racial superiority but simply because it was very difficult to immigrate or emigrate at the time.

Despite this, according to the Institute for Strategic Dialogue (ISD)—a British think tank specializing in extremism—organized far-right networks across the globe are actively promoting the Great Replacement conspiracy theory as much as possible. References to it online have doubled in the last five years, with more than 1.5 million mentions on Twitter alone (with the number of tweets mentioning the theory nearly tripling in four years from just over 120,000 in 2014 to over 330,000 in 2018 and skyrocketing since that time, according to a July 2019 ISD report).[25]

The Great Replacement has become a dominant ideological doctrine of the European far-right, which actively works to fuel racial paranoia and seeks to make white Europeans feel as though they will be "wiped out" by non-white Muslims. (The ISD also found that this conspiracy theory "got a bump" and found new life after featuring prominently in the manifesto of the Christchurch gunman.) Once obscure, the Great Replacement has now moved into mainstream Western politics; it has been referenced publicly by right-wing Western political figures including US president Donald Trump, right-wing Italian interior minister Matteo Salvini, and Björn Höcke of the *Alternative für Deutschland* (AfD) in Germany.

In February 2020, we saw this weaponized Islamophobia rear its ugly head again, this time in Hanau, Germany where ten people were murdered (and five injured) by a white supremacist terrorist at several locations—including two hookah lounges—frequented by local Kurdish & Turkish Muslims. After the hookah lounge massacre in Hanau, German police officials found a twenty-four-page manifesto posted online where the shooter predictably railed against Muslim minorities in Germany and told the world that people of certain African, Asian, and Middle Eastern origins have to be "completely annihilated" within the country. "If there was a button available that would make this become a reality, I would press it in a flash," he ominously wrote while also bizarrely claiming to have invented the Trump-ian slogan "America First" inside his rambling manifesto.

"Racism is a poison. Hate is a poison," German chancellor Angela Merkel responded in a video statement regarding the February 2020 hookah lounge massacre in Hanau. "This poison exists in our society and it is to blame for far too many crimes," Merkel said, noting the mounting evidence that the perpetrator was motivated by his right-wing anti-Muslim worldview. It is important to understand that Islamophobia and fear of "replacement" by groups like Muslims is not limited to white people in Western countries. In several Asian nations, we are now witnessing staggering levels of weaponized Islamophobia as well. In places like China and Myanmar (formerly known as Burma), they now approach genocidal levels as leaders actively try to erase Islam from within their borders.

The doctrine of "ethnic cleansing" was first officially investigated by the United Nations during the Balkan genocide in the former Yugoslavia during the mid-1990s (which was orchestrated by Serbian president Slobodan Milosevic primarily against Bosnian Muslims). Generally speaking, the term "ethnic cleansing" is legally defined as a purposeful policy designed by one ethnic or religious group to "remove by violent and terror-inspiring means" the civilian population of another ethnic or religious group from certain geographic areas. These brutal genocidal practices were used by the Nazis during the Holocaust and in places like Rwanda to ethnically cleanse populations. Practices employed in the name of genocide can include murder, torture, arbitrary arrest/detention, extrajudicial executions, rape/sexual assaults, and forced exile.

Similar to the international law guidelines on ethnic cleansing, the definition of the term "genocide" primarily resides within Article 2 of the 1948 "Convention on the Prevention & Punishment of the Crime of Genocide." Generally speaking, the crime of genocide is defined under international law to be any acts committed with the intent to destroy—in whole or in part—a national, ethnic, racial, or religious group. These acts include "killing members of the group; causing serious bodily or mental harm to members of the group; deliberately inflicting on the group conditions of life calculated to bring about its physical destruction in whole or in part; imposing measures intended to prevent births within the group; & forcibly transferring children of the group to another group."[26]

In present-day Myanmar (which is the Southeast Asian country formerly known as Burma), the Rohingya Muslims have been the victims of a coordinated government ethnic cleansing campaign under the watchful eye of 1991 Nobel Peace Prize winner Aung San Suu Kyi, who has done virtually nothing to stop the erasure of Muslims from her country. *The Economist* magazine once called the Muslim Rohingya "the most persecuted people in the world." There is good reason for that. In a pre-dominantly Buddhist country, the Rohingya are a small, though indigenous, ethnic group who have lived for centuries in the Rakhine province of Myanmar. And until recent years, they had found ways to coexist with the rest of that country's population. Although the Myanmar government disingenuously character-izes Rohingya Muslims as immigrants from neighboring coun-tries like Bangladesh, the Rohingya have been living in Myanmar since time immemorial, and virtually all external observers agree they should be considered native to Myanmar.

In 1982, the government of Myanmar passed an anti-Mus-lim citizenship law that set things in motion. It officially rec-ognized eight different races and 130 minority groups within Myanmar —but deliberately omitted the country's one million Rohingya Muslims. Since the passage of the law, many people in that country have been subjected to propaganda designed to make them feel that Rohingya are Muslim "intruders" who were brought in by British colonialists from neighboring Bangladesh.

The consequences of this hate have been horrifying.

Hundreds of thousands of Rohingya refugees have been housed in camps like Cox's Bazaar in Bangladesh, which has now become the largest refugee settlement in the world, accord-ing to the Norwegian Refugee Council.[27]

For many Western observers, it is initially incomprehen-sible to think that some of the most egregious Islamophobic incitements to violence could come from Buddhist monks in an Asian country. But a closer look reveals how anti-Muslim hate can take root in virtually any country or culture.

In Myanmar, the flames of genocidal ethnic cleansing against Rohingya were *directly* fanned by a group of right-wing Buddhists that were part of an extremist group known as "969." Positioning itself as a patriotic grassroots movement, 969's most vocal cheerleader was an extremist Buddhist monk named Wirathu who had been previously jailed by the former military junta running Myanmar for anti-Muslim violence. Wirathu told his fellow Buddhists to boycott Muslim shops and shun interfaith marriages. He openly referred to mosques as "enemy bases" and—in sentences that were not carried out in full—was sentenced to twenty-five years in prison for distributing anti-Muslim pamphlets inciting communal riots. Most notoriously, this 969 leader, for a period, even began referring to himself as the "Burmese bin Laden" and finally surrendered himself to Myanmar police in November 2020 after a year of evading arrest on sedition charges.[28]

It is hard for many Westerners to grasp just how terrifying Wirathu and his ilk have become in Myanmar.

"I am afraid to call him 'Wirathu' because even his name scares me," a Swiss documentary filmmaker once told Agence France Presse (AFP) after filming a special about the genocidal Buddhist monk. "I just call him W."[29]

The Swiss filmmaker might have been frightened, but for many in the West, the terror still does not connect on a visceral level. People are unable to see a Buddhist in a saffron robe as someone who might incite genocidal violence on a grand scale. For example, Wirathu was featured in a July 2013 *TIME* magazine *cover story* with the headline "The Face of Buddhist Terror." The accompanying story enumerated on the dangers faced by Rohingya and the tactics used by militant monks to fuel anti-Muslim violence in Southeast Asia. Despite this prominent report, the news barely made a ripple on the national stage.

Others have also tried.

"It's very sad," the Dalai Lama once famously told ABC News when pressed about the ethnic cleansing of Rohingya

Muslims by his fellow Buddhist monks. "Nowadays, even Buddhists are involved," the Dalai Lama further conceded.[30]

Yet even this concession by the highest holy man in the faith has done little to bring attention to these crimes.

The genocidal ethnic cleansing of Rohingya Muslims was not an overnight phenomenon, of course. And international agencies monitoring the world for serious crimes have done a better job of identifying and tracing its trajectory. As early as 2013, prominent human rights organizations like Amnesty International and Human Rights Watch were releasing warnings that the government of Myanmar was conducting a campaign of ethnic cleansing against the Rohingya.

Another curious aspect that further "muddies the water" when it comes to Myanmar is the role that their leader has played. There is an old aphorism which says that something must be seen in order to be believed. When it comes to how Myanmar's leadership has treated the Rohingya, it seems that because many cannot believe it, they cannot see it. Even though it's right in front of their faces!

After she became the de facto ruler of Myanmar, 1991 Nobel Peace Prize winner Aung San Suu Kyi—previously known as "The Dame of Rangoon" for being a champion of justice and human rights—stunned the global community by publicly whitewashing the genocide of Rohingya Muslims during her high-profile fall from collective grace. Because opinion of her was so high in Western countries, when reports of anti-Muslim genocide emerged, many Westerners felt that they could not be true. Most liberal Westerners assumed they must have misunderstood a nuance of the situation, or that some aspect was being "lost in translation." But nothing was being lost. The reports were accurate. Considering what most in the

West believed she stood for, the disgraced dame Aung San Suu Kyi had done a complete 180.

Eventually, Aung San Suu Kyi herself seemed to realize that some mealy-mouthed attempts to mitigate the situation might be called for if she desired to stay in power. She had the nerve to tell *BBC World News* that she thought the phrase "ethnic cleansing" was "too strong" to describe what was happening to the Rohingya Muslims in her country (even though human rights groups like Amnesty International already publicized well-documented cases of mass murder, systemic rape, and torture—all taking place on her watch).

"I don't think there is ethnic cleansing going on," she blithely told the BBC. "I think 'ethnic cleansing' is too strong an expression to use for what is happening."

In addition to human rights groups, the global community begged to differ.

The United Nations had consistently and unequivocally decried the treatment of Rohingya Muslims by Myanmar's government during her watch. The UN has further officially stated that it is "very likely" that Myanmar's military has itself committed grave human rights abuses against Rohingya Muslims, which would be tantamount to crimes against humanity under international law.

"Stop the violence," said 2014 Nobel Peace Prize winner Malala Yousafzai when prompted to comment about the anti-Muslim genocide in Myanmar. "I am still waiting for my fellow Nobel Laureate Aung San Suu Kyi. The world is waiting and the Rohingya Muslims are waiting!"[31]

In addition to Malala, at least seven other Nobel Peace Prize laureates have publicly called for the designation of the anti-Muslim Rohingya campaign to be officially labeled as a "genocide," which would trigger certain legal protections under international law and which eventually led to the International Court of Justice at The Hague condemning Myanmar's government in a January 2020 official ICJ court ruling.[32]

"In 1944, as a Jew in Budapest, I too was a Rohingya," world-renowned philanthropist George Soros once said during a ceremony in Oslo, Norway. "The parallels to the Nazi genocide are alarming."[33]

And French president Emmanuel Macron became the first major world leader to publicly declare that a "genocide" was occurring against Myanmar's Rohingya, speaking out forcefully against their treatment in September 2017.

The US Holocaust Memorial Museum also conducted exhaustive research, which found conclusive and "mounting evidence" of widespread genocide against Rohingya Muslims.

And eventually, the United Nations declared the Myanmar military's campaign against the Rohingya "textbook ethnic cleansing."[34]

In August 2018, Aung San Suu Kyi was stripped of her "Freedom of Edinburgh" award in Scotland for her refusal to condemn the genocidal violence. By late 2019, she had also had seven other major awards revoked due to her complicity. On January 23, 2020, the International Court of Justice (a.k.a. "the World Court") issued a twenty-eight-page ruling against the Southeast Asian country of Myanmar for their genocidal ethnic cleansing campaigns against one million Rohingya Muslims. In their unanimous ruling, the World Court ordered the government of Myanmar to take "all measures within its power to prevent the commission of all acts"[35] under the Genocide Convention against the Rohingya Muslim people moving into the future.

Anti-Muslim hate can come from any group. It can arise anywhere, in any culture, including in people who were formerly thought to be on the right side of history. It can impact people who are ethnically Middle Eastern, but plenty of other ethnicities too. Though many implicated in the hate, certainly, are white supremacists who are themselves white, the horrible narrative of hate, prejudice, and the Great Replacement allows Muslims to come under threat from virtually any direction, anywhere in the world.

***

The fifth victim of the 2019 New Zealand mosque massacre was a sixty-eight-year-old man named Mounir Soliman. He was one of four Egyptian victims of the Christchurch massacre. The civil engineer rarely missed any of the five daily prayers in the Al Noor mosque, which was located very close to his house. Before his untimely death, Mr. Soliman had spent twenty-two years as a quality manager at Scotts Engineering, where he was remembered as a "lovely man" in an official company statement after his passing.

***

Directly to the north of Myanmar is the People's Republic of China. It has recently undertaken one of the largest and most sinister campaigns of ethnic cleansing against Muslims in modern history. It is, truly, Orwellian in style, scope, and scale. The government's target is a very specific ethnic group known as the Uighur Muslims.

Previous to the current anti-Muslim ethnic cleansing campaign, the Chinese government had sought for several decades to restrict the practice of Islam in the western Xinjiang region. However, more than half of the twenty-four million people in this Chinese province are Uighur Muslims. According to most estimates, over one million of these Uighur Muslim men, women, and children are now imprisoned inside internment camps. The government's goal is nothing less than to erase Islamic identity from within China's borders.

Why? What does China fear? It's a hard question to answer, but very clearly they fear something. Something not present in any one of China's fifty-five other recognized ethnic groups.

Perhaps it is their language. Uighur Muslims generally speak a native Turkic language. The Xinjiang province where they live borders eight other countries, including several Muslim-majority former Soviet states, Pakistan, India, and Mongolia. Because of this, one possible reason for the program of ethnic cleansing by the Chinese central government may be that Uighurs represents an entry-point of Islam into the rest of mainland China.

In harrowing statements by survivors and escapees, Uighur Muslims who have been held prisoner inside these Chinese internment camps have claimed that they were pressured to renounce Islam, to criticize basic Muslim practices, and to sing Chinese communist party propaganda songs. There were also widespread reports of Muslims being forced to eat pork and drink alcohol (both of which are forbidden to observant Muslims), as well as reports of much worse things—torture, rape, and murder at the hands of the Chinese captors. A September 2018 Human Rights Watch report[36] found that the Chinese government was using brutal coercive practices against Uighur Muslims, which included murder, torture, arbitrary arrest/detention, extra-judicial executions, gang rapes, and systemic sexual assaults throughout these Muslim internment camps.

According to the Associated Press, the ultimate aim of the Chinese government is probably to "erase their Islamic beliefs" and reshape the identities of these people in an Orwellian manner.

In addition to banning Muslim names for newborn babies, there were also reports of forced marriages of Muslim women to non-Muslim Chinese men, and the outlawing of Ramadan activities and other religious observances. Authorities in the Chinese capital of Beijing have even bizarrely ordered Muslim halal restaurants to remove any Arabic letters and/or Islamic symbology from their food establishments.

***

The sixth victim of the 2019 New Zealand mosque massacre was a sixty-eight-year-old man named Ahmed Abdel-Ghany who opened up his own halal restaurant and food truck in Christchurch, and was known around town for selling "Egyptian Donuts."

***

The Chinese government has long campaigned to bring Chinese people of all faiths in line with hardline Communist Party right-thinking, and this often means casting religion to the side. Needless to say, it is not just Muslims who are persecuted in China today. Chinese authorities have shut down many underground Christian churches and torn down crosses deemed to be illegal by the government. But Muslims have received particular attention in recent years.

Some think that while the Uighurs have always made China nervous, it was a riot in 2009 between Uighurs and majority Han Chinese in Xinjiang that touched off China's current feeling that "something needs to be done" about Uighur Muslims.

Originating in Urumqi, the region's capital, the bloody riots left two hundred dead and massive destruction in their wake. It also gave China the grim determination that "something must be done" with these people.

Yet another—and even more disturbingly banal—possibility behind China's monstrous treatment of the Uighurs may be that they stand in the way of $1 trillion in infrastructure improvements.

Yes. You read that right.

The Chinese government is currently undertaking what it calls the "Belt and Road Initiative"—a staggering one trillion dollar infrastructure project which will ultimately connect China to Africa and Europe. (Many have called it the most ambitious road-building and transportation modernization project in human history, in terms of sheer scale.) For this project to succeed, the roads, bridges, and railways under construction will all have to pass through the heart of Xinjiang province. Whether or not it is the true cause of the despicable actions being taken against the Uighurs, the enormous one trillion dollar project may explain why many Muslim-majority countries close to China have been so silent during this ethnic cleansing campaign against 1 million of their sisters and brothers.

The kingdom of Saudi Arabia is home to Islam's two holiest cities—Mecca and Medina—and the Islamic Republic of Pakistan is the second most populous Muslim country in the world. Even so, the respective leaders of both of these prominent Muslim countries have both refused to publicly condemn China's ethnic cleansing of Uighur Muslims. As mentioned, their deafening silence may well stem from the fact that Beijing is pumping billions of dollars from the one trillion dollar "Belt and Road Initiative" into their respective coffers in Riyadh and Islamabad.

In February 2019, the controversial crown prince of Saudi Arabia-Muhammad bin Salman (often known as MBS)-traveled to China to meet with Chinese president Xi Jinping. The meeting took place during the height of increasing media attention on Beijing's persecution of Uighur Muslims. According to *Newsweek* magazine, Saudi Arabia and China have engaged in over sixty-three billion dollars' worth of trade deals just since 2018. It was likely for this reason that the Saudi crown prince—whom, I hasten to remind you, the CIA has publicly confirmed ordered the assassination of *Washington Post* journalist Jamal Khashoggi—cravenly defended China's use of "re-education" camps (a thinly-cloaked euphemism for internment camps). This might have been a chance for MBS to stand up for his fellow Muslims and attempt to turn down the long road to redemption. Instead, he proved that, as ever, he remains motivated only by an endless cupidity and thirst for power. The horrible fates befalling his fellow Muslims mean little to him if he is growing his country's influence with a powerful ally.

"China has the right to carry out antiterrorism and deextremization work for its national security," the Saudi crown prince said on Chinese television when asked about the Uighur Muslims.[37] Yet international observers were not fooled. It was clear that by asserting that the millions of Chinese Uighurs were all terrorists—a claim as absurd as it was sinister—he was giving his blessing to China's awful policies.

Not to be outdone by his Saudi counterpart, the prime minister of Pakistan —former cricket superstar Imran Khan—also gave his implicit endorsement of China's actions on-camera when speaking to a major Turkish news network in 2019.[38]

"You're doing business with China," the reporter asked the Pakistani prime minister. "Does it mean you cannot criticize them when it comes to what they are doing with Uighurs?"

"To tell you the truth, I don't know much about this situation," Imran Khan bizarrely replied to the reporter from Turkey's state broadcaster TRT World, even though his country shares a border with the Xinjiang Province. Instead of unequivocally condemning the ethnic cleansing of a million-plus Muslims in China, the Pakistani prime minister instead decided to praise China for the billions of Beijing dollars pouring into Pakistan as part of the "Belt and Road".

Imran Khan continued to tell the Turkish TV network that China had been a "breath of fresh air for us" by pumping over sixty-two billion dollars into China-Pakistan Economic Corridor (CPEC) projects. (This CPEC project will ultimately build one of the world's largest deep-sea ports situated on the Arabian Sea in the Pakistani port city of Gwadar.[39])

Even the president of Turkey himself, Recep Tayyip Erdogan—a self-proclaimed defender of Muslims worldwide—told Chinese state media that all Uighur Muslims were "living happily" there, during a visit in 2019 to China.[40] Erdogan made this ridiculous proclamation even as his own Turkish Foreign Ministry had publicly condemned the Chinese government for ethnic cleansing a few months earlier in a strongly-worded statement which stated: "It is no longer a secret that more than 1,000,000 Uighur Turks incurring arbitrary arrests are subjected to torture and political brainwashing in internment camps and prisons."

Yet, under pressure from China's power and wealth, the Turkish leader folded like a cheap table soon thereafter. It became quite clear that President Erdogan's priority vis-a-vis China was not human rights, but to strengthen economic cooperation between the two countries. It seemed that Turkey was just as hungry for a piece of Beijing's one trillion dollar pie as their Saudi Arabian and Pakistani Muslim counterparts.

Standing up against the lure of easy money is one of the most difficult things that ethical humans are called to do. But let me be clear, we *are* called to do it!

Directly to the west of Myanmar and China, the subcontinent of "South Asia" is known as a massive ethno-cultural region hugging the Indian Ocean consisting of nearly two billion people living in at least nine countries including: India, Pakistan, Bangladesh, Nepal, Bhutan, Sri Lanka, Afghanistan, and the Maldives. Now, you could literally walk into any of these South Asian countries today and virtually every red-blooded "Desi" person (someone with a South Asian background) will tell you that the undisputed "King of Bollywood" is a world-famous Indian Muslim superstar actor named Shah Rukh Khan.

Sadly, even though India's most famous Bollywood superstar actor is a Muslim, the birthplace of Mahatma Gandhi (and the largest democracy in the world with nearly 1.5 billion people) has found itself heading down a right-wing fascistic rabbit hole led by an ethno-nationalist prime minister named Narendra Modi.

Although many people know that 80 percent of India observes the Hindu religion, you might be surprised to learn that it's also home to the second-largest Muslim population on the planet (194.8 million Muslims and growing). With nearly two hundred million Indian Muslims living in the country today, Islam has now become the second-largest religion within India during our lifetimes. According to the Pew Research Center—by the year 2060—the South Asian regional superpower will have the single largest Muslim population of any country in the world (with over 333+ million Indian Muslims by that year).[41] But notwithstanding the fact that Muslims constitute almost one-fifth of the entire Indian population today, the land of Mahatma Gandhi has tragically become less and less welcoming to two hundred million of its own Desi citizens simply because of their Muslim religious identity.

The right-wing political legacy of Narendra Modi was forever tied to Islamophobia decades earlier in 2002. At the time, Modi was serving as chief minister (de facto political leader) for the western Indian state of Gujarat. During his watch as Gujarat's top government official, Narendra Modi stood silently as over a thousand-plus innocent Gujarati Muslims were brutally massacred by pitchfork-carrying anti-Muslim vigilante mobs. These carefully planned genocidal attacks of unprecedented savagery against Gujarat's six million-plus Muslim community still remain a collective trauma for nearly two hundred million Indian Muslims even today.

In the bloody aftermath of the 2002 anti-Muslim pogrom massacres in Gujarat, some of Narendra Modi's closest political aides were eventually found guilty for their roles in the genocidal horror. "Large numbers of [Muslim] girls were raped; men were cut to pieces and burned alive with kerosene. Pregnant women had their womb slit open and the fetuses smashed in front of their eyes,"[42] according to legendary historian, William Dalrymple (who once referred to Narendra Modi as "India's Vladimir Putin" during an interview with CNN's Christiane Amanpour).[43]

To give you more historical context, Narendra Modi is a proud lifelong member of the Rashtriya Swayamsevak Sangh (RSS) which is a right-wing paramilitary Hindutva nationalist group "inspired by the fascist movements of Europe," according to award-winning Indian essayist Pankaj Mishra. In a book review for *The Guardian* newspaper in London, Mishra further noted that the founder of the RSS also believed that Adolf Hitler and Nazi Germany "had manifested 'race pride at its highest' by purging the Jews" during World War II.[44]

Fast-forwarding to today, India has become one of the biggest countries in the world with many diverse minorities who have been persecuted by right-wing politicians like Narendra Modi (including 230 million-plus Indian Christians & Dalits [known pejoratively as 'Untouchables']). But as one of the poorest minorities in the country known locally as "Hindustan," recent studies have found that two hundred million Indian Muslims are statistically more likely to live in poor villages without schools or medical facilities and less likely to qualify for bank loans simply because of their Islamic faith.

A *New York Times* article once found that Islamophobia within mainstream society in India had become "so rampant that many barely muster outrage when telling of the withdrawn apartment offers, rejected job applications, and turned-down loans that are part of living in the country"[45] as an Indian Muslim today. "Relations between the communities are not normal," Rajiv Shah, former Gujarat political editor for the *Times of India*, once told the *Los Angeles Times*. "There is no interaction between Hindus and Muslims except at very high income levels."[46]

In August 2019, Narendra Modi soared to new right-wing heights when he defied international law yet again by unilaterally changing the status of the Indian-occupied region of Kashmir. An overwhelmingly Muslim region, Modi revoked Articles 370 and 35A of India's Constitution and imposed full draconian anti-Muslim crackdowns across Kashmir. In the nearby eastern Indian state of Assam, Modi's right-wing government separately launched an anti-Muslim disenfranchisement campaign and stripped citizenship rights from nearly four million predominantly Muslim residents with a blatantly discriminatory law called the Citizenship Amendment Act (CAA) in the summer of 2018.

According to Hindi-language news network NDTV India, the really scary part of this fascist trajectory is that Modi's right-wing government shortly thereafter began to build India's first "mass detention center" (which look suspiciously like internment camps to me) for Muslims who were stripped of their Indian citizenship by this absurdly Islamophobic law. According to NDTV India, this massive internment camp would be the "size of seven soccer fields" in total area to house over three thousand newly undocumented (and now stateless asylee) Muslims within these internment camps.[47]

Even Donald Trump couldn't resist visiting his right-wing buddy Narendra Modi during the last year of his presidency in a February 2020 meeting of proud self-proclaimed nationalists. Award-winning Indian Muslim journalist Rana Ayyub wrote in the *Washington Post* that Trump's first stop during his February 2020 visit with Narendra Modi was an ashram where the legendary Mahatma Gandhi once lived.[48]

With no irony whatsoever, Modi allegedly began to tell Trump about the historical significance of Gandhi's peaceful teachings on nonviolence while—at exactly the same time outside in the streets of New Delhi—a violent bloody anti-Muslim pogrom massacre was literally taking place. So while Trump and Modi were inside enjoying their right-wing bromance, global audiences worldwide watched in horror as TV cameras captured dramatic footage of baton-wielding New Delhi police officers and vigilante Hindu mobs targeting Muslims in India's capital city, leaving at least forty-seven people murdered on the streets of New Delhi.[49]

The following day, Trump publicly took the time to defend Narendra Modi's anti-Muslim citizenship bill when he told reporters about the CAA: "I don't want to discuss that. I want to leave that to India." By not even discussing it, Trump tacitly endorsed Modi's anti-Muslim policies and later told the same press corps that Modi was "incredible" on the issue of religious freedom.[50]

Donald Trump ended his February 2020 visit by bizarrely referring to Narendra Modi as "the father of India"; which is an honorific title usually reserved exclusively for Mahatma Gandhi for leading the nonviolent struggle for independence from British super-colonialism to form a secular democratic India.[51]

The complete ideological (and intellectual) opposite of Gandhi, the right-winger Narendra Modi is actually accused by many Indians of trying to establish a Hindu *Rashtra* (a Hindu-centric political state) where Muslims and other persecuted minorities (including the aforementioned 230 million Indian Christians and lower-caste Dalits) would be relegated to second-class citizen status across India.

Even the 2020 COVID-19 pandemic was used as a racist political tool to fan Islamophobia across India. In March 2020, a well-known Islamic missionary organization known as the Tablighi Jamaat (TJ) held a meeting of several thousand members in the capital city of New Delhi at the very beginning of the crisis. Almost immediately, we began to see fake news stories quickly go viral on social media and via Desi WhatsApp groups with silly conspiracy theories claiming Muslims were somehow responsible for the entire COVID-19 pandemic in India.

Understanding the need to publicly debunk this anti-Muslim conspiracy theory once and for all, a prominent four hundred-member group of Indian scientists and medical professionals known nationwide as ISRC (Indian Scientists' Response to COVID-19) quickly issued a public proclamation stating clearly that all "available data does *not* support the speculation" (emphasis added by author) that Muslims were responsible for COVID-19 at all, according to an April 2020 *Guardian* newspaper report.[52]

But sometimes facts do not matter.

Since then, we still saw mainstream Indian media outlets waste precious airtime with bogus stories wrongly asserting that scary Muslim missionaries were somehow coronavirus "super-spreaders." On social media, we saw Twitter hashtags like "#CoronaJihad," "#CoronaTerrorism," and "#CoronaBombsTablighi" trend across India as well. Defying belief, a government-run hospital inside India even publicly admitted to segregating Muslim patients from Hindu patients and then bizarrely claimed that the order came from the Indian government itself.

The *New York Times* further reported that megaphone loudspeakers at some Hindu temples across India were loudly broadcasting messages telling people not to buy milk from Muslim dairy farmers during the 2020 coronavirus pandemic because they wrongfully said it was infected with COVID-19.[53]

The legendary Mahatma Gandhi once famously told his followers "I am a Muslim and a Hindu and a Christian and a Jew—and so are all of you!" to remind them about the beautiful strength of India's diverse social fabric. During his lifetime trying to create a diverse multi-ethnic & multi-religious secular democratic India, the Mahatma (which is a Sanskrit word for "great soul") helped advocate for Hindu-Muslim interfaith harmony, uplifted the plight of lower-caste Dalits (known pejoratively as "Untouchables"), and promoted gender equality throughout South Asia for Desi women of all backgrounds.

But Gandhi's peaceful vision for a diverse, equitable, and inclusive India was shattered forever on January 30, 1948.

While "Bapu Ji" (an honorific title meaning "Dear Father" used by many of his followers) was walking with his beloved grand-nieces to address some followers in the capital city of New Delhi, Mahatma Gandhi was brutally assassinated by a right-wing extremist named Nathuram Godse; a militant Hindutva ideologue who shared a similar political ideology to India's current prime minister, Narendra Modi.

So before we leave the continent of Asia to analyze the Islamophobia of the Western world, in addition to China and Myanmar, let us also never forget that India's current right-wing authoritarian political lurch is slowly turning the world's largest democracy into an illiberal society that would make Mahatma Gandhi roll over in his grave.

We have seen how the first victims of the Christchurch massacre can serve as a prism that shows us how hate against Muslims—baseless hate, with no personal or specific concern attached—is reflected all over the world. But now I want to look specifically at the United States. It is my home country, where I was born and raised. It is also where I am concerned that anti-Muslim hate is poised to explode on a scale never before seen if policies and attitudes are not changed in the near future.

"No other nation on Earth comes close to experiencing the frequency of mass shootings that we see in the United States." These are the words that were written by former US President Barack Obama after two different mass shootings in August 2019; one occurred in in El Paso, Texas, and the other in Dayton, Ohio.[54]

"We should soundly reject language coming out of the mouths of any of our leaders that feeds a climate of fear and hatred or normalizes racist sentiments," Obama continued.

There was a reason for the former president to write in such strident tones. In the first six months of 2019, there were over five hundred bias-motivated attacks on American Muslims and their institutions across the United States.

In May 2019, a New Haven, Connecticut mosque suffered significant damage from an arson attack and a New York

OPEN YOUR EYES!"   41

man was indicted on hate crime charges for allegedly trashing a Queens mosque[55] while spewing an anti-Muslim tirade.

At least one apparent anti-Muslim mosque attack had a direct link to the Christchurch massacre in New Zealand. A few weeks before the 2019 Poway Chabad synagogue attack, an 8chan user scrawled graffiti directly referencing the Christchurch shooter and caused a fire at a nearby Escondido, California mosque.

Just a few weeks later—and only thirteen miles from the Escondido, California mosque—that same 8chan user opened fire at the nearby Poway Chabad synagogue, killing one female Jewish worshipper. In his racist manifesto, the synagogue shooter took credit for the earlier mosque fire in Escondido by providing insider knowledge of the arson in his manifesto.

This is just one example of how hate against Muslims is not only burning out of control in the United States, but also how it threatens to (and does) jump from group to group, in the same way a wild fire can jump from house to house.

According to award-winning British columnist Jeff Sparrow, one reason for this phenomenon is that the ongoing "war on terror" global narrative has effectively normalized anti-Muslim rhetoric, and this rhetoric has replicated "all the traditional tropes of anti-Semitism" that white supremacists had used before.[56] It's just directed against Muslims now. Or, at least, it is at the start.

The Christchurch killer made it clear in his manifesto that his decision to murder Muslims was entirely tactical. He regarded non-whites as "invaders," but chose Muslims simply because the growth of Islamophobia worldwide made them unpopular. He knew this, and he wanted his actions to set off a global conflagration, starting a race war in which whites would fight other ethnic groups. He thought, because of the current political climate, that Muslims were the tinder most likely to burn a global white supremacist fire.

Yet despite its importance, I don't want to give Christchurch "too much credit" either. That is to say, anti-Muslim hate had been simmering for a while, and this has been especially true here in the United States.

The Anti-Defamation League (ADL) has found that the number of white supremacist murders in the United States "more than doubled" in 2017, with far-right extremist groups and white supremacists being responsible for 59 percent of all extremist-related fatalities in the United States (which was nearly a 40 percent increase from the previous year).[57]

One of the worst mass shootings in modern American history took place in October 2017 when a sixty-four-year-old white man named Stephen Paddock killed fifty-eight people (and injured over five hundred others) during an outdoor concert in Las Vegas, Nevada. To this day, it is still unclear what motivated Paddock. A few weeks after the Las Vegas massacre, a twenty-nine-year-old Muslim immigrant from Uzbekistan named Saifullo Saipov killed eight people in lower Manhattan in New York City while allegedly shouting "Allahu Akbar" during his murder spree.

Both of these acts of mass murder were meant to instill terror in the general public, yet only one of them was called "terrorism" in the mainstream media.

Can you guess which one?

Yet there is more than anecdotal evidence to indicate a strong double standard when it comes to identifying terrorism. A 2019 University of Alabama study found that terrorist attacks committed by Muslims currently receive 357 percent more media coverage than those committed by white men.[58] In another media study by Georgia State University, researchers analyzed terrorist attacks in the United States from the years 2011 to 2015 and found that there was a 449 percent increase in media coverage when the perpetrator was Muslim compared to when the perpetrator was a white non-Muslim.[59] This same GSU study found that Muslims committed only 12 percent of attacks during the five-year period studied, but received over 40 percent of total news media coverage during that same time (an over-representation of over 340 percent).[60] In one example, the GSU researchers noted that the 2013 Boston Marathon bombing—which killed a total of three people—received almost 20 percent of all media coverage relating to American terror attacks in that entire five-year period. In contrast, media coverage of the 2012 white supremacist terrorist massacre at the aforementioned Oak Creek, Wisconsin Sikh gurdwara temple—which killed twice as many people as the Boston Marathon attack (six victims)—received only 4 percent of media coverage related to terror attacks during the period studied, even though it had twice as many fatalities.

The ways that our political leaders react to tragedies like this is very important. It sets the tone for many people, and can help define the prism through which such shared tragedies are viewed.

In the aftermath of the 2019 Christchurch massacre, American president Donald Trump was asked if he saw a worrying rise in white supremacy movements around the world. He replied with no irony whatsoever: "I don't really. I think it's a small group of people that have very, very serious problems, I guess."[61]

When I heard that, I thought: *You guess?*

The unwillingness of our American commander-in-chief at the time to unequivocally condemn white supremacists should be deeply worrying because it seems to encourage some violent

right-wing fascists to make the leap from online propaganda
into real-world action (like we saw during the January 2021 violent pro-Trump insurrection at the US Capitol). A few years earlier here in the United States, their sinister efforts saw another
notable violent culmination in the "Unite the Right" rally in
Charlottesville, Virginia in 2017. This event infamously led to
the murder of thirty-two-year-old anti-racist activist Heather
Heyer by a white supremacist from Ohio, who brutally plowed
his car into a group of anti-racist protestors—this horrific event
was captured on video.

"We're going to fulfill the promises of Donald Trump,"
said David Duke, former Imperial Dragon of the Ku Klux Klan
(KKK), speaking at the Charlottesville event. "That's why we
voted for Donald Trump because he said we're going take our
country back and that is what we're going to do. This represents
a turning point for the people of this country. We are determined to take our country back!"

Trump had been claimed by these murdering racists as one
of their own. How would he respond?

In his first press conference after the violence in
Charlottesville, Trump made a very telling statement when he
said: "We condemn in the strongest possible terms this egregious display of hatred, bigotry, and violence on many sides. On
many sides."

Here, I thought to myself: *On many sides?*

It turned out that the twenty-year-old neo-Nazi who
killed Heather Heyer had been open about his racist views
since high school. He attended the march in Virginia with
the white supremacist group known as Vanguard America.
After his capture, he was charged in Virginia state court with
murder and in federal court with hate crimes. However, it

should be noted that he was not charged as a terrorist (despite then-Attorney General Jeff Sessions initially describing the Charlottesville attack as meeting "the definition of domestic terrorism" under federal law). Yet in announcing the federal indictment ten months later, Jeff Sessions avoided using the word "terrorism" altogether. Instead, he said that the Justice Department remained resolute that hateful ideologies will not have the last word and that their adherents will not get away with violent crimes against those they target. Which is all well and good, but not the same as charging someone with terrorism.

In a study by the Southern Poverty Law Center, out of the nine hundred hate crime incidents in the first ten days following Donald Trump's election, it was found that people explicitly invoked Donald Trump's name or his campaign slogans in at least four-in-ten (40 percent) of these crimes.[62] The infamous neo-Nazi protests in Charlottesville were not the first to invoke Trump, and the aftermath did not constitute the first time that Trump had failed miserably to condemn white supremacy on national television.

During a national interview with CNN anchor Jake Tapper in February 2017, Trump refused to condemn the former KKK leader David Duke at least three different times (when he was prompted to comment) during the same interview. When asked by the CNN host point-blank if he would condemn Duke or any other white supremacists, Trump absurdly claimed that he did not know anything about white supremacists or about David Duke himself, and so would be unable to speak intelligently on the topic. When Mr. Tapper pressed him twice more during the same interview, Donald Trump said he could not condemn a group he had not yet researched.

Donald Trump also once famously said that "anyone who cannot name our enemy is not fit to lead this country." In light of his statements giving white supremacists a free pass for their terrorism—by explicitly refusing to name them—there's compelling evidence that he has helped weaponize Islamophobia. By only condemning dark-skinned people and people with minority religions, and by failing to publicly condemn the right-wing racists who terrorize our fellow Americans more and more each year, he has only added fuel to the fire.

But it would be short-sighted to argue that the current wave of hate that culminated with the Christchurch mosque massacre began with Donald Trump. Although he would thankfully lose the 2020 presidential election to Joe Biden, in order to truly understand Donald Trump, we must acknowledge that this right-wing political ideology of "Trumpism" was started long before his presidency from the days of his racist anti-Muslim birther conspiracy theories against a rising black presidential candidate named Barack Hussein Obama.

2

The Republican Jihad of Donald Trump

I think Islam hates us.
—Donald Trump to CNN Host Anderson Cooper[63]

The seventh, eighth, and ninth victims of the 2019 New Zealand mosque massacre were three members of the same family. The patriarch of the family (sixty-six-year-old Mr. Ghulam Hussain) and his sixty-three-year-old wife (Mrs. Karam Bibi)—along with their thirty-eight-year-old son (Mr. Zeeshan Raza)—were all murdered together that fateful day in Christchurch. The father was a retired official with Pakistan International Airlines (PIA), and his wife had recently traveled from their home in Karachi, over eight thousand miles away, to visit their son, a mechanical engineer who had moved to New Zealand only a year before. The tenth victim of the 2019 New Zealand mosque massacre was a sixty-six-year-old man named Muhammad Abdusi Samad. Growing up in humble surroundings in Bangladesh, Mr. Samad ultimately received a scholarship to study in New Zealand where he would earn his PhD at Lincoln University in Christchurch.

While studying for his doctorate, he joined a group of fellow Muslims to build the Al Noor Mosque in Christchurch and even became a volunteer "muezzin" (one who recites the Islamic call to prayer). "It was very important to him to tell them about the compassion and the sympathy of Islam," his son Tariq told the *Dhaka Tribune* in Bangladesh about his father's work with new Muslim converts[64]. After his death, hundreds of his neighbors in Bangladesh formed a human chain in his honor, and he was also publicly honored in far-flung places like Solon, Ohio and even in the remote Canadian province of Nova Scotia.

All these Muslims had become at one in their new home country. It was their home. It was who they were. The kind of bigotry that led to the killings in Christchurch was fueled by the idea that this had not happened. That Muslims can never fully integrate. That they are permanently the "other."

In many ways, the modern-day birth of political Islamophobia started with the 2008 election of a black man named Barack Hussein Obama to the presidency of the United States. Simply because he was African American with an unusual name, the election of the forty-fourth president allowed the forces of hate—as well as many amoral opportunists—to coalesce around a new kind of target. A new kind of "other."

From birther controversies egged on by the likes of Donald Trump, to ridiculous conspiracy theories about his secretly being a crypto-Muslim Manchurian candidate, Obama's election provided a new reason for the contemporary Republican Party to double-down on a political platform that emphasized Islam and Muslims as being un-American.

Few were quicker to see how unfounded criticism and otherness of the new president could be used for personal gain than reality television star Donald J. Trump. Trump was a fierce proponent of the so-called Barack Obama "birther conspiracy"; which is deeply rooted in anti-Muslim animus. Even while he was still the host of the NBC reality show *The Apprentice*, Donald Trump had already begun openly questioning the citizenship (and religion) of Barack Obama. During a March 2011 interview with right-wing radio host Laura Ingraham, Trump bizarrely opined about President Obama's birth certificate: "He doesn't have a birth certificate—or if he does—there's something on that certificate that is very bad for him . . . Perhaps it would be—that where it says 'religion,' it might have 'Muslim' . . . And if you're a Muslim, you don't change your religion, by the way . . ."[65]

In another interview with ABC News' *Good Morning America*, Trump also suggested that Obama was trying to conceal his religion by withholding his birth certificate because "maybe it says he's a Muslim" on it.[66]

Trump was not the only one saying these things, but he was among the most prominent voices. It didn't take much for others to start running with the story. During one of my televised appearances on NBC News' *Meet The Press* to discuss Islamophobia, I told host Chuck Todd and my fellow *Meet The Press* panelists that when there were already whisper campaigns about Barack Obama being some sort of crypto-Muslim Manchurian candidate, we did not see any prominent Republicans condemning these whisper campaigns (and did not until former Republican Secretary of State Colin Powell "actually came on this show [NBC News *Meet The Press*] to tell his fellow Republicans to shut the hell up").[67]

In response to this growing birther controversy, on April 27, 2011, the Obama White House released the long-form birth certificate of President Barack Obama in hopes of shutting the naysayers up, once and for all.[68] Nonetheless, people believed what they wanted to believe, and Donald Trump proved all too happy to continue to dubiously manufacture birther claims against Obama. All of them were deeply rooted in anti-black, Islamophobic-coded language.

"A lot of people do not think it was an authentic certificate. Many people do not think it was authentic," Trump told CNN during a heated exchange with Wolf Blitzer nearly twelve months after the release of Obama's long-form birth certificate.[69]

Perhaps not seeing the underlying danger, from time to time President Obama would address these right-wing carnival barkers in humorous ways. During the 2011 White House Correspondents' Association dinner, President Barack Obama told the packed nerd-prom audience that he would be unveiling his official birth video during the banquet—and then proceeded to show the famous opening scene from Disney's The Lion King to roars of laughter. "Now he can get back to focusing on the issues that matter," Obama pointedly said while Donald Trump grumpily sat in the audience. "Like, did we fake the moon landing? What really happened at Roswell? And where are Biggie and Tupac?"[70]

Yet Trump remained undeterred. A year later, the legendary pop superstar Madonna made what she later called an "ironic" remark on-stage suggesting that Obama was a "black Muslim" during one of her concerts. True to form, Trump wasted no time in pouncing on Twitter: "Does Madonna know something we all don't about Barack? At a concert she said 'we have a black Muslim in the White House.'"[71]

***

The eleventh victim of the 2019 New Zealand mosque massacre was a sixty-five-year-old man named Maheboob Khokhar.

THE REPUBLICAN JIHAD OF DONALD TRUMP 51

According to Radio New Zealand, Mr. Khokhar had been visiting his son's family in Christchurch for the first time when he was killed. He had only been two days away from returning to his native India. "Just two more days to go and this happened," his daughter-in-law told reporters after the massacre. "Sometimes we wish we never woke him, let him sleep and miss the Friday prayers, but he loved going to the mosque."[72]

Mr. Khokhar's fate showed the true perversion and horror of the white-supremacist terrorist creed. The extent of the damage that "othering" can do. Mr. Khokhar did not fit into the Great Replacement narrative. He was not in New Zealand to change the culture and outbreed white people. He was a tourist visiting family. Yet, for this, he was killed just as sure as all the others.

***

For opportunists like Donald Trump who were more than willing to use racism as a tool to gain power, such distinctions are likewise meaningless. There are only two kinds of people—us and them. And anything that might qualify you to move over to "them" can be anything a racist wants it to be.

As it turned out, Trump's hurtful and baseless questions about Obama's birth certificate had been only the opening sortie. During the 2016 presidential election, Trump would take his anti-Muslim jihad to new lows. During a presidential candidate forum in Iowa, Trump said of President Obama: "I don't know if he loves America." Trump was also widely criticized by the media for failing to correct a Republican supporter who publicly said that Obama was a Muslim during a September 2015 campaign rally in New Hampshire. "We have a problem in this country. It's called Muslims," the Trump supporter said into a microphone during the rally. "You know our current president [Obama] is one [a Muslim]. You know, he's not even an American. We have training camps growing where they want to kill us. That's my question: When can we get rid of them [Muslims]?"

"We need this question," Donald Trump immediately responded, chuckling. "We're going to be looking at a lot of different things," he continued. "You know, a lot of people are saying that bad things are happening. We're going to be looking at that and many other things."

To the shock of many—but to the great delight of the crowd in the immediate vicinity—Trump seemed to be hinting that he found his supporters' ideas about expelling Muslims from America to be a reasonable one. Sadly, this metastasizing growth of Islamophobic rhetoric resonated with many conservative voters.

A May 2016 opinion survey from Public Policy Polling (PPP) showed that nearly two-thirds (65 percent) of Trump supporters believe that Barack Obama is a Muslim (with only 13 percent correctly indicating that he is a Christian). Similarly, this PPP poll found that nearly 60 percent of Trump supporters still believed the birther conspiracy theories holding that President Obama was not born in the United States (with only 23 percent correctly believing otherwise). And further illustrating how detached from reality this demographic had become, the poll also found the following: that 27 percent of Trump supporters think that vaccines cause autism; that nearly one-in-four (24 percent) believe that the late Supreme Court justice Antonin Scalia was murdered; and that nearly one-in-ten (7 percent) believe that Senator Ted Cruz's father was somehow involved in the JFK assassination (with another 38 percent being "unsure" about his involvement in the assassination of President Kennedy).[73]

This is astonishing and disheartening. Trump is too canny not to have understood what he was doing. There was clearly a sizable demographic of gullible, confused, mistaken people who were apt to believe falsehoods. Trump was going to provide those falsehoods in such a way that he would win the presidency.

Even before his infamous "Muslim travel bans," the future president began diversifying his Islamophobic bona fides while still on the campaign trail. He called for increased surveillance of American mosques and also for creating a national database of American Muslims. During a November 2015 rally in Alabama—which famously included a physical altercation between an African American protester and several white Trump supporters—the Republican front-runner suggested that law enforcement should monitor Islamic houses of worship across America. Needless to say, this type of surveillance based solely on religious affiliation would obviously chill the First Amendment rights of millions of American Muslims.

Trump did not care.

"I want surveillance of certain mosques, if that's okay," Trump told the cheering Alabama crowd that day.[74]

He would double-down on these statements later in his campaign when he told FOX News Channel that, "We have to be very strong in terms of looking at the mosques." During another Trump campaign rally in Atlanta, he told the raucous crowd that, "We have to go and maybe check the mosques," as thousands of people cheered.[75]

Long before the neo-Nazi protests in Charlottesville, Virginia, in which he failed to condemn white supremacists, Trump had already begun creeping toward Godwin's Law—the maxim that someone will eventually be compared to Hitler if they are discussed online for long enough—when he reaffirmed for NBC News that he would like to require nearly ten million

American Muslims to register with a national database to monitor their movements. When he was asked whether Muslims would be legally obligated to sign into the database, Trump responded: "They have to be; they have to be."[76]

In response to this policy proposal, Trump was repeatedly asked to explain the difference between requiring Muslims to register for a national database and the World War II parallel of requiring all Jewish people to register with the Nazi German government. He simply replied four times: "You tell me." It was as though he believed the answer was obvious, but just beyond his ability to grasp.

Not all Republicans agreed with Trump or the political tactics he was using. One of Trump's Republican primary opponents, former Florida Governor Jeb Bush, called Trump's statements about Muslims "just wrong" during a nationally-televised interview.

"You talk about internment; you talk about closing mosques; you talk about registering [Muslim] people . . . That's just wrong," he told CNBC. "I don't care about campaigns. It's not a question of toughness. It's trying to manipulate people's angst and their fears. That's not strength. That's weakness."[77]

On the other side of the political aisle, Democratic presidential candidate Hillary Clinton immediately condemned Trump's Islamophobic proposals when she told her seventeen million Twitter followers that, "This is shocking rhetoric. It should be denounced by all seeking to lead this country."[78]

***

The twelfth victim of the 2019 New Zealand mosque massacre was a sixty-five-year-old man named Ali Elmadani. A retired electrical engineer born in the Palestinian territories,

Mr. Elmadani moved to Christchurch from the United Arab Emirates in 1998. During a vigil commemorating the fifty-one victims of the attack, Mr. Elmadani's daughter told the audience that her family was not angry at the white supremacist who had committed these crimes, because Islam does not teach vengeance. She also said she took comfort knowing that her father died in a place that meant the world to him. "I'm glad that's where he died. . ." his daughter told the crowd. "Surrounded by his friends and God."

***

Whether Muslim terrorists arise from a rare and criminal perversion of a peaceful faith is something that Trump and his supporters seem fundamentally incurious about. A comprehensive survey on Islamophobia by the Bridge Initiative at Georgetown University (where—full disclosure—I have served as a senior research fellow) found that Trump's anti-Muslim rhetoric led Americans to feel more hostility toward Muslims than any other religious group in the United States.[79]

And even before Trump entered the White House, a February 2016 Pew Research Center study found that almost half of Americans viewed Muslims negatively and that nearly half (49 percent) believed that "some Muslims in the U.S. are anti-American" and therefore untrustworthy, simply because of their faith.[80]

During the first year of Trump's presidency, I attended the Washington, DC launch of the Pew Research Center's nationwide study on the state of American Muslims under President Trump. The comprehensive 192-page study entitled "U.S. Muslims Concerned About Their Place in Society, but Continue to Believe in the American Dream" was the result of over forty thousand phone calls made in four different languages (English, Arabic, Farsi, and Urdu) to members of the American Muslim community.[81] Overall, the study found that Muslims were quite happy with their individual lives as Americans; but they were profoundly concerned about how Muslims were viewed by our elected leaders and by American society at the national level.

Additional key findings from this major Pew report included that—despite their generally positive attitude toward the American experience—nearly two-thirds of Muslim-Americans (64 perecent) felt dissatisfied with "the way things are going in the U.S. today" and that nearly three-quarters (74 percent) agreed that Donald Trump was unfriendly toward Muslims in America. Illustrating the real-life impact of Islamophobia on the lives of everyday Americans, the Pew researchers also found that nearly half (48 percent) of American Muslims said that they had personally experienced at least one incident of anti-Muslim discrimination in the past twelve months.

One of the few silver linings of this Pew study was that, alongside the reports of discrimination, nearly half of Muslims surveyed (49 percent) said that someone had expressed positive support for them because of their religion as well. The study also found that 55 percent of Muslims think Americans in general are friendly toward US Muslims (compared with just 14 percent who replied that Americans are unfriendly toward people of the Islamic faith).

It was an important study, and a lot to digest. For me personally, it showed we are perhaps at a tipping point. Despite all of the hate and bigotry used to propel Trump into office, American Muslims still have a rosy view of America as a whole. They believe in the American Dream, and still think it is possible to come here and have a good life and share in the bounty that America has to offer. At the same time, American Muslims showed that they are not deaf and blind either. They have heard and seen the things that Trump and his supporters have been saying, and it has hurt them. They are not made of stone. They are people. And while I do not believe they have yet been hurt irreparably, it is clear that racialized wounds sustained on presidential election campaign trails are quite real in their overall impact.

"On the one hand, this Pew report confirmed what should be obvious; Muslim Americans have experienced more discrimination since Donald Trump has assumed the presidency," confirmed Georgetown University Professor John Esposito. "This is not surprising when one remembers Trump's infamous statement to CNN's Anderson Cooper that 'Islam hates us' or his proposed Muslim Ban or numerous members of the Trump White House who said that Islam is not a religion and that Muslims cannot be loyal Americans."[82]

Yet, again, even in the face of this growing Islamophobia, the Pew study found that over 90 percent of respondents were jointly proud to be Muslim and American together.

In my opinion, this should destroy any misguided notion that Muslims cannot be loyal Americans as well. Yet these facts are up against the ideas and stereotypes that Trump has employed so effectively—and for so long—to characterize Muslims and Muslim Americans as an unfeeling "other" that cannot possibly have the same hopes for the American Dream as other Americans.

***

The thirteenth victim of the 2019 New Zealand massacre was a sixty-four-year-old woman named Linda Armstrong. A third-generation New Zealander, Mrs. Armstrong had converted to

Islam in her fifties, according to her family. "Linda had a huge heart and was willing to help out anyone who needed it, including travelers, immigrants, and refugees," the Armstrong family said in a statement after the shooting.

***

Supporting travelers, immigrants, and refugees. These are notions antithetical to Donald Trump and his masters.

Before becoming a chief mastermind at the Trump White House, former Breitbart executive chairman Steve Bannon once wrote a terribly racist movie script warning about the possibility of a future "Islamic States of America" in a bizarre film project that he called *Destroying the Great Satan: The Rise of Islamic Fascism in America.*

The *Washington Post* reported that the first scene of Bannon's unspeakably-racist movie opened with a fictitious scene of the US Capitol broadcasting the Islamic call to prayer whilst a crescent-and-star Islamic flag victoriously flies above the capitol rotunda.[83] This blatantly anti-Muslim movie project imagined a fundamental clash of civilizations between the West and Islam . . . and this was according to Steve Bannon himself.

"Islam is not a religion of peace" is just one of the many ridiculously anti-Muslim public statements that Steve Bannon has made—repeatedly and publicly—throughout his life.[84] And it would only be ridiculous if it were not also so hurtful. Bannon also once referred to Islam as the "most radical" religion in the world, and said that America is engaged in a civilizational struggle potentially leading to "a major shooting war in the Middle East" against Muslims.[85] Again, equal parts ridiculous and dangerous.

Steve Bannon has described Breitbart as "the platform for the alt-right"[86] and he regularly told listeners on the *Breitbart News Daily* radio show that we were engaged in a "global existential war" against Islam. He has also repeated claims that a "fifth column" of American Muslims had infiltrated the highest echelons of the US government, promoting the absurd "dual-loyalty" racist trope which many Jewish and Muslim (and before that, Catholic) Americans have faced in the past.[87]

One of Bannon's regular Breitbart Radio guests was long-time Trump surrogate Roger Stone, who also habitually warned of a future America "where hordes of Islamic madmen are raping, killing, pillaging, defecating in public fountains, harassing private citizens, elderly people; that's what's coming."[88]

There was no basis to these claims, yet that did not stop Stone from making them, Bannon from broadcasting them, or Donald Trump from riding them into the White House.

Another of Bannon's frequent guests was Pamela Geller—the president of Stop Islamization of America—whom he once described as "one of the top world experts on Islamic supremacism." Yet to get just one contrary opinion, the Southern Poverty Law Center (SPLC) reckons instead that Geller is the "anti-Muslim movement's most visible and flamboyant figurehead." She once publicly suggested on Bannon's show that Barack Obama's former CIA Director John Brennan might have secretly converted to Islam, without any proof whatsoever for this ridiculous claim.[89]

And on it went.

Needless to say, Steve Bannon never pushed back against any of these unfounded Islamophobic claims during his Breitbart tenure. Of course, it should also be noted that Bannon has not limited his hateful views exclusively toward Muslims. To illustrate just a handful of Bannon's other noxious views, his own ex-wife once affirmed for a court that Steve Bannon did not want his daughters "going to school with Jews" whom he referred to as "whiny brats." And his former screenwriting partner also once told *New Yorker* magazine that Bannon admired the documentary films made by the Nazi propagandist Leni Riefenstahl.[90] I think this admiration for Nazi propaganda makes sense in Bannon's case. He produced advertisements for Trump's presidential campaign using images and rhetoric that "anti-Semites have used for ages," according to the Anti-Defamation League.[91] He also once suggested that disenfranchising black voters might not be "such a bad thing,"[92] and even once proclaimed that he wanted female politicians who lead America to "be feminine" rather than "a bunch of dykes."[93]

It's clear that Bannon has a view of how Americans are "supposed" to be, and that he is willing to go to war against anyone who diverges from it in any way.

"I think that's excellent," former KKK leader David Duke told CNN after Trump announced that Steve Bannon would be his first Chief White House Strategist. "You have an individual—Mr. Bannon—who's basically creating the ideological aspects of where we [white supremacists] are going," the former Imperial Wizard of the Ku Klux Klan further added. "And ideology ultimately is the most important aspect of any government."[94]

In August 2017, Bannon finally left Donald Trump's White House to retake the helm as executive chairman of Breitbart News (and, finally, left Breitbart in January 2018 to pursue other projects). Instead of being humbled by his time as a public servant, Bannon actually seemed more emboldened.

"I feel jacked up!" Bannon once told the conservative *Weekly Standard* shortly after his departure from the White House.[95] "Now I'm free! I've got my hands back on my weapons.

I am definitely going to crush the opposition! There's no doubt, I built a fucking machine at Breitbart and we're about to rev that machine up, and rev it up we will do!"

We live in a world where men like Bannon have walked the corridors of power, and have been set loose to once more rain hate and divisiveness on the populace. He—and Trump's entire team of "deplorables"—have shown they were willing to use the ugliest stereotypes, lie often and wildly, and to create scapegoats whenever it suits their political purposes.

***

The fourteenth victim of the 2019 New Zealand mosque massacre was a sixty-three-year-old man named Mohsin Al-Harbi. A part-time imam who sometimes delivered the *jummah khutba* (Friday sermon), his employer remembered him as a "kind and caring Kiwi" and said that he decided to hire Mr. Al-Harbi because the former vacuum salesman had brought a twenty-year-old certificate from a previous employer to his job interview showing that he was the #1 vacuum cleaner salesman in the world for that company. During the chaotic aftermath of the mosque massacre, Mr. Al-Harbi's distraught wife frantically searched for her husband in the mosque and, overwhelmed by the horrific carnage, collapsed—having suffered a heart attack upon seeing her husband's lifeless body.

Hate, you see, is like a virus. It creates ripples that emanate out from those it touches directly. Though one may be targeted directly, the impacts—sometimes powerful ones—are felt by many, many others.

***

Sebastian Gorka is a Hungarian-American right-wing political activist with shady academic credentials. He went from being Steve Bannon's national security editor at Breitbart News to deputy assistant to President Donald Trump. After Trump's inauguration, Gorka received widespread condemnation for wearing a medal for the Vitezi Rend, a right-wing fascist Hungarian military organization that supported the Nazis during World War II, at Trump's inaugural balls. According to an NBC News report, at least three people (including one of Gorka's former political allies) have confirmed that he was an active member of Vitezi Rend when he lived in Hungary.[96] In addition to the inaugural balls, Gorka also wore that same controversial pro-Nazi medal during a nationally-televised interview with Sean Hannity on the FOX News Channel.[97] Although he had always denied any direct links to pro-Nazi groups, the Forward newspaper (formerly known as the *Jewish Daily Forward*) reported in April 2017 that Gorka had publicly supported a "violent racist and anti-Semitic paramilitary militia" organization in Hungary before it was later outlawed by multiple European court rulings.[98]

As you might imagine, the Islamophobia of Sebastian Gorka is about as evident as his anti-Semitism. He is a vocal supporter of Trump's infamous "Muslim Travel Bans." The *New York Times* reported that Gorka also stated that "violence is a fundamental part of Islam and emanates from the language of the Quran" itself.[99] This is not just dangerous for American Muslims, but for the country as a whole. A *Washington Post* article about Gorka's anti-Muslim ideology noted that most US counterterrorism experts dismiss Gorka's ideas on Islam as a dangerous oversimplification that could alienate Muslim allies and actually potentially boost recruitment for terrorist groups.

"He's nuts." This is former CIA terrorism analyst Cindy Storer's take regarding Gorka's views on Muslims.[100] "He thinks the government and intelligence agencies don't know anything about radicalization, but the government knows a lot and thinks he's nuts," she told the *Washington Post*.[101]

Further, in an opinion editorial for the *New York Times* piece called "The Islamophobic Huckster in The White House," two former Obama Administration counterterrorism experts wrote that the Trump administration has "framed Islam as an enemy ideology" and predicted a historic clash of civilizations, and that "Gorka is the expert they have empowered to translate their prediction into national strategy." The article also noted that "like the recently fired national security adviser Michael Flynn [who once referred to Islam as a 'cancer'], Mr. Gorka sees Islam as the problem. Declaring a religious war now would only validate the jihadist narrative," the Obama administration officials concluded.[102]

When it comes to American Muslims, Gorka has called the racial profiling of his fellow Americans "common sense" if they are Muslim, and has also accused mainstream American Muslim civic organizations of using "subversive tactics" to further nonspecific nefarious ends (without offering any proof or explanation).[103] Finally, he has defended the Muslim Travel Bans by asserting that the United States is "a Judeo-Christian nation" and that accepting Muslim refugees would be "national suicide" for America.[104]

How? Why? On what grounds? Gorka and his ilk never provide details or explanation. Perhaps this is because they have noticed that they do not have to. They have a ready-made, built-in audience that seems always willing to believe.

According to several law enforcement officials who attended an August 2016 lecture by Sebastian Gorka on Islam and Muslims, FBI agents who were present were disturbed to hear a racist diatribe from Gorka against Muslims during what was supposed to be a counterterrorism presentation. Gorka apparently told attendees at the Joint Terrorism Operations Course—an introductory-level class for participants in the FBI's Joint Terrorism Task Force (JTTF)—that "all Muslims adhere to Sharia law" and that, furthermore, law enforcement officials should be aware that there is "no such thing as 'mainstream Muslims.'"

Because of his naked Islamophobia, the FBI ended its contract with Gorka before he joined the White House as a senior presidential adviser to Donald Trump.[105] According to a *Wall Street Journal* report, it was estimated that Gorka had still received over a hundred thousand dollars from the FBI for his anti-Muslim "trainings" between 2012 and 2016.[106]

"The FBI promised to strengthen its counterterrorism training by properly vetting its instructors after a previous era of biased anti-Muslim training," according to former FBI special agent Mike German. "If Gorka is the type of instructor the FBI selects for these assignments under its new protocols, it shouldn't be surprising that Muslims remain a target of inappropriate law-enforcement attention."[107]

Like his former Breitbart boss Steve Bannon, Gorka resigned from his position at the White House with relative speed. In his resignation letter, Gorka wrote that "given recent events, it is clear to me that forces that do not support the MAGA ["Make America Great Again"] promise are—for now—ascendant within the White House." He also made quite clear that Donald Trump's August 2017 speech on Afghanistan had not been anti-Muslim enough for his liking.

"The fact that those who drafted and approved the speech removed any mention of 'Radical Islam' or 'radical Islamic terrorism' proves that a crucial element of your presidential campaign has been lost," Gorka also wrote in his resignation letter.

"As a result, the best and most effective way I can support you, Mr. President, is from outside the People's House."

***

The fifteenth victim of the 2019 New Zealand mosque massacre was a sixty-one-year-old man named Ashraf Ali. A resident of Christchurch for nearly twenty years, Mr. Ali was a regular worshiper at the Al Noor Mosque where he met his untimely demise that fateful day, along with fifty other innocent victims. One of several Fiji nationals slaughtered that day, his brother fondly remembered him as a "loving and caring man" who surrounded himself with good people and rarely missed an opportunity to offer regular daily prayers at his beloved Christchurch mosque.[108]

***

The question of who we do, or don't, keep company with can say a lot about us. There are those we may have to associate with—at our jobs, in our neighborhoods—and then there are more elective choices. It is telling that Trump's associations with the unofficial ministry of hate went well outside of White House grounds.

Beyond his immediate professional advisors, Trump also surrounded himself with entire constellations of professional Islamophobes—the kind of people who sought to promote Samuel Huntington's archaic "clash of civilizations" theory through anti-Muslim activism. One of these polemicists is Frank Gaffney, the founder of the Center for Security Policy (CSP). While the name is benign-sounding enough, in actuality the organization is a right-wing hack policy shop for peddling anti-Muslim conspiracy theories. On two different occasions, the Southern Poverty Law Center (SPLC) has called Frank Gaffney "one of America's most notorious Islamophobes"[109] and also labeled Gaffney as an "anti-Muslim extremist."[110] According to Georgetown University's Bridge Initiative, Steve Bannon once referred to Frank Gaffney as an "expert on Islam."[111] If this is the kind of perspective that Trump's administration wants to credit as "expert," then these are dark times indeed. Nonetheless, Gaffney has appeared on Bannon's radio show over twenty-five times. And it's not just Trump. Senator Ted Cruz (R-TX) once told reporters that Frank Gaffney would be on his national security advisors team because he considered Gaffney to be a "patriot" who was "clear-eyed about radical Islamic terrorism."[112]

According to my dear friend Peter Beinart in *The Atlantic*, Trump frequently cited Frank Gaffney's right-wing think tank whenever justifying his policies toward Muslims.[113]

And Trump made clear that Gaffney is not just a source, but a man to whom deference and respect should be shown.

Trump's first attorney general—former Alabama Republican Senator Jeff Sessions —once said that "Sharia law fundamentally conflicts with our magnificent constitutional order" while receiving the 2015 'Keeper of the Flame Award' from Frank Gaffney's organization.[114]

And the secretary of state under Donald Trump—former right-wing Kansas congressman Mike Pompeo—appeared on Gaffney's right-wing radio program more than twenty-four times since 2013. (Sebastian Gorka has appeared on Gaffney's radio program at least seventeen times, according to *The Atlantic*.)

Why does Trump demand that his servants show deference to this man? It is, I think, a sign of how useful Trump found Gaffney's ability to heap blame for everything on the heads of Muslims.

Gaffney has publicly refused to say whether he even considers Islam to be a religion at all.[115] During the Obama administration, he had the audacity to author a column entitled "America's First Muslim President?" in which he asserted that there is "mounting evidence" that President Obama is not only sympathetic to Muslims, but that he "actually may still be one himself." Gaffney concluded that Obama was engaged in "the most consequential bait-and-switch since Adolf Hitler duped Neville Chamberlain" in that same unhinged column.[116]

A man who will do and say anything, no matter how outrageous. . . Perhaps Donald Trump can relate.

Yet not everyone on Trump's side of the aisle is comfortable with Gaffney. The Conservative Political Action Conference (CPAC) banned him from attending their annual event following baseless attacks on two of its board members; out of thin air, Gaffney had accused them of being part of the Muslim Brotherhood.

The insanity does not stop there.

A *Vanity Fair* article reported that Gaffney has also publicly accused longtime Hillary Clinton aide Huma Abedin (who is Muslim) of sharing sympathies with Muslim terrorists. He even once called for congressional investigations against Muslim government employees whom he claimed to know were plotting a "civilization jihad" against America as some kind of bizarre fifth column.[117] During an MSNBC interview, Gaffney once claimed that former Iraqi dictator Saddam Hussein was behind the 1995 Oklahoma City bombing (even though it was actually a right-wing white supremacist named Timothy McVeigh who committed the worst pre-9/11 terrorist attack ever on American soil). In 2016, Gaffney hosted prominent white supremacist Jared Taylor on his radio show to discuss Muslim immigration. (Later, he claimed that he had no idea about his guest's white supremacist views, even though he had literally introduced his guest as "the author of six books" —including *White Identity*— which should have probably given things away).[118]

In his most extreme, Gaffney has used nakedly genocidal language against Muslims. He once told the *New York Times* that he considered Muslims to be "termites that hollow out the structure of the civil society." For any student of history, this dehumanizing rhetoric is eerily similar to the genocidal anti-Semitic rhetoric employed by Adolf Hitler's allies in the build-up to the Holocaust.[119] (In prior interviews, Gaffney had also referred to Muslims as "parasitic vermin," "rats," and as being "subhuman" without any sense of historical irony whatsoever.[120])

These are Trump's friends. There was a whole constellation of them circling him when he was president. Gaffney is just one.

***

The sixteenth victim of the 2019 New Zealand mosque massacre was a sixty-year-old man named Abdelfattah Qasem. Before serving as the board secretary for the Muslim Association of Canterbury in New Zealand, Mr. Qasem had spent much of his life in Kuwait before moving his family to New Zealand in the early 1990s during the first Gulf War, seeking a more secure place to raise his children. After the massacre, his family members remembered him as a "very happy person" who helped refugees and immigrants with language translation services upon their arrival to New Zealand.

***

Helping others. A chance to learn the language and integrate. Not in Trump's America.

One of the chief architects of Executive Order 13769 (more commonly referred to as the first "Muslim Travel Ban") was a relatively unknown thirty-something former congressional staffer named Stephen Miller. Along with Steve Bannon, Miller is credited with contributing the more radical and xenophobic lines to Trump's inaugural address outlining a civilizational clash against Muslims. In the address, Trump infamously declared: "We will unite the civilized world against radical Islamic terrorism, which we will eradicate from the face of the Earth."[121]

Trump was the one speaking, but the lines were all Bannon and Miller. We've talked about Bannon, but who is Miller, and, more importantly, why would Trump choose to surround himself with such a person?

Miller began his right-wing conservatism at an early age; his anti-Muslim views can be traced back to his high school days in southern California. Miller once wrote an editorial for his high school paper criticizing his school's ostensible philosophy of nonviolence. Young Miller wrote that "Osama Bin Laden would feel very welcome here."[122]

During his college years, Stephen Miller's opposition to Islam and multiculturalism also drew him into the orbit of infamous neo-Nazi Richard Spencer—a prominent white supremacist who had called for the "peaceful ethnic cleansing" of nonwhites and who was one of the lead architects of the infamous 2017 neo-Nazi protests in Charlottesville, Virginia.

Both Stephen Miller and Richard Spencer attended Duke University together, with the latter referring to himself as a "mentor" to Miller during their college days.[123] Spencer told The Atlantic that the two of them socialized as members of Duke University's conservative union; while Miller was an undergraduate and Spencer was a graduate student.[124] "I spent a lot of time with him at Duke," the neo-Nazi leader reminisced fondly about Miller.[125] "I hope I expanded his thinking."

"It's funny no one's picked up on the Stephen Miller connection [with me]," Spencer once candidly admitted to *Mother Jones* magazine during a sit-down interview.[126] "I knew him very well when I was at Duke. But I am kind of glad no one's talked about this because I don't want to harm Trump," the prominent white supremacist admitted.

(Miller's time at Duke was clearly formative for him, and it's evident that he understands the importance of college campus culture. Miller has worked with David Horowitz—once referred to as the "godfather of the anti-Muslim movement" by the Southern Poverty Law Center —to help organize an "Islamo-Fascism Awareness Week" on college campuses across the nation.[127])

After graduating from Duke, Stephen Miller got a job in the office of Republican Alabama Senator (and future Trump attorney general) Jeff Sessions. Before his stint with the right-wing Alabama senator, Miller also served as press secretary to former right-wing congresswoman Michele Bachmann (one of the founding members of the House Tea Party Caucus).[128]

Possibly fueled by Miller, Bachmann made global headlines for launching a public anti-Muslim witch hunt against then-Secretary of State Hillary Clinton's chief aide, Huma Abedin. Falsely charging that Ms. Abedin had ties to Egypt's Muslim Brotherhood, Bachmann questioned whether she was part of a nefarious "Muslim Mafia" conspiracy to harm the United States by influencing US foreign policy.

In an unprecedented rebuke by a prominent member of her own party, the late Senator John McCain (R-AZ) took to the Senate floor to forcefully condemn Bachmann when he said that Huma Abedin "represents what is best about America: the daughter of [Muslim] immigrants, who has risen to the highest levels of our government on the basis of her substantial personal merit and her abiding commitment to the American ideals that she embodies so fully. I am proud to know Huma and to call her my friend," John McCain told his Senate colleague that day. He continued his principled defense of Abedin by calling her "an intelligent, upstanding, hard-working and loyal servant of our country. These sinister accusations, these attacks on Huma have no logic, no basis and no merit and they need to stop now!"[129]

Nonetheless, Miller persisted.

Serving as one of Trump's primary speechwriters during a high-profile visit to Saudi Arabia in May 2017, Miller prepared to help Trump lecture over fifty leaders from Muslim-majority countries . . . about their religion of Islam! As political columnist Ed Kilgore from *New York Magazine* put it bluntly: "Yes, that's right: The president, a man who has espoused openly Islamophobic views and is known for his less-than-subtle thinking and speaking, will go to the birthplace of the religion, as a guest of a regime whose entire legitimacy derives from its role as the guardian of Islam's Holy Places, and presume to lecture Muslims on their obligation to fight 'radical Islam.'"[130]

And, of course, this was just what Trump did, seeking to harangue the Muslim leaders using language composed by an Islamophobic white supremacist. The lasting impact on the United States and its relationship with the Muslim nations cannot yet be fully known. But I'll tell you one thing: it didn't help the cause of peace.

According to *Politico*, both Steve Bannon and Stephen Miller worked collaboratively to design and implement the controversial 2017 Muslim Travel Ban. In response to the near-unanimous condemnation of the Ban within media and political circles, instead of humbling himself in the face of mounting political and legal opposition, Stephen Miller had the audacity to appear on the CBS News program *Face The Nation* and make a bizarre authoritarian declaration: "Our opponents, the media and the whole world, will soon see as we begin to take further actions that the powers of the president to protect our country are very substantial and will not be questioned!"[131]

Here, perhaps, is an important clue. A lack of questions. Trump did not like to be questioned. We wonder why he surrounded himself with men like Miller and Bannon. The answer may be found in their own words. Miller and Bannon created policies designed to inflame the base and consolidate the president's power. And they never, ever questioned him.

***

The seventeenth victim of the 2019 New Zealand mosque massacre was a sixty-year-old man named Musa Vali Suleman Patel. As a longtime imam (or "prayer leader") in the southern Pacific archipelago nation of Fiji, Mr. Patel was described as a selfless leader by friends and colleagues. Upon hearing of his death, his cousin told a British newspaper, "We can't believe it. He chose New Zealand because he believed New Zealand was the safest place in the world."[132]

People generally choose safety. This is not a trait unique to members of any race or religion. People want safety and security for themselves, but also for their families. And giving people what they want is certainly a route to power. Nations like to have leaders who are strong protectors. And for all of recorded history, opportunists like Trump have understood that they can rise on promises to protect their people from imagined threats just as much as from real ones.

***

During his 2016 presidential campaign, we saw Donald Trump at various times promise to ban all Muslims from America, refer to Mexicans as "rapists," and cast a wide variety of aspersions on people from other cultures.

Shortly after taking office, Trump made international headlines by issuing an executive order entitled "Protecting the Nation from Foreign Terrorist Entry in the United States", a.k.a.: the Muslim Travel Ban.[133] Notice that the first word of the title invokes protection. He had promised to protect the nation if elected, and now he wanted to provide evidence of taking swift action to keep his campaign promises. But what, exactly, would his new measure do?

In the first iteration of the Ban, Trump's executive order temporarily suspended all US refugee admissions and halted immigration from seven Muslim-majority countries: Syria, Yemen, Somalia, Sudan, Iraq, Iran, and Libya. Further, this initial Ban also established a "religious test" for refugees as the Trump administration ordered that Christians (and other religions) be granted priority for resettlement over Muslims.[134]

The spirit was there—albeit, a racist spirit—but the execution left much to be desired. Furthermore, Trump seemed not to have anticipated the sheer amount of resistance the Muslim Ban would get.

The Ban's haphazard implementation resulted in great confusion and chaos at airports across America. As a nationwide rebuke, thousands of vocal, anti-Trump protestors flocked to pro-immigrant rallies at major international airports across America in a show of solidarity with Muslims, Muslim refugees, and other refugees alike. Hundreds of immigration lawyers and prominent human rights organizations offered free legal counsel for impacted Muslims. Challenges within federal courts were immediately filed.

The American Civil Liberties Union (ACLU) sued Donald Trump on behalf of refugee resettlement organizations, charging that the Ban violated the First Amendment's prohibition of government establishment of religion, and also the Fifth Amendment's guarantee of equal treatment under the law.[135] Across the nation, hundreds of immigration attorneys volunteered their time to challenge what they considered to be an unconstitutional order,[136] and soon the matter was presented to federal courts in New York and Virginia where judges ordered a temporary halt.[137] Around the same time, there were at least three other federal judges who upheld the temporary ruling against the initial Ban as well.[138]

Many of Trump's supporters claimed that the order was not a "Muslim Ban" at all, because it was simply meant to protect the American public from people who originate in "terror prone" countries. Yet even Trump surrogate Rudy Giuliani admitted on national television that the president had asked him explicitly how he could make his Muslim ban legal and constitutional despite this being the case.

"I'll tell you the whole history of it . . . When he first announced it, he said 'Muslim Ban,'" admitted Giuliani during a televised interview with FOX News Channel.[139] "He called me up; he said, 'Put a commission together, show me the right way to do it legally,'" explained Giuliani.

Though it does not decrease the hurt and damage done to American Muslims—and to anyone who values a just and free society—it does provide insight into the ethos behind it.

"Donald J. Trump is calling for a total and complete shutdown of Muslims entering the United States until our country's representatives can figure out what the hell is going on!" Trump had proudly proclaimed in the third person during a 2015 South Carolina presidential campaign rally. Sound bites like these, of which there are many, allow us to make the case that he has long wanted to ban Muslims from entering the United States simply because of their religion.[140] Lest it appear that men like Bannon and Miller are the only ones who have pushed Trump in this direction, it should be clear that Trump himself had already been headed in this direction for more than half a decade. And whether this language is purely tactical, or really does reveal what's in Trump's heart-of-hearts, he has been passionate enough not to let his unconstitutional, xenophobic dream die without a fight.

About a month after the first legal defeat of Trump's Muslim Travel Ban on March 6, 2017, Donald Trump issued a second revised executive order called "Protecting the Nation from Foreign Terrorist Entry into the United States," which revoked and replaced the earlier order.[141] This new order (sometimes jocularly known as "Muslim Ban 2.0") prohibited entry into the United States by immigrants and visitors from six Muslim-majority countries (Syria, Iran, Libya, Somalia, Sudan, and Yemen). However, the seventh country, Iraq, was removed. The Trump administration said that this was because Iraq had complied with a [arbitrary and asinine, in my opinion] set of rules designed to allow states to apply to be removed from the list.

In response to Muslim Ban 2.0, the American Immigration Lawyers Association (AILA) released a statement asserting that this latest Muslim ban "will not make us safer as a nation, and thousands of refugees who have been screened for resettlement will be trapped in dangerous conditions."[142] The states of Washington, California, Hawaii, Maryland, Massachusetts, New York, and Oregon all filed lawsuits asking federal judges to stop the new order from taking effect (which it was scheduled to do on March 16, 2017).

In addition to removing Iraq from the list of banned countries, Muslim Ban 2.0 also exempted those who already had visas and green cards from the ban. However, most legal experts believed that the rule still constituted "religious discrimination" and should still be considered unconstitutional. ACLU national legal director and Georgetown University Law Professor David Cole was among many voicing this position.[143]

This attempt to redo the ban upset me personally, and I did my best to make clear why it was not appropriate.

"Donald Trump is just putting lipstick on a pig," I said during an interview with Al-Jazeera English television about this second ban.[144] "This latest executive order is just a Muslim Ban 2.0. He is sending a message that Muslims are not welcome in Donald Trump's America. Simply putting lipstick on a pig still makes it a pig."

To the credit of the American people, virtually nobody was fooled by this new application of lipstick.

A week after the state of Hawaii filed its federal lawsuit challenging Trump's Muslim ban in late 2017, US District Judge Derrick Watson issued a temporary restraining order which prevented the travel ban from taking effect. After hearing arguments from both sides, Judge Watson wrote a judicial decision finding that there was "significant and unrebutted evidence of religious animus driving the promulgation" of both the revised Muslim Ban 2.0 and the original Muslim Ban. The federal judge also noted that any "reasonable, objective observer" would conclude that Trump's ban was implemented with a "purpose to disfavor a particular religion," namely Islam.[145] One day later, another federal judge from Maryland also handed down a nationwide preliminary injunction against part of the executive order. Like his counterpart in Hawaii, US District Judge Theodore Chuang of Maryland argued the revised Muslim

Ban 2.0 order was intended to clearly discriminate against Muslims as well.

Yet on June 26, 2017, the United States Supreme Court voted 5-4 (along ideological and party lines) to allow parts of Trump's Muslim Ban 2.0 to go into effect. In allowing the ban to take effect, the conservative-heavy US Supreme Court narrowed the scope of injunctions that lower courts could put on the temporary travel ban.

The Supreme Court allowed implementation of the Muslim Ban from the six Muslim-majority nations, with an exception for people who had any "bona fide relationship with a person or entity in the United States."[146] (Specifically, these "bona fide relationships" included foreign nationals with "close family" connections in the United States.) However, Trump's own State Department initially said that the only people who counted as "close family" were parents (including in-laws and step-parents), spouses, fiancé(e)s, children (including sons-in-law and daughters-in-law), siblings, and half-siblings. According to BBC News, "close family" relationships which shockingly did not make Trump's grade included grandparents/grandchildren, aunts, uncles, nieces, nephews, and/or cousins.

There were, of course, challenges to this . . .

Just a few weeks later, a court in Hawaii ruled that the Trump administration's definition of "close family" relationships defied common sense.

"Common sense, for instance, dictates that close family members be defined to include grandparents," wrote district judge Derrick Watson in his official court opinion.[147] "Indeed, grandparents are the epitome of close family members." On January 31, 2020, the Trump administration added six more countries to the Muslim Ban travel list, slamming the door on immigrants from the African nations of Nigeria, Sudan,

Tanzania, and Eritrea, as well as Myanmar in Southeast Asia and Kyrgyzstan in Central Asia. Two of these countries (Sudan and Kyrgyzstan) are Muslim-majority countries and three others (Eritrea, Tanzania, and Nigeria) have sizeable Muslim populations nearing 40 percent. It seems quite fitting that Donald Trump would add heavily Black Muslim countries from Africa to his Ban since he once famously referred to African nations as "shithole countries" during a 2018 meeting with a bipartisan group of senators at the White House.

Yet despite numerous inconsistencies and absurdities, despite containing naked bigotry, and despite going against what virtually all Americans would regard as "common sense" the ban was not lifted. And what have been the consequences?

In the view of many—including myself—the Republican anti-Muslim jihad of Donald Trump and his right-wing political allies has actually made our world a more dangerous place. It has sadly become a normative fact that Islamophobia is now the norm, not the exception, in the United States. It has also become a central part of the Republican Party's platform, which it remains today.

The national—and global—rise in Islamophobia can be credited directly to opportunistic right-wing politicians like Trump who have stoked the "clash of civilizations" narrative to arouse animus and hatred for which there is no good reason. Frustratingly, this is only helping America's true enemies, and is threatening the freedoms enjoyed by all democratic societies around the world.

3

The Hijab Bans Heard around the World

Beauty doesn't fade when being covered by hijab.[148]

—Angelina Jolie

One of the difficulties involved in discussing the threats that Muslims face today is the tendency of those having the conversations to change the subject. For example, there are very few conversations about Islam today which do not ultimately end up touching upon the type of clothing that many Muslim women choose to wear. Instead of focusing on Donald Trump's Muslim travel bans, or the meteoric rise of right-wing white supremacist neo-Nazi groups in virtually every industrialized nation, many Westerners still cannot lower their obsessive gaze from female Muslim religious attire.

   This is a problem because it prevents us from concentrating on the subjects that truly matter.

***

The eighteenth victim of the 2019 New Zealand mosque massacre was a fifty-eight-year-old man named Ashraf Razak Ali. Lovingly known as "Babu" to his friends and family, Mr. Ali was visiting his older brother in Christchurch when both siblings were caught in the bloody barrage that day. His brother luckily survived the massacre by jumping behind a bench. "I put the top half of my body behind the bench, and the bottom half outside, thinking if he shot me, he would hit me in the foot, and there was a chance I would survive," he told reporters afterwards.[149] He frantically searched for his younger brother Ashraf for over twenty-four hours, clinging to the hope that he was one of the few survivors taken to local Christchurch hospitals. Sadly, it was not to be. His niece sent him a video the next day from an Australian media outlet which showed an excerpt from the gunman's video; a pile of dead bodies could be seen, including the corpse of his younger brother Ashraf Ali.

***

But, again, some people would like to talk about headscarves instead.

"Who imposed me to wear this head scarf? It's my personal choice," remarked Amani Al-Khatathbeh, founder of the online magazine *MuslimGirl*, during an Australian panel discussion on women in Islam.[150] "I chose to put this on my head. But, you see, that's the way that we want to talk about Muslim women, right? As if they don't have any agency, as if they can't make their own decisions and speak on their own behalf."

In August 2017, a private Facebook group comprised of right-wing anti-immigrant Norwegians was widely mocked on social media after some of their members apparently could not tell the difference between a photograph of empty black seats on a local city bus and Muslim women wearing burqas.

It was silly and absurd, but it also exposed the underpinning ignorance that drives this sentiment.

A right-wing Facebook user from Norway posted a photo of empty black bus seats to the Facebook group *Fedrelandet Viktigst* (which roughly translates into "Fatherland First") with the question "What do people think about this?" in what they ignorantly thought was a city bus full of burqa-clad Muslim women. According to media reports, other members of this racist Facebook group immediately started commenting about how "frightening," "tragic," and "scary" this scene of burqa-clad Muslim women was to the future of lily-white Norway.[151] Other Facebook members decried that such a thing could ever happen in Norway (again, it didn't) and worried that the phantom Muslim female passengers could have "weapons and bombs" under their garments.

Silly, right? Well, it was until it wasn't.

Because of this nonexistent threat from Muslim women, in June 2017, Norway announced formal legislative plans to ban all face-covering Muslim veils in universities, schools, and kindergartens across the country.

Yes, kindergartens.

And though it had strange origins, this proposed hijab ban was just the latest in a series of proposed anti-Muslim legislation by European countries (including France, Holland, Belgium, Bulgaria, and others). In the Norway hijab ban, any female Muslim employees who insisted on wearing hijab could risk losing their jobs. Further, many female Muslim students could face expulsion from their colleges and universities if they were found in violation of this ridiculous law.[152]

This kind of "hijab ban-demonium" (which I define as a panicky sort of reaction that bans Muslim women from wearing hijabs, niqabs, burqas, and/or burkinis without any regard for religious freedom issues) is a phenomenon which continues to creep across many Europe and Western societies today. Politicians from all over the spectrum are using Muslims as political footballs to further their xenophobic ideological platforms.

For example, German Chancellor Angela Merkel once publicly told attendees at a Christian Democratic Union conference that, "The full facial veil is inappropriate and should be banned wherever it is legally possible."[153] These absurdly privileged and culturally relativist comments were based in the context of growing anti-immigrant sentiment across Germany as they absorbed over one million Muslim refugees from civil wars in Syria and Iraq. Many analysts conceded that Merkel's statements were likely political calculations to pander to right-wing Germans as her favorability ratings were sinking. However, that doesn't lessen their damage to millions of Muslims across Europe.

According to Amnesty International, anti-Muslim hate crimes in Germany drastically increased in recent years because of the rise of Islamophobia. An Amnesty report found that between 2013 and 2015, there was a nearly 87 percent increase in violent racist crimes primarily targeting German Muslims. The researchers also noted a 1600 percent increase in bias-motivated crimes which specifically targeted shelters for refugees and asylum-seekers (who happened to be predominantly Muslim).[154]

For many this hatred culminated in what came to be known as the case of the "headscarf martyr"—one of the most brazen Islamophobic hate crimes in modern history and barely anyone knows her story.

In July 2009, a thirty-two-year-old Muslim woman from Egypt named Mrs. Marwa El-Sherbini was publicly murdered in a German courtroom by a Muslim-hating fanatic who stabbed her eighteen times in front of a packed chamber of horrified witnesses. Marwa had been in the courtroom giving testimony against her attacker for having previously called her a "terrorist" and "Islamist whore" in public while she was pregnant. Adding insult, as she was being publicly murdered in front of the packed German courtroom by a white man; her distraught husband rushed to her side only to be shot himself by a German police officer in the courtroom.

Although she was hailed as the "headscarf martyr" in her native country of Egypt, the case of Marwa El-Sherbini received very little media coverage anywhere else in the world. For many Muslims, this clearly illustrated the growing racist ambivalence toward bias-motivated attacks on women who are visibly Muslim across the Western world.[155]

"The 'hijab oppresses women' narrative is not only racist, it is also sexist," according to Dalia Mogahed, a former executive director for the Gallup Center for Muslim Studies. "To assume a woman's hijab was forced without asking her is to presume she views Western styles as ideal."[156] Mogahed also cited several Gallup surveys showing that about 90 percent of Muslims globally believe that hijab is a free choice by the vast majority of women who wear it all over the world.

"Oppression means the taking away of someone's power and their agency. Yet a woman in a hijab is only covering her body and hair, not her voice or intellect," she told the New York Times. "A man dressed in a full robe and head cover—like many do in the Middle East—is not said to be oppressed. To say that hijab oppresses women is to say that the source of a woman's power—but not a man's—is her body and not her mind."[157]

***

The nineteenth and twentieth victims of the New Zealand mosque massacre were a fifty-eight-year-old man named Asif Vora and his twenty-eight-year-old son, Ramiz Vora. The elder Vora had recently traveled from his native India to visit his first newborn granddaughter who was still in a Christchurch hospital. The father-son duo had journeyed to the mosque together to pray for the health of the newborn baby girl who had been placed in an incubator. According to media reports, the twenty-eight-year-old first-time father only held his daughter once in his lifetime.[158] And just like that he was gone.

***

According to some, the trend of modern hijab bans across the European Union truly began in earnest around December 2003 when then-French President Jacques Chirac called for the passing of a federal law which would effectively ban religious "dress or symbols" which conspicuously showed any religious affiliation within all public schools in France. "I believe that the wearing of dress or symbols that conspicuously show religious affiliation should be banned in schools," Chirac told an audience of four hundred guests during a live nationally-televised broadcast from the Élysée Palace in Paris. "The Islamic veil—whatever name we give it—the [Jewish] yarmulke and a cross that is of plainly excessive dimensions: these have no place inside public schools," he continued.

A French public opinion poll at the time found that 69 percent of the French public supported this ban. Chirac's ban was also supported across the political spectrum, with 75 percent of right-wing voters and 66 percent of left-wing voters both in favor of the legislation. This poll also found that 58 percent of French people polled stated that they opposed the creation of new school holidays for Jews and Muslims in France as well.[159]

In the end, Chirac got his way. Yet even after this initial hijab ban, the people of France were not satisfied with simply banning Muslim attire in schools; it was now time to ban Muslim clothing at swimming pools and public beaches, as well.

In August 2016, the mayor of the southern French coastal town of Cannes (world-famous for its natural beauty and the annual Cannes Film Festival) decided to unilaterally implement a formal ban on full-body swimsuits (a.k.a. "burkinis") worn by some Muslim women on the city's beaches. This ban stipulated the following: "Access to beaches and swimming is banned to any person wearing improper clothes that are not respectful of good morals and secularism." In bizarre remarks reported by BBC World News, the mayor of Cannes also had the audacity to proclaim: "I simply forbid a uniform that is the symbol of Islamic extremism."[160]

According to *VICE News*, the full-body swimsuits, which are now commonly called "burkinis," first appeared in the popular consciousness with British celebrity chef Nigella Lawson—who is not a Muslim—who once famously wore a burkini on Australia's Bondi Beach in 2011. Since that time (and not only to the credit of Lawson), economic analysts have found that the consumer market for Islamic modest fashion (including burkinis) has been growing steadily around the world. In fact, one report actually projected that Muslim consumer spending on food and lifestyle would soon reach $2.6 trillion.[161]

In case you were thinking that the Cannes burkini ban might have been an isolated incident, I must share that it was probably pure coincidence that it went into effect on the exact same day that another "burkini day" was summarily canceled at a public swimming pool near the French city of Marseille. The outlawing of the burkini day in Marseille prevented a group of local Muslim women from using their local public swimming pool simply because brown Muslim women wanted to wear the same swimwear that a white woman named Nigella Lawson had worn freely without any controversy whatsoever.

In the weeks and months that followed, at least twenty-nine other cities and municipalities along the French Riviera jumped on the anti-Muslim bandwagon by implementing their own burkini bans. There was almost no opposition. Even the left-wing French prime minister at the time somehow found the audacity to tell reporters that he thought that the burkini was a symbol of the enslavement of women.[162] In response to the growing controversy, the highest administrative court in France, known as the "Conseil d'Etat," suspended the burkini ban, but some defiant French cities still said they would ignore this ruling and keep handing out fines to women who wore the full-body Lycra swimsuit in public.[163]

"I find it laughable that a burkini in France is any more offensive than seeing a topless woman or some middle-aged man's butt-crack on a beach in France," was how I put it during a live Al-Jazeera English television interview on the French burkini ban controversy to over seventy-six million viewers worldwide.[164]

However, shortly thereafter, the continent of Australia made its own international headlines when some of their own politicians began using Muslim clothing as a political football. In August 2017, the head of Australia's right-wing One Nation party, Pauline Hanson, made headlines down under when she famously walked into the Australian parliament dressed in a black burqa while trying to promote her legislative motion to ban the burqa. Before addressing her colleagues, Pauline Hanson removed the burqa and stated that, "I'm quite happy to remove this because it should not belong in this parliament. I call on the Government to ban full face coverings in public places!"[165]

In response to her clearly Islamophobic stunt, the Australian attorney general at the time (George Brandis) scolded Hanson in front of her parliament colleagues, informing her that the ruling government had no intention of banning Islamic religious clothing or indulging in racist behavior that marginalized the Australian Muslim community.

"Senator Hanson! No, we will not be banning the burqa," the attorney general told the Senate (to a standing ovation). "I'm not going to pretend to ignore the stunt that you have tried to pull today by arriving in the chamber dressed in a burqa. I would caution you and counsel you to be very, very careful of the offense you may do to the religious sensibilities of other Australians." He concluded by reminding his colleagues in the Australian parliament that they have "about half a million Australians in this country of the Islamic faith. It is absolutely consistent with being a good law-abiding Australian and a strict, adherent Muslim."[166]

This "Wear-A-Burqa-To-Work" political stunt came as little surprise to political observers; Pauline Hanson was already notorious for her Islamophobic political theatrics. In the past, she had referred to Muslims as "pit bulls" and also publicly supported a Trump-style banning of Muslim immigrants into Australia.[167] In June 2017, she wrote a letter to Australian prime minister Malcolm Turnbull suggesting that, "If you need to consider a US-style [Muslim] ban, as proposed by United States President Donald Trump, then so be it."[168]

Addressing the growth of Islamophobia in her native land, Australian Muslim academic and media personality Dr. Susan Carland once wrote that "Muslims in Australia have been pushed into a corner. In a willful rejection of both facts and fairness, Muslims are screamed at for not doing enough, not saying enough, not being enough, and yet when we do, say, and be exactly what is ordered of us, our accusers stick their fingers in their ears and shout 'La la la! I can't hear you over my shouting accusations that you never condemn terrorism or accept the Australian way of life!'"[169]

***

The twenty-first victim of the 2019 New Zealand mosque massacre was a fifty-seven-year-old man named Lilik Abdul Hamid. Originally from Indonesia, Mr. Hamid had worked with Air New Zealand as an aircraft manager for over fifteen years. The CEO of Air New Zealand, Christopher Luxon, told reporters that Mr. Lilik had been a valued member of the airline's engineering team and that his loss would be deeply felt for years to come. "We called him MacGyver. He was always the first person people call, even to fix a clock," his daughter remembered about her murdered father after the Christchurch massacre. "He always knew what to do. He died in a holy place, worshipping god. That's the thing we want to remember."[170]

Daughters and fathers. A sacred connection. A personal one.

***

While we have seen the origins of burqa bans as far back as 2003, there are those who feel that the 2001 Afghanistan war is also connected. During the beginning stages of the infamous "Global War on Terror," the George W. Bush administration decided that Afghan women needed to be liberated from men forcing them to wear the burqa. However, this narrative has since been projected onto nearly one billion Muslim women worldwide. If we are liberating the Muslim women in Afghanistan . . . then why stop there? Professor Mimi Thi Nguyen from the University of Illinois examined how, in this narrative of "liberation," the Muslim burqa became symbolic for Western armies.

In an academic article for the University of Chicago's *Journal of Women in Culture and Society,* Professor Nguyen chronicled the establishment of the "Kabul Beauty School" during the Afghanistan war—overseen by the nongovernmental organization Beauty without Borders—and which was financially sponsored by the fashion and beauty industries in the United States. According to Professor Nguyen, the colonized population in Afghanistan was always considered to present potential profits vis-à-vis its untapped beauty market. By insisting on the imposition of Westernized liberal standards of "beauty" on these Muslim women, Professor Nguyen concluded that a "dispossession of agency" resulted.[171]

According to Columbia University Professor Lila Abu-Lughod: "In the common Western imagination, the image of the veiled Muslim woman stands for oppression in the Muslim world."[172] She has emphasized, however, that Muslim women who wear religious attire should not be considered as lacking personal agency. Abu-Lughod has written about how women in the United States mobilized around the plight of the Afghani woman oppressed by the Taliban—Muslim women who were represented in the media as being without agency, covered from head to toe in their *burqas*, unable to go to school or even wear nail polish. The Bush administration then used this visual as part of their moral justification for the military invasion of Afghanistan; which was *then* used for the sociopolitical subjugation of Muslim women in the Western diaspora via hijab and burkini bans.

"I would argue that the use of these images [of Muslim women in religious attire] has also been bad for us, in the countries of the West where they circulate, because of the deadening effect they have on our capacity to appreciate the complexity and diversity of Muslim women's lives—as human beings," said Professor Abu-Lughod. "Did we expect once 'free' from the Taliban that they would go 'back' to belly-shirts or dust off their Chanel suits?"[173]

Even a hijab worn symbolically by a devout Christian African American female college professor in Illinois has caused considerable tumult. In December 2015, a small evangelical school in the western Chicago suburbs close to where I grew up called Wheaton College made international headlines when it summarily fired Professor Larycia Hawkins—a tenured African American professor of political science—because she pointed out that Christians and Muslims worshipped the same Abrahamic God, and proclaimed that she would wear a hijab in solidarity with Muslim women during the Christian season of Advent. In a December 2015 Facebook post explaining her decision, Professor Hawkins wrote:

> I stand in religious solidarity with Muslims because they, like me, a Christian, are people of the book. And as Pope Francis stated last week, we worship the same God. As part of my Advent Worship, I will wear the hijab to work at Wheaton College, to play in Chicago, in the airport and on the airplane to my home state [Oklahoma] that initiated one of the first anti-Sharia laws (read: unconstitutional and Islamophobic), and at church . . . [174]

It was a brave act of solidarity by a Black female professor with Muslim women everywhere, and should have been only mildly controversial [if at all]. However, once again illustrating the unique power of the burqa to arouse hysterics, her employer immediately placed her on leave, and soon moved to fire her.

On one side of the resulting political debate, activists like the Reverend Jesse Jackson compared Professor Hawkins to civil rights icons like Rosa Parks. On the other side, we saw right-wing anti-Muslim evangelists like Franklin Graham declaiming: "Shame on her!" simply for showing empathy to Muslims.

In the immediate aftermath of Professor Hawkins' act of hijab solidarity, things got so heated on that suburban Chicago campus that a Christian student at Wheaton College who also chose to wear a hijab in solidarity with Professor Hawkins reported that another classmate slammed a door in her face and left her with cuts and bruises. Meanwhile, the *Washington Post* reported that someone had actually created an entire fake website for the Islamic Center of Wheaton which falsely suggested that the local mosque (an actual mosque) and Professor Hawkins were supporters of ISIS (which was, of course, totally untrue).[175]

The stories of brave people like Professor Larycia Hawkins show us that this racialized demonization of "the Other" will never end until we get out of our comfort zones to engage with people who are different from us. Making connections with people of other backgrounds has a real and meaningful impact on our overall worldviews. For example, a 2014 survey by the Pew Research Center found that only 27 percent of white evangelicals in America claimed to know anyone who is a Muslim (with even fewer evangelicals claiming to know someone who is a Hindu or Buddhist). That same Pew study found that nearly half (49 percent) of black evangelicals (like the aforementioned Professor Larycia Hawkins) confirmed that they actually *do* personally know a Muslim in their everyday lives. Following suit, when Pew asked these people to rate their (positive or negative) feelings about people of other faiths, it should come as little surprise that black Protestants gave Muslims higher ratings than other American religious minority groups like Mormons, atheists, Hindus, or Buddhists. At the other end of the spectrum, this Pew study found that white evangelicals gave atheists and Muslims the lowest favorability ratings possible.[176]

***

The twenty-second victim of the 2019 New Zealand mosque massacre was a fifty-seven-year-old physician named Dr. Amjad Hamid. The Palestinian cardiologist had spent much of his life in the gulf state of Qatar and had trained as a doctor in Syria. In the final years of his life, Dr. Hamid spent much of his time ministering to rural under-served communities in the mountainous areas of New Zealand's North Island. In addition to his professional acumen, his colleagues fondly remembered him for acts of kindness such as bringing fresh hot baklava from a Christchurch bakery for his coworkers. "He was well liked for his kindness, compassion, and sense of humor," the Taranaki District Health Board said in a statement after his murder. "He was the perfect man, it's a big loss,"[177] his wife said after the massacre, mincing no words.

A lifesaving physician known for acts of kindness. And yet, in the eyes of white terrorists, he was still "the other." Still somehow not worthy of life. Whether it is a head scarf, or a different religion, it is clear that some things cannot be overcome in the eyes of bigots.

***

To highlight the impact of Islamophobia on Muslim women in the West, the European Network Against Racism (ENAR)—an EU-wide network of NGOs in all European Union Member States and Iceland—published a major report called "Forgotten Women: The Impact of Islamophobia on Muslim Women" which studied policies and attitudes within eight major European countries (Belgium, Denmark, France, Germany, Italy, Netherlands, Sweden, and the United Kingdom). This exhaustive report was published with the support of the European Union (EU) and provided comprehensive insight into the many sociopolitical challenges that millions of European Muslim women face today. In regards to employment discrimination, the ENAR report found that Muslim women are subjected to three different types of penalties within employment sectors of European countries: 1) gender penalties, 2) ethnic penalties, and 3) religious penalties. Illustrating some of their key findings on gendered Islamophobia, these researchers found that 73 percent of Dutch Muslim women of Afghani descent said that they had experienced discrimination at their workplace at least once in the past. And in Germany, only 3 percent of companies had invited Muslim women for job interviews if they were wearing headscarves in their application photograph. These are only two examples, but they give you a sense of what was found. Anti-Muslim bigotry is real and impactful, and it is often based on how people appear.

"My employer asked me why I started to wear the headscarf, and I replied that it would not influence my ability to work," a twenty-two-year-old Dutch Afghan Muslim woman named Sahar told the researchers. "I am still the same Sahar and I will work the same way I did before. My employer then said that customers would now see that I am Muslim."

"'Yes,' I told her, 'but I have always been Muslim.'" Shortly thereafter, her employer terminated Sahar's employment contract for no reason whatsoever.

In the United Kingdom, the European study found that over 50 percent of female British Muslim respondents who wear the hijab felt that they had missed out on promotion opportunities because of religious discrimination. In Belgium, nearly half of employers (44 percent) admitted that wearing a Muslim headscarf had negatively influenced the selection of female Muslim candidates for possible employment.[178]

"Some media often depict a stereotypical binary representation of Muslim women either as oppressed or as dangerous and do not consider Muslim women as active agents," according to the ENAR report. "In all countries, most news stories related to Muslim women concern violations of women's rights, which contributes to constructing negative stereotypes and does not consider Muslim women as a diverse and heterogeneous group."

The researchers also studied incidents in which "stereotypical images" of Muslim women were being used within the public domain to create a fertile ground for discrimination and even violence. They found that when European media outlets reported on news stories related to Islam (positive or negative), many of these stories were often accompanied with stereotypical stock image photographs of Muslim women wearing black burqas.

These portrayals of Muslims in the media directly correlate to negative public opinion amongst the European masses. According to a YouGov poll, a striking 55 percent of British voters currently think "there is a fundamental clash between Islam and the values of British society," compared with just 22 percent—only about one in five—who say Islam and British values are "generally compatible."[179] In France, nearly 80 percent of French people polled stated that the headscarf was a problem for *vivre-ensemble* ("living together"). In Sweden, almost 65 percent of the Swedish population believed that Muslim women are "oppressed" simply by virtue of their Islamic faith.[180]

The media is generally a visual medium. Thus, it is primarily *visibly* Muslim women (wearing hijab) who are the main targets of Islamophobic violence across the West. And these crimes tend to mainly occur in "open spaces" such as on public transportation, in city streets, or at local markets and shopping centers. These are not Muslim women walking home alone in dark alleys. Quite to the contrary. These are Muslim women in places where they ought to be enjoying safety in numbers.

Why do those filled with hate feel so comfortable picking on women in public? Why women and not men?

In the Netherlands, over 90 percent of the victims of Islamophobic hate crime incidents in 2015 were Muslim women. In France, 82 percent of Islamophobic violence in 2014 recorded by the Collective Against Islamophobia targeted Muslim women. In Belgium, 64 percent of Islamophobic hate crimes in the three-year period between January 2012 and September 2015 concerned Muslim women. And in Germany, a survey found that 59 percent of female Muslim respondents claimed that they had been publicly insulted, verbally abused, or physically assaulted by strangers.

Finally, in the United Kingdom, a prominent anti-racist organization found that 54 percent of the in-person (as opposed to online) victims of Islamophobic threats and verbal abuse were Muslim women.[181]

Even the purportedly friendly nation of Canada is not immune from hate that targets Muslim women. For example, the province of Quebec once proposed a piece of legislation—known popularly as "Bill 62"—which would have made it illegal for Quebec public services to be given or received by people wearing "face coverings" (which, let's be honest, is just a euphemism for covered Muslim women). The provincial government pretended that the law was about civility and public safety. "We live in a free and democratic society," said Quebec Premier Philippe Couillard during the heated debate over the legislation. "You speak to me, I should see your face and you should see mine. It's that simple."

But was it?

"In fact, it is not that simple," wrote Toronto Star columnist Thomas Walkom in response to the premier's tone-deaf statements. Mr. Walkom said that the real aim of Bill 62 was to pander to anti-Islamic prejudice by singling out Muslim women who—for religious reasons—freely choose to cover their faces. "If U.S. President Donald Trump had proposed this particular law in his country, the outrage would have been palpable. The worst of Trumpism has come to Canada," he concluded.[182]

Canadian Muslims, also, understood acutely what the bill might have made possible.

"This is nothing new; there is certainly deja vu that we have seen this debate for seven years in Quebec, and more broadly in Canada," said Ihsaan Gardee, executive director of the National Council of Canadian Muslims (NCCM) during an interview with Al-Jazeera News on the controversy.[183]

Many anti-racism activists asserted that Bill 62 was simply inventing a solution for a made-up fictitious problem. According to Environics Research—a Canadian polling and market research firm—the vast majority of Muslim women in Canada do not even wear religious attire at all. And out of those who choose to do so, only a tiny few wear the burqa or niqab (full body/face covering) on a daily basis.

We were literally talking about fifty people out of millions, give or take. Seriously.

The entire Canadian province of Quebec has a population of 8.4 million with only "fifty to one hundred" people in the entire province of Quebec (less than .0012 percent of their entire population) who choose to wear the niqab or burqa, according to the *New York Times*.[184]

Yet the power of Muslim women's religious garb to inflame simply cannot be overestimated.

"It is blatantly discriminatory," said Professor Emmett Macfarlane from the University of Waterloo on the anti-Muslim Quebec legislation. He said that Bill 62 is a clear perversion of secularism because it is not neutral on its face since it only discriminatorily applies to Muslim women and targets specific Islamic religious practices.[185] "This is the opposite of neutrality," Professor Macfarlane said.

To highlight the disproportionate media coverage that Muslims receive today, Canadian journalist Davide Mastracci conducted research and found that this anti-Muslim bill received over 30 percent more national media coverage across Canada than the Trans-Pacific Partnership (TPP), which was a much larger global issue with far greater geo-political significance.[186]

A further disappointment was that this blatantly anti-Muslim law in Canada received only minimal resistance from Canadian politicians—including liberal Prime Minister Justin Trudeau. Anti-Muslim sentiment comes from both sides. A November 2017 public opinion poll from the Angus Reid Institute in Canada showed that a majority of Canadians (51 percent) have an overall negative opinion of Islam and Muslims as a whole and a whopping 46 percent of Canadians saying that the overall presence of Islam is "damaging" Canadian society.[187]

"We've seen this before," said Amira Elghawaby, former communications director for the National Council of Canadian Muslims (NCCM). "Who can forget former [conservative] prime minister Stephen Harper's obsession with the issue of a woman wearing a face veil while taking a citizenship oath?" She noted that Canada's conservatives had previously tried to ban face veils from people swearing an oath of Canadian citizenship.[188]

So, how did this story end?

In October 2017, the members of Quebec's provincial legislature voted 65-51 in favor of Bill 62. However, only a few months later, in December 2017, a Canadian court suspended part of the legislation after determining it was unconstitutional. More specifically, the court suspended Section 10 of the law, which forced individuals to uncover their faces to engage with public services (such as riding a city bus or seeing a doctor). This appellate ruling was issued in response to a lawsuit filed on behalf of Mrs. Warda Naili, a Muslim woman who wears a full-face covering.

"We're delighted that the Quebec Superior Court has suspended the Niqab ban—a law that tries to dictate to women what they can and cannot wear,"[189] the Canadian Civil Liberties Association said in a statement. "This is a huge victory but there's still work to be done."

Yet bigotry dies hard. The forces of xenophobia were not done.

In June 2019, the National Assembly of Quebec proposed a new anti-Muslim piece of legislation—this time called "Bill 21"—which hoped to ban certain public-sector employees (including public school teachers, judges, lawyers, police, and prison guards) within Quebec from wearing religious symbols such as niqabs, hijabs, and/or turbans. While this new Bill 21 did not specifically target Muslim women in its language, any reasonable observer could clearly see that a disparate impact of this legislation would likely be borne by Muslim women.

Even with the rise of anti-Muslim legislation in Quebec, the nation of Canada still sees itself as a pioneer in multiculturalism for its diversity policies; including allowing observant Sikh men who work as mounted police to wear their traditional turban and dagger while on duty in official uniform.[190] But the patriarchy is often present even among those who count themselves as "woke," and we have seen that things are quite different when it comes to Muslim women's agency in regards to Islamic religious attire.

Perhaps part of the problem is a lack of curiosity about Muslim women's clothing. Its position as "the other" in the Western world makes us stop there—and we fail to discern the layers of nuance that exist.

According to McGill University Professor Alia Al-Saji, even our lazy Western use of the inaccurate term "veil"—whether we interchangeably or haphazardly use it to refer collectively to hijab, burqa, and/or niqab—is evidence that we retain a kind of post-colonialist mindset linked to negative Orientalist stereotypes about Muslim women in general. According to Professor Al-Saji, the word "veil" is a term that recalls images of previous Muslim cultures which are presented in monolithic homogeneity. She rightfully notes that we should challenge ourselves to appreciate that female Muslim religious attire is historically dynamic and that it changes within culturally-distinctive modes of feminine dress in different parts of the world.[191]

***

The twenty-third victim of the 2019 New Zealand mosque massacre was a forty-seven-year-old woman named Mrs. Husna Ahmed. A native of Bangladesh, Mrs. Ahmed helped several people to safety during the mass shooting. Despite reaching a safe distance with others, she returned to the scene of the crime to look for her wheelchair-bound husband. It was then that she was killed. "She was busy with saving lives, forgetting about herself," her husband Farid tearfully remembered after the massacre about his beloved wife, Husna. He later told reporters that he had forgiven the Christchurch terrorist because of his Muslim worldview and the teachings of his Islamic faith. "I hope and I pray for him," he told reporters. "I don't have any grudge. This is what Islam taught me."[192]

***

In 2008, a seventeen-year-old American Muslim teenager named Samantha Elauf was turned down for a job at an Abercrombie & Fitch store in Tusla, Oklahoma for not complying with their "look policy" because of her hijab. According to media reports, the trendy clothing store claimed that because her hijab was considered to be "headwear" (which was forbidden), and because its color was black, the young lady was not eligible for employment.[193] Abercrombie & Fitch is a brand known for taking controversial positions on the physical attractiveness of their employees and models, but dismissing someone from consideration because of their religious garb was something entirely new. With the help of the Council on American-Islamic Relations (CAIR)—the largest American Muslim civil rights organization where I once served as its first-ever national legal director—Ms. Elauf filed an employment discrimination claim against Abercrombie & Fitch through the US Equal Employment Opportunity Commission (EEOC), which subsequently filed a lawsuit on her behalf stating she had been denied the job due to discrimination based on her Islamic religious beliefs.

It was a significant case which went all the way up to the United States Supreme Court. CAIR filed an "amicus curiae" ("friend of the court") brief in support of Ms. Elauf's employment discrimination claim, which read in part:

> Title VII of the Civil Rights Act of 1964 ensures equality of employment opportunities by prohibiting discrimination on the basis of religion. [American] Muslims and EEOC offices have reported a 'shocking' spike in anti-Muslim employment discrimination since September 2001. Despite the fact that Muslims make up only 0.8% of the country's population, around 20% of the religious discrimination complaints received by the EEOC were from Muslims.[194]

Almost seven years after she was first denied employment by Abercrombie & Fitch, on June 1, 2015, the Supreme Court of the United States ruled in favor of Samantha Elauf, finding that "an employer may not refuse to hire an applicant if the employer was motivated by avoiding the need to accommodate a religious practice." In addition to awarding Ms. Elauf a monetary award of $44,653 ($25,670 in damages and $18,983 in court costs), the Supreme Court justices said that Abercrombie & Fitch had violated the constitutional prohibitions on religious discrimination contained in Title VII of the Civil Rights Act of 1964.

"I was a teenager who loved fashion and was eager to work for Abercrombie & Fitch," Ms. Elauf told reporters after the Supreme Court ruled in her favor. "Observance of my faith should not have prevented me from getting a job. I am glad that I stood up for my rights and hope other people realize that this type of discrimination is wrong."[195]

***

The twenty-fourth victim of the 2019 New Zealand mosque massacre was a fifty-five-year-old man named Matiullah Safi. In the aftermath of the attack, his nephew told BuzzFeed News that Mr. Safi's son was finally able to confirm that his father was one of the fifty-one mosque massacre victims when he saw the white supremacist's livestream on Facebook Live. "He was showing me the video, going 'This is my dad! He got shot in the head!'" Mr. Safi's nephew recalled. "I tried to settle him down. But he was saying 'This is my dad! I know him and what kind of clothes he wears!'"[196] The fifty-five-year-old father had fled his war-torn homeland of Afghanistan hoping to find a safer place to live in Christchurch, New Zealand. "Death was still a bullet," his nephew said after the mosque massacre. "Even coming to the safest place in the world."

***

Notwithstanding the rise of anti-hijab movements around the world, we are also witnessing the meteoric rise in the multibillion dollar "modest fashion" industry, which I believe will continue to empower future generations of Muslim women to express themselves and their faith in the many different ways that they may choose. A few years ago, a survey found that Muslims worldwide spend a staggering $266 billion on clothing and footwear (more than the total fashion spending of Japan and Italy combined, for example). Not long into the current decade, it is expected that Muslim fashion spending may balloon to a staggering half a trillion dollars.

"Globally, the Muslim population is a youthful and growing demographic," said Professor Reina Lewis, author of *Muslim Fashion: Contemporary Style Cultures* and an authority on Muslim clothing. "This makes Muslims a very important consumer segment for anything. The market for Islamic com-modities started out looking at 'food' and 'finance.' I've been saying for the last few years that 'fashion' is going to be the 'third F'—and this is indeed what is beginning to happen."[197]

In 2014, the fashion giant DKNY unveiled a women's fashion collection for Ramadan, and Tommy Hilfiger launched its own Ramadan capsule collection the following year. We have also seen other fashion giants like Oscar de la Renta, Zara, and Mango launch their own modest-friendly fashion lines specially-themed for female Muslim consumers.[198]

I am cautiously hopeful that the marketplace in the coming decades—if nothing else—will help to push away the bigotries associated with Muslim women's fashion, and help to widen the range of clothing choices that the world is willing to embrace.

"At a time of heightened tensions around how a multicul-tural society can live in harmony, fashion is experimenting with the aesthetic of [the] covered woman, which has itself become a kind of visual shorthand for Islam," according to London's *The Guardian* newspaper.[199] "Is there a connection between mod-est dressing as a cultural and political issue, and modesty as a trend?"

Halima Aden is a rising international fashion model. She is also a former Kenyan refugee who came to America when she was only six years old.

And this supermodel wears a hijab.

It is always interesting to me how the global fashion indus-try—which has historically been built off the commodification of women's bodies in just about every way you can think of—has now begun to promote brown-skinned hijabi Muslim women among its ranks. Is this a good or bad thing? It is good in the sense that a Muslim woman wearing garb in which she feels appropriately modest is not seen as flummoxing or surprising, but rather as part of contemporary fashion (albeit on the "mod-est end" of the spectrum). Are fashion companies self-interested, seeking to "cash in" on new markets and consumers? Of course, they are in it for a buck. But this may be, realistically, the best scenario we can hope for.

And there are signs that a positive change is already underway.

Halima Aden was the first hijabi Muslim woman to grace the cover of an American women's beauty magazine (*Allure*), and she was also the first Miss Minnesota pageant contestant to compete in a hijab and burkini in November 2016. Since that time, she has gone on to walk in Kanye West's Yeezy, Season 5 show at New York Fashion Week, and also made history as the first hijab-wearing woman on the cover of *Vogue* magazine.[200]

Trailblazers like this are important. They tell the industry, and the world, that these things can be done.

***

The twenty-fifth victim of the 2019 New Zealand mosque mas-sacre was a fifty-four-year-old man named Ashraf El-Moursy Ragheb. One of several Egyptian nationals killed in the attack, Mr. Ragheb owned a souvlaki shop in Christchurch. At a pub-lic service honoring the victims of the massacre, Mr. Ragheb's fourteen-year-old daughter took the stage to proclaim her love for her deceased father, and the featured musical guest, legend-ary British singer Yusuf Islam (formerly known as Cat Stevens), told the audience about the "love and kindness that has sprung up right here in New Zealand" in the aftermath of the attack on Muslims like Mr. Ragheb.

***

Love and kindness. These are the way forward. These are the way to understandings between cultures. These are the tools that can help us to understand the many varieties of female (and human) empowerment. In addition to the fashion industry, hijab-wearing Muslim women are also beginning to make political history across the Western world. In November 2016—during the same election that gave Donald Trump the presidency—a thirty-four-year-old black Muslim female refugee named Ilhan Omar also made history by becoming the first Somali-American Muslim women to be elected as a state legislator in Minnesota.[201] Yet just a month after she was elected, Ms. Omar told *Mother Jones* magazine that she was confronted by a taxi driver who called her a "filthy" ISIS supporter, while threatening to rip off her headscarf.

On June 5, 2018, Ilhan Omar filed to run for the US House of Representatives from Minnesota's fifth congressional district after six-term incumbent Keith Ellison (the first Muslim ever elected to Congress) announced that he would not seek reelection. In the November 2018 general election, Ilhan Omar won with 78 percent of the vote. She and former Michigan state representative Rashida Tlaib (D-MI) were the first Muslim women ever elected to Congress and they joined my friend Congressman Andre Carson (D-IN) as the three Muslim members who serve in the US House of Representatives today. (Congresswoman Omar received the largest percentage of the vote of any female congressional candidate in Minnesota state history, and she was sworn in on a copy of the Quran owned by her grandfather.)

"Being an immigrant, a refugee, Muslim—all of those things represent an otherness that is not typical or easily confined into the social fabric of this country," Congresswoman Omar stated during an interview for *TIME* magazine's *Firsts: Women Who Are Changing the World* issue, conducted shortly after her historic election.[202] "I ended up pushing all of the negative things aside because I kept thinking, regardless of whether we win or lose, this will shift the narrative about what is possible [for Muslim women everywhere]."

The Islamic headscarf has always been a powerful symbol of Muslim women's defiance against the male gaze, against colonialism, and against Islamophobia as we know it today. Now in the West, it has become a racially politicized garment; there is every reason to think it will sadly remain at the center of a socio-political tug-of-war for the foreseeable future.

However, in country after country, we have seen that the legal right of Muslim women to freely wear the headscarf in workplaces, and public spaces, is generally being upheld by the highest courts. It is a fundamental religious freedom and human right.

True, with the meteoric rise of right-wing nationalism throughout Europe in recent years, we have seen countries like Germany, Austria, and The Netherlands impose legislative restrictions on hijab within the public square. Yet Muslims are committed to fighting the marginalization of Muslim women within their respective societies.

In the past handful of years, there have been challenges to be sure. In some cases, these involve legal language used to target female Muslims *generally,* when it is deemed impermissible to target them *specifically.*

In March 2017, right-wing politicians across Europe welcomed a ruling by the EU's highest court which allowed companies to effectively ban employees from wearing visible religious symbols, including hijabs. In its first decision on the issue of women wearing Islamic headscarves in the workplace, the European Court of Justice in Luxembourg had ruled that religious garments could be banned; but only as part of a general policy barring all religious and political symbols.

In reaching its legal decision, the court found rationalizations in three of its conclusions. First, it ruled that any prohibition on employees wearing Islamic headscarves at work that arises from a more general ban on political, philosophical, or religious symbols does not constitute direct discrimination under EU law. Second, it concluded that it is legitimate for an employer to want to display a policy of religious or political neutrality in relation to employee dress, but only for workers coming into direct contact with its customers. Third, it ruled that employers cannot use the expressed wish of a customer not to receive a service from an employee wearing an Islamic headscarf as grounds for differential treatment.[203]

In light of this never-ending obsession with female Muslim religious clothing—and how it intersects with other xenophobic sociopolitical trends in Western society today—I think it is safe to say that the resolution of this issue will involve a marathon, and not a sprint. Global observers continue to wonder about the collective fate of millions of female Western Muslims as they seek to make a life for themselves, to practice their faith, and to engage—at their own pace—with Western notions of modesty and propriety without feeling uncomfortable. The forces reaching out to Muslim women on this issue may be a strange and motley crew, but they are also a powerful one. I believe that the market-driven forces that want to sell clothing to Muslim women—coupled with the political, social, and cultural advocates for a spectrum of fashion that can include women of the Islamic faith—have the power to win in the end. And though there will be some setbacks along the way, I believe that eventually they will.

4

Is It Time for the Muslims to Leave Europe?

I hate Islam! The ideology of a retarded culture . . . [204]

—Dutch Politician Geert Wilders

After the January 2015 *Charlie Hebdo* terrorist attack in Paris, an interesting thought experiment was posed in *The Atlantic* by Jeffrey Goldberg.

Goldberg's piece was entitled "Is It Time for the Jews to Leave Europe?"[205]

Looking to the other side of the Abrahamic aisle, Goldberg chronicled the rise of anti-Semitism in contemporary Europe, and considered the ways it has mirrored the rise of Islamophobia. Goldberg also did not shrink from considering the hate crimes that have been perpetrated against European Jews, by white nationalists, by Muslim extremists, and by other groups. Near the end of the article, Goldberg tells the story of a conversation between Joe Biden and a top Israeli official, in which the Israeli confides to Biden that Jews in Israel have a secret that gives them strength in times of challenge. And the secret is "we have nowhere else to go."

When it comes to the Jews and Muslims of Europe today, it may fairly be asked if the religious and cultural bigotry we are seeing is based upon the mindset that Europe is not for "you" (Jews and Muslims) because you have somewhere else to go.

In his article, Goldberg further observed that, in the 2010s, many European societies ignited heated culture wars that seemed to be aimed at their own Muslim communities. There were many reasons for this—not the least being the influx of Muslim refugees from Iraq and Syria. But these new culture wars seemed to call for a kind of quick referendum—a referendum on the future of Muslims within the European Union. It is as if many in Europe would like to "settle" the continent's attitude toward Muslims quickly, before they have a chance to settle and integrate. The motivations behind this attitude are ones that we have seen before.

Even the most optimistic global analysts concede that overall anti-Muslim sentiment within European societies has now normalized to the point where millions of young Muslims have been relegated to second-class citizenry. This is even true for millions of European Muslims who are born in the EU.

The increased hostility toward European Muslims has directly resulted in widespread anti-Muslim discrimination, political marginalization, and an upsurge in Islamophobic hate-crimes. The politicized institutionalization of Islamophobia across Europe in the last few decades or so—from the 2009 Swiss national referendum ban on (all four) mosque minarets in the "neutral" country of Switzerland, to the litany of anti-Muslim headscarf bans in France and other EU nations—evince an "other-izing" of almost 10 percent of Europe's entire population.

Any coherent plan for the future of European Muslims will have to address over fifty years of ongoing societal discrimination faced by young and diverse EU Muslims (especially when it comes to employment discrimination and religious freedom). It will also have to address the upsurge of anti-Muslim hate that has manifested in recent years.

***

The twenty-sixth victim of the 2019 New Zealand mosque massacre was a fifty-four-year-old man named Mohamad Mohamedhosen. A native of the African island nation of Mauritius, Mr. Mohamedhosen was a graphic designer who had previously lived in England before moving to New Zealand two years before his untimely murder at the Linwood Mosque.

It did not matter that Mr. Mohamedhosen had a British pedigree or the kind of skill set that gained him entry into mainstream business culture. His religion was enough to "other-ize" him. And that was enough to seal his fate.

***

On the flip side of the European integration divide, we have also seen groups like ISIS peddle their own warped version of Islamophobia by stating that they intend to destroy the "gray-zone" of peaceful coexistence between Muslim communities and Western societies. To illustrate this point, the terrorist group's online magazine *Dabiq* once stated that the *Charlie Hebdo* attack in Paris had "eliminated the gray-zone" of coexistence in Europe.[206]

Groups like ISIS often gauge their operational success based upon whether they see an uptick in anti-Muslim hate crimes after one of their brazen attacks. In addition to causing generalized mayhem, these groups also want to simultaneously watch Western nations lash out against their Muslim minorities (which they see as resulting in potential recruitment for themselves). Although Muslims as a whole tend to get collectively blamed every time one of these idiots commits a criminal act, it should be noted that most experts strongly agree that the overwhelming majority of young extremists become radicalized online as 'lone wolves' and not inside of any mosque. Take, for instance, the *Charlie Hebdo* attackers in Paris. They were not only radicalized online, but were already seasoned lawbreaking deadbeats. They had long criminal histories, and most had spent time in prison.

Digging into their pasts after the attacks, European investigators found that the criminals were actually "lazy" non-observant Muslims. They did not associate with the Muslim community around them, and many of them did not even have jobs. In interviews, their own family members characterized them as irreligious deadbeats who spent their time smoking marijuana in bars and "never went to the mosque."[207] Their relatives further divulged that these extremists had never even read the Quran before. Suffice it to say, these are hardly the images of devout "holy warriors" drunk on over-immersion into their religion that the Western media likes to portray. These were criminal assholes that were very far from their faith and looking to kill people for no reason.

European counterterrorism experts consistently find that homegrown, self-proclaimed jihadists consistently have one thing in common: no serious Islamic religious training at all. According to Professor Olivier Roy—a world-renowned expert on French Muslims—there is actually an inverse relationship between Islamic religious piety and attraction to violent groups like ISIS. "This is not so much the radicalization of Islam as the Islamicization of radicalism," Professor Roy once trenchantly observed about this phenomenon, according to the London Review of Books.[208]

***

The twenty-seventh and twenty-eighth victims of the 2019 New Zealand mosque massacre were a fifty-one-year-old man named Naeem Rashid and his twenty-one-year-old son, Talha Naeem. As captured in the terrorist's Facebook livestream video of the massacre, the elder Mr. Rashid sees his son being gunned down by the attacker and immediately runs directly toward the white supremacist, trying to tackle him. Sadly, Mr. Rashid was also gunned down and died from his injuries. Mr. Rashid had been a university professor in Christchurch, and had moved to New Zealand from his hometown of Abbottabad, Pakistan. The prime minister of Pakistan (former cricket superstar Imran Khan) tweeted after the mosque massacre that Mr. Rashid was "martyred trying to tackle the white supremacist terrorist"[209] and further stated that Mr. Rashid's courage would be recognized with a posthumous national award by the Pakistani government.

"I blame these increasing terror attacks on the current Islamophobia post-9/11 where Islam and 1.3 billion Muslims have collectively been blamed for any act of terror by a Muslim," Prime Minister Khan added.[210] Shortly thereafter, United Nations Secretary-General Antonio Guterres reiterated "the urgency of working better together globally to counter Islamophobia and eliminate intolerance and violent extremism in all its forms."[211]

***

The question of when an act of terror—if ever—can be said to represent or speak for a larger population is a difficult one. Yet sadly, we have seen far too many in the Western world prove willing to take things at face value when it comes to collectively blaming Muslims. To assume that someone who says he speaks for all Muslims does in fact speak for them. I suppose it is easier than actually thinking, but it does not create a worldview that correlates to the truth of things.

Although Europe's Islamophobia has historically been relegated to right-wing circles in the past, we are now seeing anti-Muslim sentiment continue to seep into the political mainstream, largely based on these ideas that ISIS-like attackers can speak for Muslims as a whole. Adam Shatz from the *London Review of Books* has written that center-right political circles now openly talk about a "Muslim fifth column" across Europe. To give you a sense of what this means in terms of the normalization of Islamophobia within mainstream European politics, a leading figure in former French prime minister Nicolas Sarkozy's centrist political party once proposed interning four thousand suspected Islamists in "regroupment" (a.k.a. internment) camps with no controversy whatsoever.[212] The fact that such a proposition was greeted without any outrage shows just how prevalent anti-Muslim sentiment has seeped into the European mainstream.

Because of the pervasiveness of anti-Muslim feeling across the political spectrum, many anti-Muslim hate crimes often go unreported. For far too many victims, weaponized Islamophobia is now simply part of everyday life for them. Muslims do not expect the governments of the countries where they live to take crimes against them seriously. The European Union Agency for Fundamental Rights (FRA) recently found that well into the twenty-first century, very few European Union

(EU) countries had even recorded hate crimes with "anti-Muslim" or "Islamophobic" motives inside their official databases.[213] Although the Council of Europe *does* now graciously place Islamophobia under their definition of racism and xenophobia, many experts agree that Islamophobia should be treated similarly to anti-Semitism by European law enforcement agencies across the continent.

Anti-Semitism and Islamophobia are both unique and similar. A yin and a yang. They are analogous in that they are both projects of majority exclusion, religious stigmatization, and racialized scrutiny by right-wing ultranationalist politicians, organized neo-Nazi hate groups, and conservative media outlets. The modern history of anti-Semitism arose with modernity itself, over a hundred years ago, in a Europe obsessed with maintaining the Christian "purity" of nation states. This kind of thinking led to the worst mass genocide in modern human history: the Holocaust.

Like anti-Semitism, Islamophobia is not new to Europe.

The French term "Islamophobie" first appeared in print in a 1910 book entitled *La Politique Musalmane dans l'Afrique Occidentale Francoise*. In that book, the author criticized the anti-Muslim views of France's colonial administrators working in former Muslim-majority colonies such as Benin, The Gambia, and Senegal in western Africa.[214] "Islamophobie" was also used in a biography on the Prophet Muhammad (peace be upon him) that was completed in 1916 by another Frenchman named Alphonse Etienne Dinet. The author dedicated his book to the brave Muslim soldiers in the French army who died in battle during World War I.[215]

So Islamophobia may not have been present *to the extent* that anti-Semitism has been present in Europe's history . . . but it has always been present.

The good news is that in many parts of Europe today, anti-Semitism and other forms of racism are rightfully condemned and punished. However, Islamophobia still remains the one racist ideology which can still often go unpunished, or even encouraged. Recent global events have allowed Europe's far-right ultra-nationalists to make Islamophobia this century's ugly form of European xenophobia which is tolerated by the general public at-large.

Once known exclusively for their rabid anti-Semitism, many right-wing ultranationalist political parties across Europe have now added Muslims to their mix of targets. And as the pull of these ultra-right groups gets stronger, the center shifts. Europe's mainstream constitutional democracies—most of which describe themselves as "liberal" societies—have nonetheless started to impose very illiberal laws related to their Muslim citizens. Quick examples include the wholesale banning of mosque minarets and Muslim headscarves in some European countries; which directly violates the European Convention on Human Rights (not to mention each country's own respective constitution which guarantees religious freedom and other international law doctrines governing the rights of minorities).

Marine Le Pen—the political leader of France's xenophobic far-right National Front political party (known in French as *Front National* or FN)—is the daughter of the very famous anti-Semitic racist, Jean-Marie Le Pen. Jean-Marie is now in his nineties, but still serves the FN in emeritus positions, and the father-daughter team still disseminates hatred throughout the continent. Most people know that it was Nazis and their right-wing allies throughout Europe—not just in Germany—who were responsible for fanning the flames of anti-Semitism that led to the Holocaust. Yet Jean-Marie Le Pen told Muslims just where he stands when he once bizarrely claimed—with no irony whatsoever—that Muslims were exclusively responsible for anti-Semitism.[216]

Although his daughter has been more politically astute than to repeat her father's transparent anti-Semitic and anti-Muslim views word-for-word, Marine Le Pen's own brand of racism nearly won her the 2017 French presidency; she eventually lost to Emmanuel Macron in a nationwide run-off election. Her far-right party has publicly called for limiting Muslim immigration to France, and has called for measures that would essentially force Muslims to erase their Islamic identities in public life. In recent years, she has also begun imitating one of her father's more dangerous ideas—suggesting that Muslims are to blame for anti-Semitism in France.

As in the United States and other Western nations, Marine Le Pen has sought to appeal to disenfranchised, poor, and rural voters by convincing them that foreign elements bringing different cultures and religions into their country are the reason for their hardships. Politicians like her have become the pseudo-official voice of the "New Right"; and ultra-nationalist parties have now managed to establish themselves within mainstream French partisan politics.[217] These movements have repackaged old conspiracy theories and racist ideologies into new millennial contexts to gain appeal with disenfranchised white voters.

Every year, it seems to get worse. Mainstream support for Le Pen's party has increased by 12 percent since she took over the party's leadership from her father in 2011. Do not underestimate the growth of a couple of political percentage points per year.

Following World War II, racist, right-wing parties in France (and throughout Europe) languished in unpopularity on the fringes of the political sphere. They had almost no influence in major European national elections at all.[218]

Then, as the twenty-first century dawned, something began to change. A rightward political shift began, and many of these formerly isolated right-wing parties began to gain ground. There's no question that part of this was due to Europe becoming less "white" and more "brown." As early as 2002, Jean-Marie Le Pen received the second-highest percentage of the popular national vote in France. At the time, political experts thought this was an aberration. Little did they know it was the beginning of a long-term electoral trend.

Political parties in France have been sitting at an ideological fork in the road for years. Politicians want to say things the people want to hear, and they want to get elected. Former centrist French prime minister Nicolas Sarkozy seemingly set the tone for a shift rightward when his party (the Union for a Popular Movement [UMP]) changed the focus of their campaign platform to immigration and "law and order" (both of which tacitly centered on Muslim identity in France). When Sarkozy did this in 2007, the young right-winger Le Pen claimed issue ownership which then thrust her into the French political mainstream. Rather than taking votes away from Le Pen, Sarkozy's move only bolstered the legitimacy of Le Pen and her party by moving the French political center further to the right. This craven political move only helped solidify her right-wing party as a legitimate, mainstream party for the foreseeable future in France.[219]

Ever the political opportunist, Le Pen next began raising "security concerns" with regard to immigration issues, mostly focusing on French Muslims of North African origin. This successfully tapped into unresolved post-colonialist feelings of the white French populace regarding the Algerian War. And to shield herself from charges of outright Islamophobia, Le Pen couched her rhetoric in economic and political terms—and steered away from cultural identity. This was effective, and further broadened her political base away from the racist fringe and into to the bourgeois mainstream. A public opinion poll published in *Le Monde* newspaper found that 46 percent of French people agreed that Marine Le Pen is "the face of patriotic conservatives, with traditional values," while a lesser 43 percent believed that she leads the "nationalistic, xenophobic extreme right" fringe party in France.[220]

The French concept of *laïcité* is a strict form of hyper-secularism which is designed to keep religion completely out of public life. This principle has been more or less entrenched within French culture from around 1905 to the present. Historically, it is generally agreed that it was adopted to quell the influence of the Roman Catholic Church over a century ago. However, today the religious lines are beginning to become blurred in regards to this concept. I believe that *laïcité* remains, but that its focus has shifted almost exclusively to Muslim identity in France, pure and simple.[221]

Before the French parliament passed the 2004 legislative ban against Muslim headscarves in schools, only about 14 percent of female Muslim students in France wore the headscarf at all, according to *The Economist* magazine.[222] Still, the government felt the obsessive need to regulate this very, very small percentage of the student population. In addition to public schools, this initial French ban also covered government institutions. But it grew from there.

Soon thereafter, these French hijab bans shifted to the private sector as well, with a 2014 legal ruling against a female Muslim daycare nursery employee's right to wear a hijab. Although that court ruling suggested that it should not be considered a complete ban on hijabs, it nonetheless set a dangerous legal precedent.

This pervasive anti-hijab sentiment within French society has also allowed other public and private organizations to "take matters into their own hands" with no repercussions. Some French Muslim women wearing hijab have reportedly been barred from entering clothing stores and even denied service at high-end restaurants. Similarly, some French Muslim women have been refused ID cards from Paris metro ticket offices— despite a court judgment by a French tribunal stating there were no grounds for refusal for subway tickets. A Muslim woman was even once kicked out of a Paris opera house after several cast members performing *La Traviata* "strongly" objected to the presence of a Muslim woman in the audience wearing a headscarf.

"A singer spotted her in the front row during the second act," said Jean-Philippe Thiellay, director of the Bastille Opera. "Some performers said they didn't want to sing" with a veiled Muslim woman in the audience and they kicked her out of the opera house.[223]

Bravo.

Although formal and informal clothing restrictions ostensibly impact Jewish and Muslim religious attire equally, there is simply no question that the goal is to chill Islamic identity. Marine Le Pen has made this clear in public speeches. "The meaning of the proliferation of the veil in France is not to be placed on the same plane as the wearing of the *kippah* [or yarmulke]. We know very well that the proliferation of the wearing of the veil— and in certain neighborhoods, the burqa—is a political act," she remarked.[224]

"France is a rather conservative country," former French ambassador to the United States Pierre Vimont once told me during an interview in the French Embassy in Washington, DC. "France has always found it rather difficult to reform itself in a peaceful and progressive way. They would rather go for big changes like revolutions." Because of its admittedly conservative jingoistic history, the rise of immigration from predominantly Muslim North African countries has given France an identity crisis of sorts. The country is called to balance its constitutional traditions of *Liberté, Egalité, Fraternité* (liberty, equality, and fraternity) with the influx of Muslim minorities who are turning into a demographic majority in some places inside France.[225]

During our interview, Ambassador Vimont (a lawyer himself) offered his own two cents on the controversial legacy of France's hijab bans. "This was a bone of contention in many of our schools," he said. "Some of the heads of our schools wanted to prevent children from getting in with their hijabs and [were] therefore forbidding it, [while] others wanted to accept it."

"I, myself, had my doubts," Vimont admitted to me. "If you try to look at it from a very pragmatic way, you have a lot of wise people who worked together and came out with this proposal that they thought hijab should be forbidden in schools. [However] we are still being very tolerant with freedom of religion and the right for every person to practice their religion in total freedom."[226] If one thing is clear, it is that in contemporary France, the position of something like a hijab ban on the political spectrum is difficult to identify. French people from all sides variously agree and disagree with it. The center has shifted. Ideas such as banning the clothing worn by a very specific minority group are increasingly mainstream.

Although the year 2020 was mainly focused on the COVID-19 coronavirus global pandemic, that year also saw the latest societal chasm between the government of France and its nearly ten million French Muslim citizens. In October 2020, a forty-seven-year-old French schoolteacher named Samuel Paty was gruesomely murdered by an eighteen-year-old Chechen teenager in the northern Paris suburb of Éragny. According to officials, the teacher had shown his students the controversial anti-Muslim cartoons from the *Charlie Hebdo* magazine which apparently motivated the teenage attacker.

Just two weeks later, three people were killed inside a church in the southern French coastal city of Nice by a twenty-one-year-old man who had come to the country from Tunisia just a few weeks earlier. According to his own family members, the Nice attacker was not a religious person and had a long criminal history of "violent behavior and drug use"[227] which had brought him to the attention of local police even before the November 2020 attack inside the church.

At the time facing an existential political challenge from right-winger Marine Le Pen, French president Emmanuel Macron wasted no time in scapegoating Muslims by ridiculously claiming that the religion of Islam as a whole is in "crisis all over the world today" to pander to racist tendencies of centrist white French voters in his attempt to cravenly win the April 2022 French presidential election against his right-wing political nemesis.

"The last thing the world needs amid a resurgent COVID-19 pandemic is a clash of civilizations. Yet this is what French President Emmanuel Macron seems intent on fomenting," according to essayist Pankaj Mishra in a *Bloomberg News* column entitled "Macron's Clash of Civilizations is Misguided" during the 2020 controversy. "To put it soberingly: Macron has staked France's global reputation on crude mockery of a figure revered by more than 1.5 billion Muslims."[228]

True to form, the usual chorus of selectively-outraged Muslim political leaders wasted no time in their wholesale condemnation of France's anti-Muslim crackdown. Turkish President Recep Tayyip Erdogan swung first and publicly questioned Macron's mental health (which immediately pro-voked France to recall its ambassador from Turkey). Shortly thereafter, Pakistani Prime Minister Imran Khan publicly stated that the French government "encourages Islamophobia" and we saw widespread boycott protests of French products in countries like Kuwait, Qatar, Libya, and Bangladesh.

Nonetheless, the illiberal rightward lurch in France against ten million Muslims continues.

In December 2020, a far-right politician in the French parliament introduced a piece of legislation effectively creating "internment camps" for French Muslims. The proposed legislation[229] presented by Guillaume Peltier, a right-wing political ally of Marie Le Pen, has been criticized by human rights activists because it calls for the creation of "administrative detention centres" (a.k.a. internment camps) to house people that have not committed crimes but are considered "radical" by the French government.[230]

At this rate, this ongoing anti-Muslim fixation from the French government could realistically lead to future generations of over ten million French Muslims feeling like strangers in their own land. Can you imagine the collective trauma of millions of young French Muslim girls and boys who are being made to feel like "permanent second-class citizens" inside their own country while their white French neighbors obsessively mock their religion and then force them to laugh at it themselves?

The historical irony with France's political hypocrisy toward Muslims is that we are witnessing craven milquetoast centrist politicians bending over politically for Marine Le Pen's right-wing political party (which was actually co-founded by well-known Nazi collaborators, by the way).[231] Furthermore, you might also remember from earlier in this book that the modern-day ideological grandfather of the white supremacist "Great Replacement" conspiracy theory (the former erotic novelist-turned white supremacist Renaud Camus) still lives freely in side France spewing his white supremacist venom to his racist minions around the world.

For these reasons, before we take you to another part of the globe, let us never forget the ten million French Muslims who are slowly becoming second-class citizens in their own country while the ideological grandfather of modern white supremacy comfortably flips through his own erotic novels inside the library of his fourteenth-century castle in the "enlightened" European country of France.

***

The twenty-ninth victim of the 2019 New Zealand mosque massacre was a forty-seven-year-old man named Mohammed Imran Khan. Outside of his family, the three C's of curry, cricket, and community were the most important things in his life. A restaurateur who owned the well-known Indian Grill eatery in Christchurch, Mr. Khan took great pride in preparing his prized meal—Hyderabadi rice biryani—a delectable specialty from his native India. "He was a good friend to me, I'm going to miss him a lot," the restaurant's head chef told reporters after the massacre. "It brings a sense of calm to me that when he was taken away that he was praying to God."[232]

Whether it is food, clothing, or other parts of their culture, immigrants bring their unique, authentic selves with them when they enter a new culture. How those cultures react to what immigrants bring is more than a little telling.

***

Although Islamophobia is growing all over Europe, it surprises many to know that a leading voice of European Islamophobia actually hails from Holland, a place renowned for its tolerance, art, and scholarship. In the seventeenth century, Andalusian Muslim scholar Ahmed ibn Qasim Al-Hajari described lengthy discussions on religion with pluralistic Dutch scholars in Amsterdam.[233] In the late sixteenth and early seventeenth centuries, The Netherlands was home to both Jews and Muslims, and was described as a place of "unlimited freedoms to all sorts of religions" in a Europe still finding its identity.[234]

Yet today, one of the most high-profile politicians in the country is an anti-Muslim zealot named Geert Wilders. He has been described as an "opportunistic Islamophobe" by former US Ambassador to The Netherlands Cynthia Schneider.[235] His goofy, platinum blonde bouffant hairstyle has been compared to Donald Trump's. But unlike Trump, Geert Wilders has been a legitimate political force in Holland for a long, long time. And during his tenure, Wilders has always served as the leader of Holland's anti-Muslim political party, ironically named the "Party for Freedom."

Founded in 2005, the Party for Freedom has gradually grown into the fourth-largest party in Holland. It is now an unabashed political platform for Islamophobic anti-immigrant sentiment in The Netherlands. Like other right-wingers once relegated to the batshit fringes of society, Wilders is now accepted within mainstream Dutch politics. He carries considerable political sway. During the 2012 national elections in Holland, the ruling coalition actually had to get Geert Wilders' political support in order to gain power.[236] This would have been unthinkable just a few years earlier.

In the early 2000s, Geert Wilders made a racist proposal to ban the construction of new mosques in The Netherlands.

At the time, it was still mostly seen as the eccentric dream of a silly Dutch extremist. It was not taken seriously. But now, both Wilders and his proposals are. Like Donald Trump, he is now called a "populist" and his xenophobic rhetoric is no longer dismissed as "crazy talk." Hard as it is for many to believe, he is now taken very seriously. It is quite possible that Geert Wilders could one day become Holland's prime minister, a chilling prospect for millions of Dutch Muslims and other minority groups.

Like Marine Le Pen in France, Geert Wilders appeals to a growing nonspecific, impersonal fear of immigrants—particularly those from Muslim-majority countries—and he stokes this irrational fear of the "Islamization" of the West. As we have seen in so many places —including the United States—Wilders is not particularly sure why more Muslim residents would be so bad . . . but he is still very, very sure that they would be.

"I'm not against immigration because I believe all the people who immigrate are not bad people," he once said. "But they bring along a culture that is not ours. Islam is not there to integrate; it's there to dominate!"[237]

Again, domination is very unspecific. How? Why? What form would this forecasted domination take?

Though his charges have never been very specific, Wilders has nonetheless used his political platform to promote a hatred of everything related to Muslim identity. He once even compared the Quran to *Mein Kampf* by Adolf Hitler.[238] From there, he has vacillated between proposing that the Quran be banned outright, to asking that a special tax be levied on it.

In 2011, Wilders was tried and acquitted by a Dutch court on criminal charges of inciting hatred against Muslims; an outcome that only increased his popularity.[239] When Wilders addressed a Dutch crowd in The Hague after his party made gains in the March 2015 election, he showed that the trial had not changed him by making chillingly ominous remarks about the future of Muslims across Europe: "I ask all of you, do you want in this city, and in the Netherlands, more or less Moroccans?!" he shouted. Though a bit convolutedly phrased, his sentiment was crystal clear.

The audience chanted, "Less! Less! Less!"

Wilders ominously replied with a sinister smile: "Then we will arrange that!"[240]

Wilders is important because he is inspiring other Islamophobes, and not just in Europe. As word of his exploits spreads, he has increasingly garnered a following in the United States. In a dozen American states, Geert Wilders had been quoted and cited by right-wing lawmakers in the course of proposing legislation to combat the boogeyman "threat" of Sharia law and Muslim immigration.[241] Wilders seems to like this international attention, and has found himself welcomed by a certain set of the population whenever he visits the United States. And when he speaks to our right-wing media, he minces no words.

"Islam wants to kill or subjugate us," Wilders once proclaimed on the FOX News Channel during one of his American tours.[242]

"We have had enough of the Islamisation of society," Wilders once barked in another interview. "Immigrants have to adopt our values, not the other way around."[243] He also insisted that "we don't hate Muslims, but they have to integrate."

This growing popularity of politicians like Wilders and Le Pen is emblematic of a trend across the EU mainstream. Europeans are become increasingly intolerant and hostile toward both native-born European Muslims and more recent immigrants from the Middle East. The xenophobic movements of the day can no longer be characterized simply as "radical right-wing" fringes. These movements are garnering mainstream political support across Europe.

The British think tank Demos has summed up this growing trend nicely: "Formerly on the political fringes, these [anti-Muslim political] parties now command significant political weight in the parliaments of Austria, Bulgaria, Denmark, Hungary, the Netherlands, Sweden, Latvia and Slovakia, as well as the European Parliament."[244] Because of their growing political market share, far-right Islamophobic racists are going to be a part of the political scene in Europe for the immediate and foreseeable future. They are not going to fade away, or get tired and go home. European politicians have realized that inciting hate against some of Europe's most vulnerable immigrant minorities can be a path to electoral power. Because of this, it will be difficult to make meaningful change and turn back the tide of hate. Nonetheless, it is what must be done if we wish to preserve the virtues of tolerance, enlightenment, and openness for which Europeans are historically known.

***

The thirtieth victim of the 2019 New Zealand mosque massacre was a forty-six-year-old Turkish man named Zekeriya Tuyan. Shortly after the massacre, Turkey's foreign minister took to Twitter to confirm the murder of their citizen in this "treacherous terrorist attack." Diplomatic relations between Turkey and New Zealand became temporarily strained after Turkish President Recep Tayyip Erdogan then showed graphic video clips of the massacre during rallies denouncing Islamophobia. In response, the government of New Zealand banned the video and said that anyone caught sharing it could face up to fourteen years in prison.

To smooth relations between the two countries after this silly political row, New Zealand's Foreign Minister Winston Peters traveled to Turkey to speak at an emergency session of the Organization of Islamic Cooperation (OIC) executive committee meeting convened by Turkey to address Islamophobia. Though relations between New Zealand and Turkey were somewhat restored, the case of Mr. Tuyan shows how just one Islamophobic act can have massive global geopolitical repercussions. It shows why stopping hate crimes—of all types, against all people—should be a serious priority for governments everywhere.

***

Muslim communities in non-Muslim majority countries are generally a collection of fractured diasporic minority subgroups composed of people from diverse racial, ethnic, and socioeconomic backgrounds. In the United Kingdom, recent census data showed that approximately 2.7 million people (or 4.8 percent of the total population) define themselves as "Muslim." This would make Muslims the second largest religious group in Great Britain after Christians (who represent 59.3 percent of the population). To break down the Muslim population a little further, a survey taken right after 9/11 showed that those of Pakistani origin made up 42.5 percent of the British Muslim population; Bangladeshis, 16.8 percent; Indians, 8.5 percent; and "other white" Muslims represented 7.5 percent of the population. This "other white" category used by British census researchers included people of Turkish, Arabic, and North African origin who did not define themselves as nonwhite; Eastern European Muslims from Bosnia and Kosovo; and white Muslims from across Europe. Finally, 6.2 percent of the UK

Muslim population identified as black African, 5.8 percent as other Asian, and 4.1 percent as British.

Even with this diverse heterogeneity, it is still understandable that British Muslims are primarily associated with the South Asian subcontinent, given the fact that South Asians make up over 67 percent of the British Muslim population.[245]

Even though British Muslims represent only a small percentage of the UK population, it has been this small population whose "national loyalty and integration has been of greatest concern" to the UK government. However, many academics have noted that despite concerns regarding British Muslims' loyalty, all of the available empirical evidence—and survey after survey— actually suggests that the vast majority of UK Muslims do proudly "feel British" when it comes to their national identity while also being proud of being Muslim.

The British Home Office Citizenship Survey once found that 43 percent of UK Muslim respondents identify "very strongly" with Britain and 42 percent "fairly strongly"(meaning that 85 percent of British Muslims felt quite proud of their British national identity). According to experts, later surveys even suggested that British Muslims identified more strongly with Britain than the remaining British public at-large (including white British citizens).[246]

In October 2015, British Prime Minister David Cameron announced that anti-Muslim hate crimes were going to be "recorded as a separate category for the first time" by police in England and Wales. Thankfully, this long-overdue move finally brought crimes against Muslims in line with anti-Semitic attacks (which had been recorded in a separate legal category for some time). Cameron was acting for a reason. In the twelve-month period between July 2014 and July 2015, the London Metropolitan Police Service reported a 70 percent increase in hate crimes against Muslims, according to BBC News.[247]

"I want British Muslims to know we will back them to stand against those who spread hate, and to counter the narrative which says Muslims do not feel British," Cameron stated. "And I want police to take more action against those who persecute others simply because of their religion."[248]

The new policy resulted in London police charging at least 816 Islamophobic offenses in the first year alone. According to Tell Mama—a British NGO that monitors Islamophobia and anti-Muslim hate crimes—nearly 60 percent of the Muslim hate-crimes across the United Kingdom targeted "visibly Muslim" women, who wore Islamic religious attire of some sort signaling they are Muslims.[249]

Yet in that same time period, there was also a surge in anti-Semitic hate crimes in the United Kingdom as well, rising by a whopping 93 percent. I think this is important to note, because it shows that the trend is toward a generalized rise in hate. It is impacting Muslims and Jews, but it has the potential to spread to other minority groups as well.

At an international symposium called the "Transatlantic Discourse on Integration" sponsored by the European Forum for Migration Studies at the University of Bamberg in Germany, I once told an audience of prominent European journalists, civic leaders, and government officials in Berlin that any intellectu-ally-honest debate on Western Muslims must aim to "rebuild the bridge of trust that unfortunately has been burning." I also noted that politicians speak of "Muslim assimilation," but that the term "integration" is more inclusive and also more apt, because it acknowledges a two-way street between dominant Western cultures and minority communities; they both have responsibilities toward one another other.[250] I also shared that there is more work to be done. I believe the failure of European governments to fully integrate their diverse Muslim populations—especially second and third generation European Muslim children—has contributed to the social, political, and economic marginalization of Muslims across Europe.

This is quite evident in Germany today. The country now has the second-largest Muslim population in Western Europe. Yet out of the approximately four million Muslims living in Germany, only half of them are legal citizens. Needless to say, this creates a large swath of the Muslim population who are denied access to basic social, educational, and governmental services.[251]

Additionally, Germany has also seen fit to pass their own litany of legislative bans on Muslim (and Jewish) religious practices including ritual circumcision, Islamic headscarves, mosque minarets (which is a tower typically built into or adjacent to mosques), and ritually-slaughtered meat to conform to halal (and kosher) religious standards. In meaningful ways, millions of Muslim citizens still do not enjoy the same religious freedom privileges as white Christians across the European Union.

As predominantly-white European populations continue to age and shrink in number demographically, the idea that dark-skinned Muslims are becoming a larger percentage of European populations is creating growing unease. According to the Pew Research Center, Muslim communities across Europe are generally younger than other demographic groups. The median age for Muslims in Europe was around thirty-two-years old, while all other Europeans were about eight years older with a median age around forty. This growing age disparity is expected to increase even more in the decades to come.[252]

Europe has a longstanding history of racism and xenophobia, when it comes to attitudes toward Jewish and nomadic Roma people (who are also pejoratively known as "gypsies" around the world). Groups like Pew and others have consistently found that anti-Semitic attitudes toward Jewish people are still widely prevalent across European societies, although Jewish people are not seen as negatively today in Europe as Muslims are.[253] According to Pew, at least half of the population polled in European countries like Italy, Greece, and Poland admitted to harboring overall negative opinions of Muslims who live within their respective countries. One spot of good news was that, even despite the rise of Marine Le Pen, Pew further found that the highest overall positive rating was actually in France, where 76 percent of people surveyed said that they had a favorable view of Muslims.[254] Strangely though, the French population still over-estimates the number of Muslims in France because an Ipsos-Mori poll once found that French citizens thought that their country contained a population that was 31 percent Muslim (even though only 8 percent of France is actually Muslim).[255]

***

The thirty-first and thirty-second victims of the 2019 New Zealand mosque massacre were a forty-four-year-old man named Khaled Mustafa and his sixteen-year-old son Hamza Mustafa. As refugees from war-torn Syria, the Mustafa family had moved to New Zealand because they could not join their extended family in the United States because of Donald Trump's Muslim Travel Ban. A horse trainer by profession, Mr. Mustafa regularly brought his sons to Friday prayers with him every week at the Deans Avenue mosque. The matriarch of the family remembered receiving a frantic phone call from her sixteen-year-old son Hamza during the massacre. "He said 'Mum, there's someone come into the mosque and he's shooting us!'" she remembered.[256] "After that, I heard shooting and he screamed and after that I didn't hear him. His phone was on [for another twenty-two minutes], but I couldn't talk to him. After that someone picked up the phone and told me 'Your son can't breathe, I think he's dead!'"

The example of the Mustafa family shows that bans and prejudices against Muslims have real impacts and alter the destinies of families across the globe. And tragically, it also shows that even countries that are "safe and welcoming"—at least in comparison to others—are not always so. And that those exceptions to the rules can be unspeakable.

**

As we consider the future of Muslims around the world—and in Europe especially—we should always consider the millennial generation, and the ones to come after it. However, it can be challenging to discern when young people are, or are not, simply parroting the views of the households in which they are being raised. A survey of six thousand British schoolchildren—the largest of its kind in the United Kingdom at the time—found that over 60 percent of British children surveyed believed that Muslim asylum seekers and immigrants were "stealing jobs in the UK." Furthermore, 35 percent of young people across Britain believed that "Muslims are taking over our country," and about 28 percent of respondents believed that jobs being taken by foreign workers might prevent them, personally, from reaching their own career goals in the future. (All this is according to *The Guardian* newspaper in London.[257])

In Scandinavia, young people are determining the future of nations, but the dominant culture is still a conflicted one. Weaponized Islamophobia is finding its way into the land of

IKEA, especially. In the 2010s, there were hundreds of anti-Muslim attacks, including several major arson attacks, against Swedish mosques in a single week alone.[258] Fearing for their safety, the country's Muslim community took to the streets in a major demonstration to ask for increased security from their government. "We want to send the message that these attacks are a problem for all of society, and not just Muslims," according to Sweden's Islamic Association.[259] Allies held aloft banners that read "Don't touch my mosque!" and placed hundreds of red paper hearts on the door of a mosque that had been targeted by racist graffiti.[260] Sweden is a generally progressive and tolerant country, but it is important to note that major Islamophobic events have still taken place there.

The neighboring Scandinavian country of Denmark has a smaller Muslim population, and in the estimation of many, it seeks to keep its Muslim population tiny by imposing some of Europe's strictest immigration regulations.[261] The country's stinginess on granting refugee status for asylum seekers is so concerning that the United Nations High Commissioner for Refugees (UNHCR) has publicly condemned Denmark's anti-immigrant policies in the past.[262] At the local level, Denmark's "ritual meat ban" was introduced as an "animal welfare initiative" that banned religious animal slaughter without first stunning the animal to render it insensitive to pain. On its face, this law discriminated against both Denmark's orthodox Jewish and Muslim communities who follow strict religious traditions in which animals must be dispatched quickly in kosher and halal methodologies, respectively.

Both Jewish and Muslim groups across Denmark publicly insisted that their method of religious slaughter for both halal and kosher meat is in many cases more humane than electrocuting and stunning animals (as most slaughterhouses do) and they joined their legal efforts in order to have the decision reversed by the European Court for Human Rights. In response, the conservative Danish government pointed to the fact that neighboring Sweden and Norway had both already banned the practice of slaughter without stunning of animals; although they did state that kosher and halal foods could be imported into the country from abroad. Rabbi Pinchas Goldschmidt, head of the European Conference of Rabbis, argued that the Danish ban was a "further erosion of religious liberties in Europe" for both Jewish and Muslim communities across the continent.[263]

The famously "neutral" country of Switzerland—long praised for its tolerance and forward-thinking nature—has roughly 150 mosques nationwide, with only four minarets among them across the whole country. There are about four hundred thousand Muslims in all of Switzerland—most of them from Kosovo and Turkey—among a total population of about 7.5 million people.[264] Nonetheless, the Swiss government would have you think that Muslims are trying to build mosque minarets on every peak of the Swiss Alps! In 2009, a national referendum put forth by the right-wing Swiss People's Party (SVP) proposed legislation to ban mosque minarets across the country.[265] It passed with 57.5 percent of the vote.[266] It also put Switzerland in breach of international conventions on human rights and religious freedom.

The Swiss minaret ban was yet another case of anti-Muslim paranoia being ridden to electoral victory for the far-right in Europe. The organizers of the Swiss anti-minaret campaign had successfully turned a nonexistent dispute over minarets (all *four* of them!) into a symbolic referendum on the future of Muslims in Switzerland. "Minarets are [Islamic] symbols of power," claimed right-wing Swiss politician Ulrich Schluer at the time.[267]

So, sadly, we see that the creeping Islamophobia in Europe has even tainted idyllic "neutral" countries like Switzerland.

According to the Pew Research Center, the total number of European Muslims is projected to continue to increase and this would remain true even if all Muslim immigration stopped today. For example, even if all immigration were halted at this very moment, the population of Muslims would still increase from 4.9 percent to 7.4 percent of the population of Europe by the year 2050, due to simple demographic change. This increase in European Muslim populations will occur mainly because Muslims tend to be younger (by thirteen years, on average) and because they also have higher fertility rates (usually at least one more child per family, on average).[268]

According to the Brookings Institution, there are many other smaller European countries with their own far-right political movements inspired by racist political cues about Muslim demographic change which came directly from Donald Trump's playbook. Many of these smaller European societies will continue to use Muslims as a political football for the foreseeable future. We can see this in countries like Italy, Poland, and Hungary.

In Italy, the two major populist parties currently in power—one right-wing and the other center-left—advance different ideas regarding the optimal relationship between "native Italians" and Muslim minorities, but they still share a convergent prognosis by centering Muslim identity inside their political arena. And although Muslims represent less than 0.1 percent of Poland's entire population, we have seen that Islam and Muslims continue to increasingly feature in the country's political debates as well. Nearby in Hungary, Donald Trump's buddy (right-wing Prime Minister Viktor Orbán) and his conservative Fidesz Party have kept Muslim immigration on the top of Hungary's political agenda.[269] In the 2018 elections, the question of Muslim refugees was central in the campaign, with Orban using the issue not just to solidify his base, but also to expand his support across the country.

Let us end our European tour here. What we have seen should give us pause and make us think deeply.

Europeans seemingly do not wish to acknowledge a simple but unavoidable truth—and certain politicians have found that they can ascend to power by pandering to the idea that this truth can be ignored. That truth is simply this: Muslims are not going away anytime soon.

Just as diverse Jewish communities were eventually integrated into Europe's social fabric; so too will European Muslims be. This integration will not bring negative impacts for Europe, but will instead enrich European nations in a variety of ways, and build on their history of tolerance and pluralism. Whipping up fear of nonspecific terrors that Muslims will supposedly bring with them might be good for getting elected in the short term, but it bears no correlation to the vibrant and diverse future which awaits the Europe of the future.

5

Sharia Is Coming! Sharia Is Coming!

I believe Sharia is a mortal threat to the survival of freedom in the United States.

—Former US House Speaker Newt Gingrich

During the first term of Barack Obama's presidency, I was quoted extensively in a *TIME* Magazine cover story on Islamophobia called "Does America Have a Muslim Problem?" The magazine story dealt with the aftermath of the proposed Park51 Islamic community center in lower Manhattan (which was infamously dubbed the "Ground Zero Mosque" by right-wing haters seeking to block its construction). In addition to the Park51 controversy, the *TIME* article also highlighted nearly half a dozen other mosque projects across the United States which faced copycat smear campaigns and bitter opposition from right-wingers.

"Islamophobia has become the accepted form of racism in America," I was quoted as saying in the August 2010 *TIME* Magazine cover story. "You can always take a potshot at Muslims or Arabs and get away with it." At the time, a joint *TIME*-Abt SRBI poll found that 46 percent of Americans believe Islam is more likely than other faiths to encourage violence against non-believers. Only 37 percent claimed to know a Muslim American. Overall, 61 percent opposed the Park51 project, while just 26 percent were in favor of it. Just 23 percent said it would be a symbol of religious tolerance, while 44 percent said it would be an insult to those who died on 9/11.

The project was so politically radioactive at the time that Barack Obama eloquently defended the American Muslim community's constitutional right to practice its faith—and by inference, to build their mosques where legally permitted—during a White House dinner. But the very next day, President Obama backtracked stating that he was not, he clarified, commenting on the "wisdom of making the decision to put the mosque there."[270]

The heated debate around the high-profile Park51 Islamic Community Center in New York City's lower Manhattan was a catalyst for anti-Sharia movements not just in the United States, but across the Western world as well. Both anti-Muslim opponents (and even well-meaning liberal supporters) inaccurately referred to Park51 as the "Ground Zero Mosque" and that only galvanized anti-mosque movements across the world. Yet the debates over this proposed space simply bore no relation to reality. The Park51 project was an Islamic community center created to propagate interfaith dialogue, and its location bore no intentional relation to the site of the September 11 attacks.

Yet debate over the Park51 Community Center quickly became absurd, with anti-Muslim forces claiming that it would represent an Islamic "victory" flag planted in the ashes of the

Twin Towers. A proposed NYC bus advertisement objecting to the project actually depicted a plane flying toward the World Trade Center's towers with a rendering of the Islamic community center on the right. It was clear that no implication, extrapolation, or exaggeration would be considered too absurd or insane.

The "Ground Zero Mosque" controversy was important because many other high-profile anti-mosque campaigns across the West still seek to use it as a model to chill the religious freedom rights of millions of Muslims today.

One such copycat anti-mosque campaign took place in 2010 in the southern college town of Murfreesboro, Tennessee, near the campus of Middle Tennessee State University. Anti-Muslim protestors here similarly denounced plans for a large mosque proposed near a residential subdivision. The faux controversy began when hundreds of angry anti-Muslim protesters turned out for a contentious county board meeting on the proposed Murfreesboro mosque project. The protests and subsequent court challenges ended up delaying the construction of the mosque for nearly five years.

Just a few months before the Murfreesboro kerfuffle began, members of a right-wing Tea Party group in Temecula, California decided to take loud barking dogs and racist anti-Muslim picket signs to Friday Muslim prayers at a neighborhood mosque that was seeking to build a new worship center on a vacant lot nearby. Many of them cited the "Ground Zero Mosque" as their inspiration when asked what motivated them to commit this brazenly cruel act of anti-Muslim intimidation.

In Wisconsin, several Christian ministers in Sheboygan decided to lead a noisy fight against Muslim community members who sought permission to open a mosque in a former health-food store bought by a local Muslim doctor. These ministers were urged on by the precedent set in Manhattan that mosques could be challenged successfully.

And even in a progressive New England city like Bridgeport, Connecticut, several local Muslim community leaders had to ask local police for increased security so that they could worship in peace after an angry Islamophobic mob protested outside their local mosque.

In Texas, nearly a dozen members of a group calling itself Operation Save America angrily confronted peaceful Muslim worshippers at the Masjid An-Noor mosque and yelled what congregants described as "hate-filled slogans" against Muslims seeking to simply worship in peace.[271] Once more, the "Ground Zero Mosque" was heavily cited as their inspiration.

The fact that this is accepted perplexes me to no end! Can you imagine if we woke up one morning to news of an effort by a network of heavily armed self-described "patriots"—many of them carrying loaded semi-automatic guns— to block the construction of temples and organize over twenty nationwide simultaneous armed protests outside Jewish synagogues? Or what about African American churches? I think most reasonable people would be horrified at the prospect of mass intimidation at these minority houses of worship across the country.

What we have to ask ourselves, then, is why is it different for Muslims? What aspect of the propaganda have we collectively accepted such that we are not alarmed by this happening to innocent Muslims?

In recent years, this activity has not abated. The double standard against Muslims remains. In October 2015, a nationwide network of right-wing anti-Muslim "patriot" groups orchestrated nearly two dozen coordinated armed protests at Islamic mosques across America. I believe these racist bullies intended nothing less than to silence the First Amendment rights of nearly ten million American Muslims.

Did that produce the same degree of outrage as protests against Jews or African Americans might have?

Not so much.

This nationwide campaign was euphemistically called the "Global Rally for Humanity" and encouraged "fellow patriots" to unite in protest of the growth of Islam in America. As I wrote in *The Atlantic* at the time: "These would-be 'patriots' are nothing more than gun-wielding bullies trying to intimidate religious minorities from freely exercising their First Amendment rights by pointing their loaded semi-automatic Second Amendment rights directly into synagogues, temples, and mosques around the country."[272] Simply put, for these haters, if Muslims are allowed to build their houses of worship and participate in a free society—just as Jews, Hindus, Black Christians, and others have been allowed to do—then Muslim extremists have "won" somehow.

***

The thirty-third victim of the 2019 New Zealand mosque massacre was a forty-year-old man named Haroon Mahmood. A native of Pakistan, Mr. Mahmood had worked as a banker before moving to New Zealand to become assistant academic director of Canterbury College in Christchurch. Before his murder, he was only two months away from earning a PhD in finance. He was eventually laid to rest in a mass burial along with twenty-five other Muslim victims of the New Zealand attacks. Two months after the Christchurch massacre, Mr. Mahmood's wife and two children accepted his PhD posthumously from Lincoln University in an emotional graduation ceremony. "It was hard, but it was wonderful to see them come," Vice Chancellor Bruce McKenzie told Radio New Zealand. "It was very moving. There were a lot of tears."[273]

Mr. Mahmood had become a New Zealander and had exemplified some of the finest traits and achievements in the estimation of any culture. And still he was killed for simply being a Muslim.

***

Many haters of Islam and Muslims often make the ridiculous argument that mosques are somehow inherently "breeding grounds" for extremism in the West. I urge anyone considering this silly argument to consult the massive two-year joint study by Duke University's Sanford School of Public Policy and the University of North Carolina which found that American mosques are, actually, a deterrent to the spread of extremism. Echoing these findings, a related *New York Times* article found that many mosque leaders in America had actually put significant effort into countering extremism by building youth programs, sponsoring public forums, and scrutinizing educational materials taught within their mosques.[274]

Going back to the "Ground Zero Mosque" controversy for a moment, certain right-wing vocal critics of the project —a coalition that included conservative American political figures like Sarah Palin, Newt Gingrich, and other Tea Party activists— attacked the Park51 project on the grounds that it would create extremists. When, in fact, we now know the opposite to be true. Former Republican vice presidential nominee Sarah Palin infamously asked people to "refudiate" (sic) the Park51 project on Twitter. Right-wing televangelist Pat Robertson publicly pledged to organize legal efforts and fundraising campaigns to block its construction. All because they believed it would do the opposite of what it would actually do.

This would be amusing if it were not also so hurtful.

There were only a few brave vocal supporters of the proposed Park51 project at the time. These were true champions of American pluralism and religious tolerance. They included New York City Mayor Michael Bloomberg. During an emotional press conference on the controversy, Mayor Bloomberg bravely told TV cameras: "Whatever you may think of the proposed mosque and community center, lost in the heat of the debate has been a basic question: Should government attempt to deny private citizens the right to build a house of worship on private property based on their particular religion? That may happen in other countries, but we should never allow it to happen here." Bloomberg choked back tears as he spoke these words.

"This nation was founded on the principle that the government must never choose between religions, or favor one over another. There is no neighborhood in this city that is off-limits to God's love and mercy," Bloomberg concluded.

For those who duplicitously claimed that the Park51 center was being built on sacred hallowed ground, in fact, the unassuming lower Manhattan building in question was actually an old Burlington Coat Factory store. This new hundred million dollar Park51 community center to be built in its place would have included bookstores, restaurants, art galleries, basketball courts and, yes, even a Muslim prayer room.

I still wonder how any reasonable person could be opposed to that.

Another unsung hero in the Park51 debate was CNN host Fareed Zakaria. Without any obligation whatsoever, Mr. Zakaria decided to return an award (and ten thousand dollar cash honorarium that came with it) to the Anti-Defamation League after the group bizarrely joined the opposition to the Park51 community center. In a *Newsweek* column called "Build the Ground Zero Mosque," Mr. Zakaria wrote that "If there is going to be a reformist movement in Islam, it is going to emerge from places like the proposed institute. We should be encouraging groups like the one behind this project, not demonizing them. Were this mosque being built in a foreign city, chances are that the U.S. government would be funding it."[275]

As Jeffrey Goldberg from *The Atlantic* noted: "Americans who seek the marginalization of Muslims in this country are unwittingly doing the work of Islamist extremists. We must do everything possible to avoid giving them propaganda victories in their attempt to create a cosmic war between Judeo-Christian civilization and Muslim civilization. The fight is not between the West and Islam."[276]

Georgetown University Professor John Esposito—once called the "most influential Islamic scholar in the United States"[277] by The *International Herald Tribune*—told me during an *Esquire* interview that many of these anti-Muslim activists are regularly employing hate speech and dangerous invective aimed at Islam and Muslims as a whole. Professor Esposito told me that these people duplicitously conflate Islam and Muslims as a whole with terrorism for general American public consumption in a hyper-partisan social media landscape. Yet community centers such as the one proposed in Manhattan would stand to break these stereotypes and prove how untrue they are. Perhaps that is why white nationalists fear them.

"The result [of prevailing attitudes] has been the growth of Islamophobia—a widespread suspicion of mainstream Muslims and discrimination towards Muslims based on their religion or race—that has led to hate crimes and other acts of violence," Professor Esposito elaborated. He added that these anti-mosque protests are just the tip of a growing racist iceberg, concluding: "Especially troubling is the fact that opponents and protesters were not simply uneducated or marginalized bigots, right-wing political commentators, and hardline Christian pastors, but also American politicians who belong to mainstream political parties as well."[278]

Many other experts agree with this position.

"I think most Americans are exposed to anti-Muslim messages in the media and elsewhere," this, according to Professor Christopher Bail, author of a groundbreaking media study tracking the prevalence of anti-Muslim groups in US news coverage. "The danger, I believe, is that many Americans have not been exposed to the positive messages of Muslim organizations because they receive so little media coverage. We learned the American media almost completely ignored public condemnations by prominent Muslim organizations in the United States."[279] Instead, Professor Bail noted that American media tends to disproportionately focus on Muslims almost exclusively in a negative media framework.

To illustrate this point, a January 2019 study published in *Justice Quarterly* by researchers from the University of Alabama found that the constant negative framing of Muslims primarily within a "national security" framework generally led media outlets to over-emphasize acts of terrorism committed by Muslims over those committed by white people. The study showed that terrorist attacks carried out by Muslims received 357 percent more media coverage than those committed by other groups (like white supremacists). This clear anti-Muslim bias in news coverage of attacks based on religion might explain why members of the American public tend to fear Muslims, and see Muslims as aggressors who are looking to "conquer" rather than just being normal Americans of a different religion trying to raise their families.

A major study from the Media Portrayals of Minorities Project (MPoMP) at Middlebury College analyzed the portrayals of ethnic and religious minority groups in major American daily newspaper databases. Out of all the minority groups analyzed, this Middlebury study found that Muslims were by far the most negatively portrayed minority group in America. "In brief," the Middlebury researchers wrote, "Our analyses show that coverage of Muslims stands out as being both the most frequent and the most negative by a wide margin," compared to overall newspaper coverage of African Americans, Asian Americans, Latinos, and Jewish people.

This September 2019 report also highlighted the fact that although 17 percent of articles about Jewish people analyzed mentioned anti-Semitism at least once, only 2 percent of articles about Muslims mentioned the word Islamophobia anywhere at all.[280] Many people rightfully see Donald Trump's Muslim Travel Ban as a clear reflection of rising "anti-Muslim sentiment" or "institutionalized Islamophobia"; and there are fewer and fewer questions as to how these feelings arise.

"Muslims have been a positive force in United States history since the [nineteenth] century," according to Duke University Professor Chris Bail. "Before the September 11 attacks, Muslims might have been described as a 'model minority' with above average levels of education and income. They were so inconspicuous that they were routinely confused with Latinos. Needless to say, the September 11 attacks changed everything."[281]

***

The thirty-fourth victim of the 2019 New Zealand mosque massacre was a thirty-eight-year-old man named Kamel Darwish. A dairy farmer by profession, Mr. Darwish had only arrived in

Christchurch a few months before the attack from his native country of Jordan. His brother had convinced him to move to New Zealand because he said that there was no safer place to raise a family. The double tragedy for the Darwish family occurred one day after Kamel's funeral, when his sixty-five-year-old mother Saud Adwan died suddenly of a massive heart attack less than twenty-four hours after burying her son. "She came yesterday to attend the funeral," according to a family friend. "Apparently this morning she passed away because she couldn't deal with the sorrow and sadness of losing her son."[282]

***

Any red-blooded American with a basic high school education knows that the Supremacy Clause of the US Constitution states that the Constitution and the laws of the United States are the only things which constitute the "supreme Law of the Land." This simply means that no other law in the world (either foreign or domestic) can trump our American constitution.

Certainly not Islamic Sharia law.

And yet . . . fear of it remains something that politicians have realized they can manipulate for their own right-wing political agendas.

"Anti-Sharia law initiatives could be in future election cycles what anti-gay marriage initiatives were before," Marc Ambinder from *The Atlantic* magazine once wrote. "That is, a cultural wedge issue that the [Republican Party] uses to ensure that hard-core conservatives enthusiastically flock to the polls." To illustrate this point, Ambinder noted that former Republican presidential candidate Newt Gingrich once told conservative activists at the Value Voters Summit that, "I am opposed to any efforts to impose Sharia in the United States, and we should have a federal law that says under no circumstances in any jurisdiction in the United States will Sharia be used in any court to apply to any judgment made about American law."[283]

Of course, we already have laws making clear that Sharia law will not be imposed: the highest constitutional kind.

Gingrich also once called Islamic law a "mortal threat to the survival of freedom in the United States" and likewise unnecessarily declared his opposition "to any efforts to impose Sharia in the United States,"[284] as if bearded mullahs were already gathering ominously on the steps of the US Capitol to make everyone eat from their yummy halal food trucks!

In addition to Gingrich, other right-wing presidential wannabes have jumped on this anti-Muslim fear-mongering bandwagon over the years. For instance, former Republican congresswoman Michele Bachmann (R-MN) once declared that Sharia "must be resisted across the United States."[285] Another 2012 presidential hopeful, pizza magnate Herman Cain (who died in July 2020 of COVID-19), once condemned the "attempt to gradually ease Sharia law and the Muslim faith into our government" during one of his campaigns.[286]

By whom? When? How?

Sometimes I think these batshit crazy politicians learned a dangerous lesson from Gingrich and others who came before them. They regurgitate absurd and ridiculous claims about Islam or Muslims as a sinister, aggressive force—and there is no substantive negative consequence to making them.

For example, Newt Gingrich once bizarrely suggested that the US Supreme Court had somehow become an Islamist sleeper cell, for the love of God! He further accused two liberal Supreme Court justices (Justice Stephen Breyer and Justice Elena Kagan) of insufficient vigilance against the threat of Sharia, stating that "no judge should remain in office who tries to use Sharia law to interpret the United States Constitution."[287]

It was insane. It was laughable. And yet Gingrich suffered no substantive negative political condemnations for making these outrageous anti-Muslim claims.

A public opinion poll from the Public Religion Research Institute (PRRI) found that more than one-third of white evangelicals (34 percent) in America believe that Muslims wish to establish Sharia law within the United States (which, again, would clearly violate the Supremacy Clause of the US Constitution, and is therefore impossible). Not surprisingly, the percentage was even higher—52 percent—among respondents who said that they rely on FOX News Channel as their primary source of news.[288]

"The suggestion that Sharia threatens American security is disturbingly reminiscent of the accusation, in nineteenth-century Europe, that Jewish religious law was seditious," wrote Yale University Professor Eliyahu Stern in an opinion piece for the *New York Times* bluntly titled "Don't Fear Islamic Law in America." Professor Stern noted that the conspiratorial fear that Jewish law bred disloyalty was not limited to political elites in Western societies either. He noted that leading mainstream European philosophers propagated these fears at the time with their noxious anti-Semitic personal views. For instance, the famous German philosopher Immanuel Kant had once argued that the particularistic nature of "Jewish legislation" made Jews "hostile to all other peoples." Fellow German philosopher Georg Wilhelm Friedrich Hegel similarly contended that Jewish kosher dietary rules and other Mosaic laws barred Jewish people from identifying with their fellow Prussians and called into question their ability to be loyal civil servants in government.

"Most Americans today would be appalled if Muslims suffered from legally sanctioned discrimination as Jews once did in Europe," Professor Stern cogently added in his *New York Times* piece. "Still, there are signs that many Americans view Muslims in this country as disloyal."[289] He further cited a Gallup poll which found that only 56 percent of Protestants in America believe that Muslims are "loyal" Americans today. He juxtaposed that astonishing figure with another Pew Research Center poll which found that American Muslims demonstrated the highest level of integration among major American minority religious groups; expressing greater degrees of pluralistic tolerance than did Protestants, Catholics, or Jewish people in America today.[290]

"In fact, for most of its history, Islamic law offered the most liberal and humane legal principles available anywhere in the world," Harvard Law Professor Noah Feldman wrote for the *New York Times Magazine*. "One reason for the divergence between Western and Muslim views of Sharia is that we are not all using the word to mean the same thing. Although it is commonplace to use the word 'Sharia' and the phrase 'Islamic law' interchangeably. In fact, 'Sharia' is not the word traditionally used in Arabic to refer to the processes of Islamic legal reasoning or the rulings produced through it: that word is *fiqh*, meaning something like Islamic jurisprudence. Westerners typically imagine that Sharia advocates simply want to use the Quran as their legal code. But the reality is much more complicated," Professor Feldman concluded.[291]

Muslims thinkers and scholars have also made this exact same point over and over again.

"Some of the biggest misperceptions about Islamic law are that it proposes a scheme of global domination," asserts Imam Zaid Shakir, cofounder of Zaytuna College in Berkeley, California—the first Muslim liberal arts college in America.

During an interview, Imam Zaid further told me that many Westerners mistakenly believe that Islamic law "is not amenable to change in the face of changing circumstances, that it is a system that oppresses women and that by definition, it is an enemy of western civilization." In fact, he added, the mainstream doctrines of Sharia law actually forbid the un-Islamic practices that so many Westerners fear.

"For example, Sharia forbids members of a Muslim minority in Western societies from engaging in clandestine acts of violence and paramilitary organizing or from acting as political or military agents for a Muslim-majority country. Furthermore, Islamic law also forbids the disruption of public safety,"[292] Imam Zaid clarified for me.

All of this context might come as a surprise to the many people who know little about Islam—whether they are extremists who profess to be devout Muslims or right-wing Islamophobes who seek to politically exploit anti-Muslim fear around the world for their own political gains.

"In times of economic distress, people tend to be more susceptible to charlatans and demagogues telling them who to blame and who to fear," said Matthew Duss, an old friend of mine who served as longtime foreign policy advisor for Senator Bernie Sanders (I-VT), in a 2017 interview with me on the subject of anti-Sharia hysteria. "America has been through this sort of thing before with various minority groups, but we've always come through it stronger in the end. Hopefully within a few years, the idea that all American Muslims want to turn America into an Islamic state will seem as stupid as the idea that a Catholic president would take orders from the Vatican."

He likened the growth of anti-Sharia hysteria to the 'Team B' phenomenon that was prevalent in the 1970s. Under Team B, prominent US neoconservative political figures sought to issue a set of exaggerated and hysteria-inducing claims promoting anti-Soviet conspiracy theories during the Cold War era. "As we now know, these claims were just wildly overstated, to a hysterical degree," he continued. "I think there's a clear similarity in the way that anti-gay marriage referendums during the 2004 presidential campaigns and current anti-Sharia efforts are being used to stir up the conservative base" in American politics for the foreseeable future.[293]

***

The thirty-fifth victim of the 2019 New Zealand mosque massacre was a thirty-seven-year-old man named Osama Abukwaik. A civil engineer from the Gaza Strip who spent many years in Egypt as a refugee, Mr. Abukwaik decided to move to New Zealand so he could save up some money for his children's education. After the Christchurch massacre, his older brother living in California remembered him as a kind and decent man who had finally found a home in New Zealand after a lifetime of being a stateless Palestinian refugee. "I have never been to New Zealand," his brother said after the mosque shootings. "But now, Christchurch will always have a piece of me buried in it."[294]

***

We see in examples like this who it is that Islamophobia hurts, but who benefits from it, and in what ways?

The Center for American Progress (CAP) once prepared a comprehensive report entitled *Fear Inc.: The Roots of the Islamophobia Network in America*, which explored the multi-million dollar Islamophobia industry in the United States. The CAP report found that over a seven-year period alone, at least seven well-endowed American foundations and conservative donors provided over forty-two million dollars to anti-Muslim activists in America. According to CAP's findings, these wealthy right-wing funders of Islamophobia included the Richard Mellon Scaife Foundation, Donors Capital Fund, Lynde & Harry Bradley Foundation, Newton & Rochelle Becker Foundation/Charitable Trust, Russell Berrie Foundation, Anchorage Charitable Fund, and the Fairbrook Foundation. The majority of the forty-two million dollars went to five prominent anti-Muslim activists: Frank Gaffney (Center for Security Policy), David Yerushalmi (Society of Americans for National Existence and the American Freedom Law Center), Daniel Pipes (Middle East Forum), Robert Spencer (Jihad Watch), and Steven Emerson (The Investigative Project).[295]

Out of everyone in the above litany, David Yerushalmi (along with Islamophobic zealot Pamela Geller) has been the most outspoken advocate for anti-Sharia legislation in the United States. Thanks to his share of the forty-two million dollar Islamophobia pie, Yerushalmi was able to use his right-wing think tank—euphemistically named the Society of Americans for National Existence (with the hilarious acronym "SANE")—to draft boilerplate template language for anti-Sharia legislation as early as 2007, making adherence to "Sharia" a felony punishable by up to twenty years in prison.

According to the Anti-Defamation League (ADL), David Yerushalmi has a long "record of anti-Muslim, anti-immigrant and anti-black bigotry"[296] and this has been present throughout his career. For example, in addition to his naked Islamophobia, the ADL reported that Yerushalmi once called African Americans "the most murderous of peoples."[297] And yet these are the people receiving millions of dollars to fund institutes! Can it be any wonder? Racism literally pays!

I want to also note that Yerushalmi is closely aligned within the anti-Sharia movement with the flamboyant anti-Muslim activist Pamela Geller. The Anti-Defamation League has stated that Geller presents "herself as an expert on Islam, promoting the theory that there is an Islamic conspiracy to destroy American values and culture."[298] The ADL further stated that "much of her pseudo-expertise on Islam is built on exploiting public fears of a grand Muslim conspiracy that will reach every neighborhood across the country if left unchecked."[299]

The Southern Poverty Law Center, which also lists Geller's organization—the American Freedom Defense Initiative—as a hate group, once noted that Pamela Geller has "seized the role of the anti-Muslim movement's most visible and influential figurehead. Her strengths are panache and vivid rhetorical flourishes— not to mention stunts like posing for an anti-Muslim video in a bikini." The SPLC further determined that Geller is prone to publicizing other racialized conspiracy theories, including once absurdly claiming that President Barack Obama was the "love child of Malcolm X."[300]

"When you've got folks who are looking for the worst in Islam and are promoting that as the entire religion of 1.5 or 1.6 billion people, then you only empower the real extremists," wrote Brian Fishman of West Point's Combating Terrorism Center in a *New York Times* article on the rise of these anti-Muslim fear mongers.[301] With millions of dollars coming from right-wing foundations, these Islamophobic hucksters have succeeded in pushing hatred of Muslims into the Western mainstream. This is directly tied to the numerical growth of anti-Sharia legislative bills proposed across the country in the last few decades.

As evidence of this, I note that the Southern Poverty Law Center has determined that at least 120 anti-Sharia legislative bills have been introduced in forty-two states since 2010. In the year 2017 alone, there were at least thirteen different states which introduced anti-Sharia legislation; with the states of Texas and Arkansas actually passing some form of such legislation into law.[302] In June 2017, Texas governor Greg Abbott signed into law House Bill 45, which prevented the use of "foreign laws" (the neutral-sounding vanilla term which actually refers to Sharia law) in domestic civil cases within the Lone Star State. This was signed into law just four months after Arkansas adopted similar legislation.[303]

These ideological extremists vying for funding from supportive right-wing multi-millionaires and billionaires are having real impacts in the real world. The conclusions could not be clearer.

According to the Haas Institute at the University of California-Berkeley, most of the boilerplate language from these anti-Sharia bills was directly copied from "The American Laws for American Courts Act." This was the title for a boilerplate template piece of legislation shopped around to conservative state legislatures by the anti-Sharia advocacy group the American Public Policy Alliance, and written by—you guessed it—the aforementioned David Yerushalmi himself.

Although the generic text of "The American Laws for American Courts Act" talks about protecting the United States from "foreign laws" broadly, the most cursory look at the right-wing organization's website reveals its true intentions against Muslims.[304] The website of APPA repeatedly warns of the dangers of Sharia law, with no mention whatsoever of any other type of "foreign law" that we ought to fear.[305]

In response to these growing legislative attacks resulting from these newly-moneyed activists, the American Civil Liberties Union (ACLU) joined a legal challenge against a proposed amendment to the Oklahoma Constitution which would have targeted the religious practices of American Muslims. Although the right-wing political co-sponsors of this terrible Oklahoma legislation publicly admitted that there had been literally zero instances of so-called "Sharia" threats in the Sooner State, they still nonetheless decided to call their stupid proposal the "Save Our State Amendment," which ultimately passed with over 70 percent of the vote.

"Obviously, it's not possible to impose Sharia Law on American criminal courts under the Constitution. That was simply propaganda," declared Mark Potok of the Southern Poverty Law Center.[306] "So, they created a fear-mongering, hate-generating tactic, aimed at Muslims in America, that was very effective, and now a number of states have actually adopted the anti-Sharia legislation . . ."

Thankfully, an Oklahoma federal court struck down this unconstitutional Oklahoma state amendment in a later ruling. In this legal challenge, the ACLU and the Council on American-Islamic Relations (CAIR) jointly challenged the constitutionality of this Oklahoma amendment on behalf of the executive director of CAIR's Oklahoma chapter. "This law unfairly singled out one faith and one faith only," said Ryan Kiesel, executive director of the ACLU of Oklahoma. "This amendment was nothing more than a solution in search of a problem. We're thrilled that it has been struck down."[307]

To prove that anti-Sharia legislation is directly tied to moneyed right-wing American political movements, the University of California-Berkeley's Haas Institute further highlighted the fact that the majority of anti-Sharia legislations in recent history were introduced in calendar years prior to midterm and/or presidential election cycles (to ensure turnout from conservative Republican voters). For example, they showed that fifty-six anti-Sharia bills were introduced in 2011, thirty-five bills

were introduced in 2013, and thirty-five bills were introduced
in 2015. By contrast, fourteen, twenty-five, fifteen, and fourteen anti-Sharia bills were introduced in the election years of
2010, 2012, 2014, and 2016, respectively.[308] This phenomenon
highlighted a trend among conservative Republican lawmakers
to push anti-Muslim legislation in the run-up to midterm and
presidential election cycles to help get out the conservative vote
across America.

"Islamophobia affects democracy in at least three ways,"
said Dalia Mogahed, co-author of the book *Who Speaks for
Islam: What a Billion Muslims Really Think*. "Firstly, the anti-
Sharia legislation movement is really part of a larger problem,
as the same lawmakers that are targeting Muslims are targeting other minorities as well. Secondly, Islamophobia hurts our
democracy in that it scares people," she continued. "Fear makes
people more accepting of authoritarianism, conformity, and
prejudice. And thirdly, it manipulates people, and manipulates
the public to consent to policies that they would otherwise not
agree."[309]

Islamophobia may help politicians get an edge in their
midterm election campaigns, but it rides on the backs of one of
America's most vulnerable and marginalized groups.

However, as a silver lining, more and more legal experts
from across the ideological spectrum are continuing to publicly
denounce these anti-Sharia bills. The American Bar Association
(ABA) published a formal letter of dissent condemning these
bills categorically, and said: "The American Bar Association
opposes federal or state laws that impose blanket prohibitions
on consideration or use by courts or arbitral tribunals of the
entire body of law or doctrine of a particular religion."[310] The
ABA further challenged this anti-Muslim hysteria by adding
that, "American courts will not apply Sharia or other rules (real

or perceived) that are contrary to our public policy, including, for instance, rules that are incompatible with our notions of gender equality."

Needless to say, this rise in anti-Sharia legislation is directly impacting the physical safety of Arabs, Muslims, and/or South Asians. It is not the only factor, but it is doubtless a part of it. When legislation or legislators seek to repudiate a group's belief system, you can bet that people are going to feel they have more of a green light to go after that group. For example, hate crimes against Muslims increased by 67 percent in 2015 according to FBI statistics—a year when many of these anti-Sharia bills were on the table. In Oklahoma, three American Muslim students once attempted to visit conservative Republican representative John Bennett in the state capitol since they were his constituents. However, before agreeing to meet with his own constituents, the right-wing lawmaker bizarrely demanded that they first fill out a ridiculous anti-Muslim questionnaire about Islam which included dumb questions like "Do you beat your wife?"[311] Like many other right-wing Republican lawmakers today, this Oklahoma legislator had a long history of expressing anti-Muslim views. According to the *Tulsa World* newspaper, he once called Muslims a "cancer in our nation that needs to be cut out" and even refused to apologize for those blatantly Islamophobic remarks—even though he probably would have been voted out of office if he had made these statements about virtually any other minority group in America.[312]

At this rate, these right-wing Western politicians will keep attacking minorities and people of color with impunity unless our allies publicly shame them for using tired old racist conspiracy theories from the propaganda playbooks of yesteryear.

***

The thirty-sixth victim of the 2019 New Zealand mosque massacre was a thirty-six-year-old man named Junaid Ismail. Born
and raised in Christchurch, the native Kiwi Muslim ran a corner
dairy store with his twin brother Zahid (who thankfully survived
the mass shooting that fateful day). Speaking through tears, in
the aftermath Zahid told reporters "I would rather that I went
than him. I'm the naughty twin; he was the better one."[313] Mr.
Ismail's cousin told a television reporter after the massacre: "I
couldn't find a more softly spoken, shy, beautiful personality.
Whenever you met Junaid, you had to re-evaluate who you were
as a person. He had that kind of effect on people."[314]

Yet that is the thing about acts of terror. It can take the very
best of us, the very worst of us, and anyone in between.

***

Truth be told, there is no better way to scapegoat nearly two billion global Muslims collectively than by insinuating that we are
all card-carrying members of some sinister global Muslim mafia.
To illustrate this point, the "Muslim Brotherhood Terrorist
Designation Act" is a bizarre annual piece of legislation first
introduced by right-wing US Senator Ted Cruz (R-Texas) which
calls for labeling the Muslim Brotherhood as a "foreign terrorist
organization" (or "FTO") by the US State Department.[315] Not
to be outdone by his erstwhile Republican primary opponent,
Donald Trump threatened to issue his own unilateral executive order directing the State Department to examine whether it
should designate the Muslim Brotherhood as a foreign terrorist
organization (FTO) while he was president as well.[316]

The Muslim Brotherhood is a social, religious, and political
organization founded by an Egyptian schoolteacher in 1928. It
was originally focused on social programs such as feeding the

hungry and providing medical attention to the unwell. Over the years, it has taken many different political positions and has sometimes splintered. Today, while many of its members are orthodox conservatives, adherents come from across the ideological spectrum and identify with different eras in the party's history. (Consider Republicans today who identify with Abraham Lincoln contrasted with those Republicans today who identify with Donald Trump.)

By invoking the "Muslim Brotherhood" as a monolithic smear against Muslims who challenge their policies, I believe that right-wing politicians like Ted Cruz and Donald Trump are not genuinely trying to keep America safe; instead, they simply want to criminalize American Muslim civic life as a whole. They are trying to find a solution to a nonexistent problem, and I am not the only one to see it. A *Washington Post* article called "How an obscure U.S. policy effort could hurt American Muslims" highlighted how previous bipartisan presidential administrations (both Democrat and Republican) have *never* previously viewed the Muslim Brotherhood as a "foreign terrorist organization."[317] Instead, the *Washington Post* reported that these new Republican efforts to designate the group are politically-based and would "have a far-reaching impact on American Muslims at a time when Muslim community leaders say the religious minority is facing the worst harassment" in the United States today.

Michele Dunne, director of the Middle East program at the Carnegie Endowment for International Peace, has stated that if these right-wing politicians are successful in their pursuits, it would be the first time in American history that a group was designated as an FTO ("foreign terrorist organization") based purely on "ideological" grounds.[318]

"It is wrongheaded and dangerous to tar all [Muslim] Brotherhood members with one brush," the *New York Times* editorial board wrote in one collective voice condemning the move by Republicans.[319] "It appears to be part of a mission by the president and his closest advisers to heighten fears [of Muslims]." The *Times* editorial board further pointed out the historical fact that the Muslim Brotherhood officially "renounced violence decades ago," similar to the Irish Republican Army (IRA) fully renouncing violence in 1994.[320] They concluded their *New York Times* editorial by asserting that Trump's talk about branding the Brotherhood as a terrorist organization did nothing but "fueled darker fears of an administration intent on going after not just terrorists but Islam" and jeopardizing the civic lives of seven million American Muslims as well.

"Designating the Muslim Brotherhood as a Foreign Terrorist Organization in fact plays into the hands of ISIS and other terrorist groups," said Georgetown University professor John Esposito. "It will be used by the terrorists as a propaganda recruitment tool against the United States. Declaring the Brotherhood as a terrorist organization would fuel an anti-Muslim witch hunt that the US has not experienced since the McCarthy anti-communist era."[321]

Once again, we see ourselves ruled by men (and women) who do not mind putting the world into unnecessary danger when and if it will further their own near-sighted political ends.

***

The thirty-seventh victim of the 2019 New Zealand mosque massacre was a thirty-six-year-old man named Mohammed Omar Faruk. The construction worker from Bangladesh was only a few months away from becoming a father, but he never lived to see the birth of his child. "He was the only one to look after his family," his roommate said after the massacre. "He always dreamed of returning home, but was killed in Christchurch."[322]

Unlike Mr. Faruk, several members of the Bangladesh national cricket team—who were in town for a match against New Zealand's national team—just avoided the massacre by arriving late to the Christchurch mosque that fateful day. Afterward, they expressed shock and dismay at the killing of one of their countrymen, and wondered at the forces which could have caused such a horrible thing to occur.

***

For many years, the "Islamophobia industry" has looked for characterizations and slanders that would further its ends, and not just in the United States. For years, politicians around the world have used the "Muslim Brotherhood" label as sloppy shorthand to defame any Muslim civic organization, politician, and government official that they did not like. For instance, here in the United States, the Muslim Brotherhood smear has been used in the past to attack prominent American Muslims like former Democratic congressman Keith Ellison (who now serves as attorney general of Minnesota), longtime Hillary Clinton aide Huma Abedin, and even Gold Star father Khizr Khan, who famously criticized Donald Trump on primetime national television at the 2016 Democratic National Convention. Abroad, however, it is used just as often by a myriad of political opportunists.

According to the Southern Poverty Law Center, Trump's threat to issue an executive order on the Muslim Brotherhood during his presidency was squarely "aimed at American Muslims and controlling them while at the same time continuing to demonize Islam."[323]

"Let me be extremely clear," said J. M. Berger, a counter-terrorism analyst at George Washington University's Program on Extremism. "This initiative is concerned with controlling American Muslims, not with any issue pertaining to the Muslim Brotherhood in any practical or realistic sense."[324] In fact, counterterrorism experts have consistently acknowledged that there is no hard evidence at all to support a Muslim Brotherhood designation apart from one murky unauthenticated "1991 memorandum" written in Arabic by a mystery man allegedly affiliated with the Brotherhood. This dubious memo is seen by the Islamophobia industry as proof of the organization's nebulous influence in the United States.

"This [alleged 1991] memorandum, of which there is only one known copy, has been widely discredited and called a fantasy,"[325] wrote Georgetown University law professor Arjun Singh Sethi in a *Washington Post* piece.

Pulitzer Prize winner David Shipler also investigated this sketchy 1991 memorandum for the *New Yorker* when he wrote that "virtually all the alarm over the coming Islamic takeover and the spread of Sharia law can be traced back to an old document of questionable authority and relevance entitled *'An Explanatory Memorandum on the General Strategic Goal for the Group in North America.'*" Mr. Shipler also wrote that this dubious memo is still regularly cited on numerous right-wing websites, and also in articles, videos, and training materials, which quote one another in circular arguments about the Muslim boogeyman coming to take over America.

"The memo, however, is far from probative," Shipler finally concludes.[326] "It was never subjected to an adversarial test of its authenticity or significance. Examined closely, it does not stand up as an authoritative prescription for action." As The Bridge Initiative at Georgetown University once nicely summed up about this sketchy 1991 memorandum: "This document should not be taken seriously."[327]

New York Times bestselling author Reza Aslan once told me during an interview that this murky 1991 Muslim Brotherhood memo "reeks of the Protocols of the Elders of Zion." For those unfamiliar, the Protocols were a debunked anti-Semitic conspiracy theory alleging a late nineteenth-century secret meeting at which Jewish leaders—pejoratively referred to as the "Elders of Zion"—planned their takeover of the world.[328] "It legitimizes the Islamophobia industry's delusional rhetoric of jihad taking over America; much like the Protocols of Zion purported Henry Ford's anti-Semitic paranoia of a Jewish plan for global domination," my friend Reza Aslan told me during an interview. "Even worse, it recycles the Protocols' abysmal legacy as a smokescreen that validates pre-existing suspicions of a population with even more racist rhetoric and propaganda."[329]

***

The thirty-eighth victim of the 2019 New Zealand mosque massacre was a thirty-five-year-old man named Shahid Suhail. "Mama! Where is Baba?" their two-year-old daughter reportedly[330] frantically asked when her father never came home after Friday prayers that day. Like many of the other mosque massacre victims, Mr. Suhail was buried along with twenty-five other Muslim worshipers in a mass burial which was broadcast live on New Zealand television. "The remains of my brother are in this soil," his brother explained about why he moved his entire family to Christchurch after his brother was massacred. "We have an emotional attachment to this land now. Suhail is buried here and when the kids grow up, we can show them this is where he lies and where he sacrificed himself for the peace and love of his new country."[331]

***

Even the CIA thinks it's a terrible idea to designate the Muslim Brotherhood as a foreign terrorist organization. According to a summary of a finished intelligence report for policymakers that was shared by a US official with POLITICO, several CIA experts publicly warned that designating the Muslim Brotherhood may actually "fuel extremism" and further damage relations with America's allies.[332] The CIA document—published internally on January 31, 2017—also noted that the Brotherhood had already publicly "rejected violence as a matter of official policy." They also noted that the Brotherhood had openly "opposed Al-Qaeda and ISIS" in public condemnations as well over the years.

"I think it would be an incredibly stupid thing to do," said Daniel Benjamin, who served as the State Department's coordinator for counterterrorism under Secretary of State Hillary Clinton, on the Muslim Brotherhood designation. "The top reason being that it's not a terrorist group."[333]

***

The thirty-ninth victim of the 2019 New Zealand mosque massacre was a thirty-five-year-old man named Hussein Al-Umari. After his death, his younger sister told PEOPLE magazine that when the gunman entered the mosque—instead of running away—her older brother actually ran towards the shooter yelling "GET OUT OF HERE!" as he died trying to tackle the white supremacist. "It wasn't surprising to me at all," she told PEOPLE magazine about her brother's bravery. "I honestly have no idea how he had the courage to do that. It makes me very proud. When the first round of shots were happening, he actually had a chance to run away. You know fight or flight? He fought. The majority of people—even me—would probably run away. It just makes me so proud that my brother had the chance to run away, but he didn't."[334]

***

Many experts believe that this attempted Muslim Brotherhood designation by right-wing Republican actors is simply a political smokescreen to criminalize American Muslim civic life in the age of Donald Trump. Prominent groups like the American Civil Liberties Union (ACLU), Center for American Progress, and Human Rights Watch have all publicly stated that any such designation would directly threaten the constitutional rights of millions of American Muslim men, women, and children everywhere.

"Designating the Muslim Brotherhood as a 'foreign terrorist organization' would wrongly equate it with violent extremist groups like Al-Qaeda and ISIS," said Laura Pitter, senior US national security counsel at Human Rights Watch. "Muslim-affiliated groups that promote civic values and protect civil rights are crucial to US democracy," she added. "Threatening their rights threatens the rights of all Americans."[335]

If Republicans were ever successful in designating the Brotherhood as a foreign terrorist organization, it would cast a cloud over a vast number of US-based Islamic charities and Muslim civil rights organizations.

"The designation would have a chilling effect on Arab and Muslim civic life and society," said Abed Ayoub, legal director for the American-Arab Anti-Discrimination Committee (ADC). "This is absolutely a political move on the part of the Trump administration. The designation is just one part of the Administration's agenda aimed at criminalizing Islam and Muslim Americans."[336]

***

The fortieth victim of the 2019 New Zealand mosque massacre was a thirty-four-year-old man named Syed Jahandad Ali. Originally from Lahore, Pakistan, Mr. Ali was a senior software developer and father of three young children. A statement from his company after the Christchurch massacre stated: "Syed Jahandad Ali has deeply touched the lives of his friends, colleagues and wider technology community through his knowledge and skills. We are devastated to have lost a very loved colleague."[337]

***

I once wrote a May 2019 opinion piece for the *Washington Post* that argued that this next-level Islamophobia—the kind based on these chilling designations—is history repeating itself yet again. Many of us forget that millions of Irish Catholics immigrating to the United States during the nineteenth century were smeared as "papists" with loyalties only to the Vatican. The Know Nothing Party strove to discredit and dehumanize them. Similarly, the Jewish community has dealt with a longstanding history of starkly naked anti-Semitism in modern American history; Henry Ford's newspaper published conspiracy theories about "international Jewry" as regularly as daily weather reports. In the current decade, Donald Trump's attempts to

smear Muslims—by saying things like "*I think Islam hates us!*"
to CNN's Anderson Cooper[338] and trying to ban Muslims from
entering the country—are just the latest such bias-motivated
policies targeting religious minorities today.

The term "scapegoats" is a biblical term from the Book of
Leviticus. It refers to a literal goat that was let loose in the wilder-
ness on Yom Kippur after the high priest symbolically laid all of
the sins of society on its undeserving head.

Since time immemorial, we have always chosen scapegoats
to blame for our society's problems (real or imagined). From the
Holocaust to Japanese internment camps to Jim Crow America,
we always seem to have needed a proverbial boogeyman.[339]
Although the presidency of Donald J. Trump is thankfully over,
the metastasizing growth of the right-wing political ideology
known as "Trumpism" is alive and well today. So if we allow
Islamophobia to keep spreading in our communities, it will only
lead to the further disenfranchisement of millions of Western
Muslims who seek to debunk the archaic "clash of civilizations"
orientalist theory once and for all.

6

Turning Over Samuel Huntington's Grave

Islam's borders are bloody, and so are its innards . . .

—Samuel Huntington

The forty-first victim of the 2019 New Zealand mosque massacre was a thirty-three-year-old man named Atta Elayyan. In addition to serving as CEO for a local tech company in Christchurch, Mr. Elayyan was also the starting goalkeeper for the New Zealand national futsal team, which is a sport similar to soccer and played with five-person teams on a basketball-style court. "Atta was a great man and well-liked by everyone," his teammate Josh Margetts told ESPN after learning of his friend's murder. "There are no words to sum up how we are all feeling. There is a huge hole in our hearts as we come to terms with the loss of a great person. He will be sorely missed."[340]

Part of a team. One of us. Not one of "them."

***

In one of his final media interviews ever before his death in December 2008, Professor Samuel Huntington sat down for an exclusive interview with *Islamica* Magazine—which later became the *Islamic Monthly*, where, full disclosure, I have served as senior editor for over a decade. In that final interview of his lifetime, Professor Huntington discussed his final parting thoughts on the controversial "clash of civilizations" theory which he so-famously coined. Since our magazine was the only Muslim publication to which Professor Huntington ever granted a formal interview during his lifetime, we wanted to use the unique opportunity to provide him a platform to clarify his "clash of civilizations" theory (which ideological extremists on both sides of the global political aisle have used to promote their own myopic worldview). Only a few weeks after our interview, Huntington suffered a stroke and retired to Cape Cod, Massachusetts where he passed away shortly thereafter.[341]

"I think it is a mistake—let me just repeat—to think in terms of two homogenous sides starkly confronting each other," Professor Huntington told us. "Global politics remains extremely complex and countries have different interests, which will also lead them to make what might seem as rather bizarre friends and allies."

"I think it's hard to talk about the Muslim world and Christian world as distinctly separate blocs," Huntington continued. "There will be association and partnerships between some Muslim countries and some Christian countries. Those already exist. And they may shift as different regimes come and go and interests change. I do not think it is all that useful to think in terms of those two 'solid blocs' [i.e, the Muslim world and the West]."[342]

During his long tenure as the Albert J. Weatherhead III University Professor at Harvard University, Huntington identified these simplistic categories as the major (and reductive) global "civilizations" in existence today: Western (which includes the United States and Europe), Latin American, Islamic, African, Orthodox (with Russia as a core state), Hindu, Japanese, and "Sinic" (which includes countries like China, Korea, and Vietnam).[343]

In response to Huntington's clash of civilizations theory, one of his fellow Harvard colleagues (and winner of the 1998 Nobel Prize for Economics) Professor Amartya Sen published an entire book refuting the "clash of civilizations" theory called *Identity and Violence: The Illusion of Destiny*. In his book, the Nobel laureate highlighted that no single civilization anywhere is a reductive monolithic entity and that a human being's individual "identity is not destiny."[344] Professor Sen's central idea is that "identity is not destiny," which means that each individual human being has the personal agency to construct their own respective identity outside of the confines of their civilization's sociopolitical entrenchments. Professor Sen further contends that Huntington's clash of civilizations theory originated from the "miniaturization of human beings"; Huntington simplistically reduced everything to "choice-less identities" created to fit into his reductive monolithic civilizational boxes. In Sen's opinion, this has only further divided the human race along demographic lines.[345]

In speaking about political movements around the world, Professor Huntington told us during his final interview that, "I think fundamentalism is what you said: this radical attitude toward one's own identity and civilization as compared to other people's identities and cultures." He noted almost predictively:

"Certainly, here in the United States, we have had our own fundamentalist movements."

And regarding minorities within Western societies, Huntington conceded that, "The larger society has to recognize some degree of autonomy for the minority: the right to practice their own religion and way of life and to some extent their language." When asked directly about whether he believed his clash of civilizations theory had been duplicitously and disingenuously used by polemicists for their own myopic right-wing political agendas, Professor Huntington immediately responded: "Oh absolutely, all the time!"

"I am not an expert on Islam," Professor Huntington finally admitted during this final interview of his lifetime. When asked directly about the one single thing that most people around the world would be surprised to learn about him, he smiled and simply replied: "A lot of people tend to think I am a dogmatic ideologue; which I am not."[346]

Only a few weeks after our interview, he passed away at the age of eighty-one. There are billions of people around the world who sincerely pray that his clash of civilizations theory can and will be buried along with him.

**

The forty-second victim of the 2019 New Zealand mosque massacre was a thirty-three-year-old man named Zakaria Bhuiya. One of five Bangladeshi nationals who were murdered in the Christchurch attack, Mr. Bhuiya had just recently gotten married in his native country, and he had helped rebuild his local mosque after a 2011 earthquake. "Zakaria was a respected member of our team and a dear friend of ours,"[347] his employer said in a statement posted on a fundraising page for his surviving widow.

Respect and inclusion. Why is it only in retrospect that we let others know how we feel?

***

Today's Republican party and other ultra-nationalist conservative political movements have embraced many aspects of Samuel Huntington's clash of civilizations theory. During the presidency of Donald Trump, he seemed to openly embrace this racialized global framework, which views the world in broad aforementioned civilizational groupings—like Western, Islamic, Sinic, Latin American, etc. As I have highlighted throughout this book, many members of the Trump administration openly viewed immigration by brown-skinned folks as a "demographic threat" to white Anglo-Protestant American culture.[348] Some of his White House advisers also believed that war with China is inevitable given its rising global power status as a Sinic civilizational powerhouse.[349] And Russia, leader of the "Orthodox" grouping in the Huntington civilizational framework, is seen by Trump as a natural ally in these higher-order conflicts because of President Vladimir Putin's shared embrace of cultural traditionalist nationalism (also known as ethno-nationalism).[350]

According to my friend M. Arsalan Suleiman—former Acting US Special Envoy to the Organization of Islamic Cooperation (OIC) under President Barack Obama—this clash of civilizations ideology animated many of the Trump administration's most identifiable policies.[351] These policies included the debates over the US-Mexico border wall, immigration reform, refugee resettlement, the Muslim Travel Bans, undermining the Iran nuclear deal, possible Muslim Brotherhood terrorist designation, aggressive posturing vis-à-vis China, and efforts to ally with Russia.

Suleiman believes that exposing the fundamental flaws of this framework is critical to fostering a rational, fact-based assessment of US foreign policy.

To highlight the disastrous impact of this Trump-ian thinking, I note that a leaked National Security Council (NSC) memo written by then-NSC Director of Strategic Planning Rich Higgins outlined the conspiratorial manner in which the Trump administration believed that Islamists, the Muslim Brotherhood, and the fifty-seven-member Organization of Islamic Cooperation (OIC) were allegedly working together as monolithic Muslim enemies seeking to undermine Donald Trump in an absurd mafia-like manner with no proof offered whatsoever.

It is in the best interest of Trump and his right-wing Republican friends to believe that this is true, no matter how ridiculous it sounds. And so they are willing to believe. And so, regrettably, are their followers.

***

The forty-third victim of the 2019 New Zealand mosque massacre was a thirty-year-old man named Farhaj Ahsan. A master's graduate of the University of Auckland, the young engineer had moved to Christchurch from Hyderabad, India nearly a decade before the massacre. "Nobody was imagining that in New Zealand—which is a peace-loving country—such a situation would arise," his grieving father told BBC World News after learning of his son's brutal murder.[352]

But the unthinkable can happen. It can happen when powerful people choose to believe and propagate absurdities, simply because it is politically expedient to do so.

***

"Contrary to what some assert, Islam is fully compatible with modernization," is how former US Treasury Secretary Larry Summers put it in a *Foreign Affairs* article challenging Samuel Huntington. His piece was entitled "The Fusion of Civilizations: The Case for Global Optimism." Summers bolstered his thesis by highlighting globalization accomplishments in Muslim-majority nations like Malaysia, where women now outnumber men 65 percent to 35 percent in national colleges and universities. He also noted that Gulf States like Qatar, Saudi Arabia, and the United Arab Emirates (UAE) now feature satellite campuses of major Western universities. Finally, he noted that the fifty-million-plus-member Nahdlatul Ulama—the largest religious organization in Indonesia (the most-populous Muslim country in the world)—has repeatedly condemned extremist groups like ISIS. All of these facts further chip away at Huntington's archaic clash of civilizations theory.[353]

The concept of "tribalism" beats at the heart of the late Samuel Huntington's theory. He once wrote that civilizations are the "ultimate human tribes" and that the clash of civilizations is a "tribal conflict on a global scale." You see, according to Huntington, instead of improved diplomacy in a rapidly globalizing age, human relations between nations from different civilizations will actually be hostile and "trust and friendship will be rare."[354] Wars will break out along civilizational fault lines.

Huntington sometimes wrote unbelievable things like "To the Asians, American concessions are not to be reciprocated, they are to be exploited."[355]

In glaring contrast to Donald Trump, former president Barack Obama represented the opposite end of the clash of civilizations spectrum—and President Obama would most certainly not credit statements such as the one above.

During a major address to the members of the Turkish parliament, President Obama told his audience in Ankara: "Let me say this as clearly as I can: The United States is not—and will never be—at war with Islam. We will be respectful, even when we do not agree. And we will convey our deep appreciation for the Islamic faith, which has done so much over so many centuries to shape the world for the better—including my own country."

Obama concluded by saying that, "The United States has been enriched by Muslim Americans. Many other Americans have Muslims in their family, or have lived in a Muslim-majority country—I know, because I am one of them."[356]

In his own inaugural address, Obama had noted: "To the Muslim world, we seek a new way forward, based on mutual interest and mutual respect."

Many people know that Barack Obama lived in Indonesia from 1967 to 1971. During his run for the presidency, he endured endless racist whisper campaigns about him being some sort of a "Crypto-Muslim Manchurian Candidate." As a result, Obama sometimes kept his political distance from the American Muslim community. During his presidential campaigns, the "Obama is a secret Muslim" conspiracy theory had become so politically radioactive that two American Muslim women in Michigan were removed from an Obama event in Detroit *by his own Democratic campaign volunteers* who were worried about the optics of their hijabs during a group photo.

Over forty years ago, the late Palestinian academic Edward Said once wrote of Islamophobia that, "I have not been able to discover any period in European or American history since the Middle Ages in which Islam was generally discussed or thought about outside a framework created by passion, prejudice and political interests."[357]

We are surrounded by evidence that Professor Said's statement still remains true today.

Although the most powerful engines of Islamophobia (and anti-Semitism) squarely rest within right-wing conservative circles—and always have—any intellectually-honest conversation about this topic must also examine disdain for Muslims within some Western liberal political circles as well. The specter of liberal Islamophobia seems to revolve around a general dislike for the way religious practices of Muslims can clash with perceived Western liberal orthodoxies.

Here in the United States, Democratic Party stalwarts like Hillary and Bill Clinton have not been immune from perpetuating anti-Muslim narratives in the past. For instance, during his nationally-televised speech at the 2016 Democratic National Convention (DNC), former president Bill Clinton told millions of Americans: "If you are a Muslim and you love America and freedom and you hate terror, stay here and help us win and make the future together. We want you!" In response, former Comedy Central Daily Show correspondent Hasan Minhaj (himself a Muslim) told the *Huffington Post* that Bill Clinton's strange remarks about Muslims were one of the motivating reasons that he created his Emmy Award-winning one-man political satire show *Patriot Act* on Netflix.

"I remember standing there and being like, 'Bill, I hate to tell you this. I don't know any terrorists,'" Hasan Minhaj said. "He thought our only value was to help find terrorists, right? He will never understand where I'm coming from and the things my community has had to go through," he added.

Minhaj concluded that an angry internet post about the remarks was not the way to go, and he was not "gonna get my humanity from Bill fucking Clinton. We have to claim that shit on our own terms. So I just started working on the Netflix show" as his personal response to growing Islamophobia around the world.[358]

Two presidential election cycles before Bill Clinton's 2016 DNC speech, his wife Hillary Clinton was embroiled in a fierce 2008 primary campaign against Barack Obama. During that election, Hillary's campaign pounced on the opportunity to capitalize on the whisper campaigns about Obama being a secret Muslim. In February 2008, many Americans might remember that there was a high-profile photograph of Barack Obama wearing traditional white African attire (with matching white turban) during a trip to Kenya which was leaked to the press.

According to numerous media reports, this photograph was actually leaked by staffers inside the Hillary Clinton campaign to the *Drudge Report*. According to *The Guardian* newspaper in London, a Clinton staffer had emailed them the photograph with the caption: "Wouldn't we be seeing this on the cover of every magazine if it were [Hillary]?"[359]

Obama's campaign manager at the time, David Plouffe, was rightfully furious and described this leaked photo as "the most shameful, offensive fear-mongering we've seen from either party in this election." He described the circulation of the picture by Clinton's campaign as part of "a disturbing pattern" against Obama and Muslims. "It's exactly the kind of divisive politics that turns away Americans of all parties,"[360] Plouffe added.

Just a few months before this leaked photograph, another junior Hillary Clinton staffer had resigned after they had forwarded an email suggesting that Obama was a Muslim.

Fast-forwarding to the third presidential debate of the 2016 presidential debate, Hillary Clinton said that the United States needed "to work with American Muslim communities who are on the front lines to identify and prevent [terrorist] attacks."

Again, this was not a new talking point at all; Clinton had consistently employed that same tired national security framework language about Muslims during her presidential runs. She again singled out over seven million American Muslims in the first and second presidential debates when she said, "We need American Muslims to be part of our eyes and ears on our front lines" against terrorism.

Like Hasan Minhaj's beef with Bill Clinton's framing of American Muslims in a purely counterterrorism framework, Hillary Clinton's perpetuation of this anti-Muslim trope has had the insidious political effect of marginalizing the political agency of millions of Muslims within the American political arena today.

"It's weird how politicians keep telling me I'm on the front line of fighting terrorism when I'm just trying to get through a sugar detox," replied St. Louis Post-Dispatch columnist Aisha Sultan concerning Hillary's remarks about Muslims. "I'm not being flippant about the role American Muslims should play about reporting anything dangerous they hear whether in a mosque or anywhere else. We all bear that responsibility. But I've never heard anyone talk like that. And, I don't hear candidates telling white Americans to be on the front lines to fight school shootings," Sultan continued.[361]

According to Professor Deepa Kumar, author of Islamophobia and the Politics of Empire, one of the critical distinctions between right-wing Islamophobia and liberal Islamophobia is "the way liberal Islamophobia works [. . .] it roundly criticizes Islam-bashing, thereby preempting charges of racism, but then it goes on to champion programs that target and vilify Muslims."[362] Using her framework, Professor Kumar noted that a liberal might obviously condemn hate crimes against Muslims, but on the flip side support illiberal policies like the New York City

Police Department's longtime spying program on US Muslims, Arabs, and South Asian communities after 9/11.

***

The forty-fourth victim of the 2019 New Zealand mosque massacre was a thirty-year-old man named Mojammel Hoq. He had moved to Christchurch from Bangladesh three years earlier to pursue a career in the healthcare industry. He hoped to earn enough money to get married. According to his family, Mr. Hoq was excited to marry his fiancée back home in Bangladesh and ultimately dreamt of opening up a dental clinic for the poor. "He was such a nice human being," his cousin told reporters after the massacre. "He was humble and competent. He always appreciated all kinds of people. This has left a big hole in our hearts."[363]

Selflessness. Service to others. Qualities that all countries would love to find in their immigrants, but which did not save the life of Mr. Hoq.

***

Shortly after President Obama was elected, a bipartisan group of about thirty-five prominent Americans—which included former Secretary of State Madeleine Albright and former Republican Congressman Vin Weber—created a report titled "Changing Course: A New Direction for U.S. Relations with the Muslim World." It purportedly contained concrete ways in which to improve US-Muslim relations while moving forward into the new century. At the time, Moroccan Ambassador to the United States Aziz Mekouar called the report "a most constructive blueprint for building relationships of cooperation between the United States and the Muslim world." The report suggested that the US partner with Muslim governments, multilateral institutions, and philanthropic organizations to make education a more powerful engine for employment and entrepreneurship within the greater Muslim world.

Former US Secretary of State Madeleine Albright spoke about the report at a dinner that I attended alongside eighty ambassadors, journalists, and political leaders in suburban Washington, DC.

"When I became Secretary of State, we did not have Muslims employed in the State Department," Albright told us that evening. "I went back to my notes, when I was writing my book, and I had various notes which read, 'Learn more about Islam.'"[364]

Yet since that time, many people have become quite skeptical about Albright, mostly because of her infamous CBS News *60 Minutes* interview on the impact of Iraqi sanctions on millions of innocent Iraqi children. During that interview, when asked by CBS News' Lesley Stahl about the effect of sanctions against Iraq ("We have heard that half a million children have died. I mean, that's more children than died in Hiroshima. And, you know, is the price worth it?") Secretary Albright flatly replied on-camera: "I think this is a very hard choice, but the price—we think the price is worth it."[365]

At a panel at Georgetown University Law Center in Washington, DC, I once had the opportunity to personally ask Madeleine Albright about her infamous CBS News interview. After identifying myself to Secretary Albright and the packed Georgetown auditorium crowd as a magazine columnist and human rights lawyer, I personally asked her whether she still stood by those statements that she made in the CBS *60 Minutes* interview.

In response to my question, she said, "Well, I'll begin by answering the question about the Iraqi children. I've answered this question many times and it's always interesting that what I say doesn't seem to penetrate. I was interviewed and I said something genuinely stupid. I have said it was stupid. Obviously, I regret any loss of life. I have said this so many times. I know that if you Google me, that I'm there as a war criminal," she joked in response to my question. "I can explain. It was a stupid statement and I regret having made it and I've said it so many times that I would appreciate if you would actually put that in writing somewhere."[366]

Your wish is granted.

***

The forty-fifth victim of the 2019 New Zealand mosque massacre was a twenty-seven-year-old man named Areeb Ahmed. A chartered accountant for the global consulting firm PricewaterhouseCoopers (PwC), Mr. Ahmed was originally from Pakistan's largest city, Karachi. The New Zealand office of PwC set up a crowdfunding page, which raised over $120,000 for Mr. Ahmed's family after his death. "There are really no words," said PwC New Zealand CEO Mark Averill after the massacre. "Areeb was a much loved member of our team and it seems so unfair that his life has been cut short in such awful circumstances. His smile, warmth, dedication, respect and humor will be deeply missed. PwC's thoughts and prayers are with his family, the Muslim community and their families, and all people affected by this terrible event."[367]

***

In the age of Donald Trump, the collective dehumanization of Muslim lives has been taken to the next level by the global "refugee" crisis. It is the worst humanitarian crisis since World War II. The terminology used to describe what is happening is fraught with questions—such as whether we should refer to those impacted as "refugees" or "migrants" and why that even matters. It matters because these terms have very different meanings and legal implications under international law.

To be clear, many of the (mainly right-wing European) Western politicians who use the term "migrants" to describe the influx of millions of predominantly-Muslim people entering into the West are deliberately doing so to avoid using the term "refugees" (which would automatically trigger legal protections under international law).

According to the 1951 UN Refugee Convention, a "refugee" is defined as someone who, owing to a "well-founded fear of being persecuted for reasons of race, religion, nationality, membership of a particular social group or political opinion, is outside the country of his nationality and is unable or, owing to such fear, is unwilling to avail himself of the protection of that country."[368]

But on the other hand, people considered "migrants" can freely leave their country of origin for reasons that could include employment, education, or any other kind of effort to improve their life. Unlike refugees, people who are considered "migrants" (or immigrants) do not possess the "well-founded fear" legal standard that refugees legally fulfill according to international law.

To put it in everyday terms, if I left my comfortable home in suburban Washington, DC and decided to move my family to Paris, I would legally be considered a "migrant" because

I moved for a better life without any fear whatsoever. On the other hand, if someone flees their home in a war-torn country like Syria and ends up in Paris, that person should then be classified as a "refugee" because they were in fear for their own safety when they fled to Paris. The important legal distinction here is that this hypothetical refugee would now automatically be granted more legal protections under international law and European Union treaties than I would. These legal protections would allow them to apply for asylum under EU law much more easily.

"This is a primarily refugee crisis, not only a migration phenomenon," UN Secretary General Antonio Guterres has remarked in the past about this humanitarian catastrophe.[369]

Vitally, it would be a violation of international law to deport refugees back to their home countries under the international legal doctrine of *non-refoulement*, which forbids the rendering of a true victim of persecution back to their home country.

This is why we have seen so many anti-Muslim political leaders labeling refugees as "migrants" instead.

Right-wing Hungarian Prime Minister Viktor Orban once contended that the "overwhelming majority" of Syrian and Iraqi refugees were actually "economic migrants" and not refugees; thus allowing him to deport anyone that he chose from Hungary.[370] Since the vast majority of refugees on the planet are Muslim, this global debate about whether to frame these destitute populations as "refugees" or "migrants" is now very narrowly focused with Islamophobia lurking nearby.

"Every European country is a product of migration and population flows. Yes, Europe has been predominantly Christian, but countries have been able to integrate Muslims, and those who have not, have frankly been faulty of their social welfare policy," was how Human Rights Watch Executive Director Kenneth

Roth put it during an interview with Voice of America.[371] "There is a real need to stand up against that Islamophobia," he continued. "It is based on this false conception of European history that there is such a thing as ethnic purity."

So although it might seem like semantics, we should understand that there is clear anti-Muslim motivation involved when right-wing political leaders try to minimize the worst humanitarian crisis since World War II as a "migrant" issue and not a massive "refugee" global crisis.

***

The forty-sixth victim of the 2019 New Zealand mosque massacre was a twenty-five-year-old woman named Ansi Alibava. She and her husband were young newlyweds from India who had borrowed money to move to New Zealand the year before so that she could complete a master's degree in agribusiness management at nearby Lincoln University. "Right before the main prayer, I heard a single shot firing and I thought that some kids outside might have popped a balloon," her husband later recounted. "But then people started falling over me, I saw people with blood on their shirts," he continued.[372] After he escaped through a broken window, Ms. Alibava's husband returned to the mosque parking lot and eventually found his wife's dead body lying outside.

"For these victims to be attacked because of their religion is inconceivable," said Lincoln University Acting Chancellor Bruce McKenzie.[373] Two months after the Christchurch massacre—in May 2019—Lincoln University posthumously awarded her master's degree. Ms. Alibava's body was then repatriated to India so that her family could be given her well-earned diploma along with their daughter's casket.

What should your country do with populations of minority "others" within your nation's borders? It is a question that has dogged nations since the beginning of time. The way leaders have answered the questions has spoken to the content of their personal—and their respective nation's—character.

***

Did you know that Donald Trump once refused to condemn the internment camps where over 140,000 Japanese Americans were held during World War II?

"I would have had to be there at the time to tell you, to give you a proper answer," Trump once told *TIME* magazine during an interview about the brutal practice of Japanese internment.[374] "I certainly hate the concept of it. But I would have had to be there at the time to give you a proper answer." The point, he said, was that war requires difficult choices. "War is tough. And winning is tough," he continued when asked to clarify his thoughts on placing 140,000+ innocent Japanese-Americans in camps simply because of their ethnicity.

The term "propaganda" was originally coined by the Jesuits in the seventeenth century; it was the name given to the Vatican committee charged with propagating the Catholic faith to the rest of the world.[375] However, it did not become part of everyday global vernacular until the beginning of World War I, when many Western powers began to use the new techniques of "mass advertising" and "public relations" to rouse popular support for their causes. Not to be outdone by our European allies, the American government entered into the propaganda fray shortly thereafter, flooding the US population with jingoistic, one-sided information.

At the beginning of our involvement in World War I, President Woodrow Wilson believed that he had only two choices when it came to communicating with the public. He could either lean toward a policy of censorship and silence, or flood the media with pro-war jingoistic propaganda. President Wilson felt it politically prudent to resort to the latter choice of pro-war propaganda.

In 1917, President Woodrow Wilson created the Committee on Public Information, better known as the "Creel Committee"—named after its chairman and pro-war journalist George Creel—which subjected Americans to a massive campaign of pro-war propaganda and public relations blitzes. In the Committee's advertising campaigns, they often depicted the stereotypical German as "the Hun," or "a blood-thirsty savage," dehumanizing them completely.[376] What is by far the most enduring image of the Committee's work is the "I Want You!" recruiting poster with a stern, finger-pointing, white-bearded Uncle Sam calling for Americans to join the US Army.[377]

The concept of "nativism" generally refers to the sociopolitical policy—especially in the United States in the nineteenth century—that favored the interests of established inhabitants over those of immigrants.[378] In modern American history, the application of this policy began with the many Irish immigrants, settling in Manhattan, who were being persecuted for their Catholic faith and immigrant status by the predominantly German Protestant "natives" (as seen in the 2002 Martin Scorsese Academy Award nominated movie "Gangs of New York" starring Daniel Day-Lewis & Leonardo DiCaprio).

After the conclusion of World War I in 1919, there were approximately eight million Germans and German Americans living in the United States; they were roughly 10 percent of the American population.[379] Many of them now felt vilified.

For the safety of their community, many German Americans began to Americanize the spelling of their last names (changing "Schmidt" into "Smith," for example). A city ordinance in Cincinnati, Ohio during World War I had called for the removal of German pretzels from local restaurants. Another city law in Pittsburgh, Pennsylvania prohibited the public playing of German composer Ludwig von Beethoven. In many situations around the United States, many German language books were removed from public libraries. Is it any wonder that these German Americans felt unsafe?

During World War II, much of the West Coast of the United States saw considerable anti-Asian sentiment, culminating in the denial of citizenship to Asian Americans (upheld by the United States Supreme Court in the case of *Ozawa v. US*[380] and the Immigration Act of 1924,[381] which barred Asians from attaining American citizenship). In making far-reaching decisions on how to deal with Japanese Americans, President Franklin Delano Roosevelt relied on the analysis of General John Dewitt, commander of Western Defense Command, whose infamous racist quotes include: "Once a Jap, Always a Jap"[382] and that the "Japanese race is an enemy race."[383] Because of General Dewitt's racially-motivated recommendations, by June 1942, more than 120,000 Japanese persons (more than 70 percent of them American citizens)[384] had been forced from their homes into ten internment camps scattered in the inhospitable desert regions of the West for the duration of the war.[385]

Even though most Americans know about the World War II internment of Japanese Americans (and Donald Trump's prevaricating thoughts on it), the race-based anti-immigrant legacy of our nation was already cemented in the prior century. Sixty years before WWII, the Chinese Exclusion Act of 1882 was the first major law restricting immigration to the United States solely based on someone's ethnicity. This racist legislation was enacted in response to irrational economic fears; native-born Americans were attributing their own unemployment and declining wages to the influence of Chinese workers (and later Japanese and all other Asian ethnicities) whom they also viewed as racially inferior. The Chinese Exclusion Act was signed into law on May 6, 1882 by President Chester A. Arthur and effectively halted Chinese immigration to the states for ten years. It also prohibited Chinese people from becoming US citizens, even if they already legally resided in America.

"Beginning in 1882, the United States stopped being a nation of immigrants that welcomed foreigners without restrictions, borders or gates. Instead, it became a gatekeeping nation,"[386] said Professor Erika Lee of the University of Minnesota, an expert on the Chinese Exclusion Act.

"In the process, the very definition of what it meant to be an 'American' became even more exclusionary," she continued.

As I mentioned, the Chinese Exclusion Act was the very first time in American history that immigrants were barred solely because of their ethnicity. In 1882, when Congress passed the law, there were 39,600 men and women from China living in the United States.

When it comes to modern equivalents, Professor Lee minces no words. She once told National Public Radio (NPR) that today's equivalent of the Chinese Exclusion Act was Donald Trump's well-known Muslim Travel Ban. "The fact that we don't explicitly name Muslims [in Trump's executive order] is more of a reflection of how our racial sensibilities have changed over the past 135 years, in terms of being more polite in our racism," she told NPR on the 135th anniversary of the Chinese Exclusion Act.[387]

It took over sixty years for the Chinese Exclusion Act to finally be repealed (by the Magnuson Act of 1943). During World War II, China became a military ally. Nevertheless, at first the 1943 Magnuson Act still allowed only 105 Chinese immigrants every year into America, reflecting persisting anti-Chinese racism in the United States. It was not until the Immigration Act of 1965—which eliminated previous national-origins policy—that truly free Chinese immigration to the United States was allowed to begin.[388]

***

The forty-seventh victim of the 2019 New Zealand mosque massacre was a twenty-five-year-old man named Ozair Kadir. Like his older brother, he dreamed of becoming a commercial pilot one day. With this in mind, Mr. Kadir had moved from India to Christchurch to join the International Aviation Academy of New Zealand as a pilot-in-training. "For the rest of their careers, every time they fly, they will remember Ozair," said Jeremy Ford, chief executive of International Aviation of New Zealand. "It's affected all our students and instructors deeply. I've heard a few students saying things like 'I'll fly through the skies with you Kadir.' Ozair's presence will be sadly missed by all staff and students at the Academy. Our love, thoughts and prayers are with his family who are now in New Zealand preparing to take Ozair home."[389]

Their hopes and dreams are like ours. They are beloved and respected like we are. In a strong, real sense, we are the same. Why did it take a mosque massacre with fifty-one murdered victims to see it?

One answer is because hatred against Muslims runs deep.

***

A recent CNN/Opinion Research Corporation survey found that nearly half of Americans (46 percent) have an unfavorable opinion of "the Muslim world." Another recent survey, this one from the Pew Forum on Religion and Public Life, found that almost four in ten Americans will admit to having "unfavorable views of Islam." And an ABC News Poll once found that more than one-third of Americans believe that mainstream Islam "encourages violence as a basic teaching."[390]

Islamophobia is implacable. Even after events such as Christchurch that can momentarily open up the world—including the United States—to empathy, it slowly creeps back. The same old encouragements to bigotry from opportunistic politicians rear up again. And once again, they begin to influence the public in a sinister direction. This pervasive anti-Muslim sentiment directly affects our legal policies toward Arabs, Muslims, and South Asians.

This is, sadly, where we are now.

A Cornell University poll found that 44 percent of Americans still believe that some curtailment of civil liberties may be necessary for Muslims living in the United States. Similarly, over one-fourth of Americans surveyed (26 percent) believed that US mosques should be targeted with increased surveillance by law enforcement agencies. And to aid in that effort, nearly 30 percent of Americans thought that undercover law enforcement agents should monitor the constitutionally-protected activities of American Muslim civic organizations.[391]

And this is during peacetime. These are the numbers we see when there has been no recent inciting event.

Nearer to 9/11, a USA TODAY/CNN/Gallup poll found that over half of Americans (53 percent) were in favor of requiring all Arabs (and by extension Muslims)—including those who are US citizens—to undergo added intensive security checks before boarding airplanes simply because of their background. The same poll found that nearly half of Americans (46 percent) actually favored requiring Arabs and Muslims to carry special ID cards on them at all times.[392]

Shortly before Donald Trump's election, the Bridge Initiative at Georgetown University conducted a special, comprehensive report called "The Super Survey: Two Decades of Americans' Views on Islam & Muslims." As the title suggests, it highlighted twenty years of aggregated public opinion polls related to Islamophobia and anti-Muslim sentiment.[393]

As you have seen, I am a person who is data-driven, and who believes we can learn a lot from polls like this. So you can imagine how excited I was.

Anyhow, this Georgetown "Super Survey" report—which synthesized 480 polling questions taken from 179 different public opinion polls over a period from 1993 to 2014—distilled a wealth of information to create a portrait of how Americans have come to view Muslims (both positively & negatively) over the years.

The survey found that there is "no other religion which so regularly figures into evening news cycles or discussions about American foreign policy" than Islam. The Georgetown researchers found that there is no other religion which occupies such a "significant chunk of our social interaction online, spurring memes and counter-memes, hashtag campaigns and Twitter wars, sincere conversations and snarky agitations, viral videos and virulent diatribes" than Islam as well.

At the macro level, this major Georgetown study found that Muslims in America now outnumber Episcopalians, and that by the year 2030, the American Muslim population is expected to be

on par with the US Jewish community in terms of total population. They also noted that American Islam is the most diverse of
any religious group in the country; the American Muslim population represents diverse demographic groups, including millions of African American Muslims, many of whom are descen-
dants of slaves (as well as immigrants from at least seventy-seven
countries around the world).

The survey also revealed that one of the reasons for such
high levels of Islamophobia in the West today is because people
simply do not know any Muslims personally. Generally speaking, they don't encounter them in their everyday lives. Nearly six
in ten Americans claimed that they do not know a Muslim. (A
separate Harvard University study found that Muslims received
three times as many "cold" ratings as Catholics and nearly four
times as many cold ratings as Protestants, versus positive "warm"
ratings, from their fellow Americans of different faiths.)[394]

But let us continue to flesh out this picture.

Many Americans know that Judaism, Christianity, and
Islam are the three Abrahamic religions; they all believe in the
same monotheistic god of Abraham. Despite this common unify-
ing religious heritage, many Americans still do not see Muslims
as part of the social fabric of the United States. A major Pew
Research Center study once found that two-in-three Americans
(65 percent) said Islam was totally "different" from their own
religion (with only 17 percent saying that it was "similar" as a
fellow monotheistic Abrahamic faith).[395]

I think that one of the great consequences of this intransi-
gent "Other-izing" of Muslims is that there is little to no outrage
when they are treated differently than other people.

In 2010, a twenty-year-old California college student named
Yasir Afifi took his car to get an oil change. While the car was
being serviced, Mr. Afifi noticed a strange black box attached

to the car's underbody. Two days later, as he left his apartment complex, he was approached by a group of FBI agents who asked where he had put their tracking device which they had planted on his car.

"It seems very frightening that the FBI placed a surveillance-tracking device on the car of a twenty-year-old American citizen who has done nothing more than being Muslim," an American Civil Liberties Union (ACLU) representative told *WIRED* magazine.[396]

Alas, human righs groups like the ACLU are some of the few organizations willing to speak out in cases of blatant Islamophobia like this one. Most Americans, when they heard the case of Mr. Afifi—if they heard of it at all—simply shrugged their shoulders and went about their day.

Across America, law enforcement agencies feel untethered when it comes to "crossing the line" with law-abiding Muslims. These agencies have spent decades secretly "mapping" Muslim communities and planting spies inside mosques, Muslim-owned businesses, and halal restaurants. In one egregious example, in southern California, an undercover FBI informant was once a paid snitch who seduced Muslim women who attended the local mosque as part of a larger entrapment scheme to infiltrate Muslim houses of worship and ensnare Muslim individuals involved in fictitious "terror" plots which never even existed.[397]

This correlation between negative public opinion views and allowing the gross mistreatment of Muslims continues to this very day.

Between December 2014 and July 2015, at least nine Muslims were shot and killed in probable hate crime attacks across the United States and Canada. But only one of those brutal anti-Muslim murders—the high-profile February

2015 execution-style triple murder of a twenty-three-year-old University of North Carolina-Chapel Hill dental student (Mr. Deah Barakat) along with his twenty-one-year-old wife (Mrs. Yusor Abu-Salha) and her nineteen-year-old sister (Ms. Razan Abu-Salha)—received any major national media coverage at all. This was mainly because the white male shooter (who was sentenced to three life sentences in June 2019) had posted anti-Muslim memes on social media and bizarrely claimed he brutally executed the three Muslim students inside their own home because of a "parking dispute."[398]

This uptick in anti-Muslim hate crimes across the West is dangerous for the future of pluralistic societies everywhere. But what is most dangerous is the intractable attitudes that Muslims "must be up to something," and if they are unfairly surveilled or even killed, then they "must have deserved it." None of us will get equal justice under the law when politicians and hatemongers spew myths and slurs suggesting that Muslims are not, and cannot ever be, equal.

***

The forty-eighth victim of the 2019 New Zealand mosque massacre was a twenty-four-year-old man named Tariq Omar. An avid soccer player, Mr. Omar coached several teams in the Christchurch United Football Club junior league. The soccer club's academy director called Mr. Omar a "beautiful human being with a tremendous heart"[399] after learning of his friend's brutal murder. Originally hailing from Singapore, Mr. Omar had been dropped off at the mosque for Friday prayers on that fateful day by his mother Rosemary. Mr. Omar went inside while she looked for a parking spot. As Rosemary was parking the car, she heard loud gunshots. As terrified worshipers fled into the street, she ran through the crowd and found her son's lifeless body inside the mosque.

This is the consequence of hate. This is the consequence of the idea that someone is always "the other."

***

Once during one of my three-hundred-plus National Public Radio (NPR) interviews over the years, I observed that the meteoric rise of this "new Islamophobia"—urged on by the likes of Donald Trump—is actually feeding into the ISIS meta-narrative and even potentially creating new recruits for them.[400] I was thinking of a piece Robert Wright once published in the *New Yorker* called "The Clash of Civilizations That Isn't." In this trenchant piece, he argues that the Trump administration risks creating a self-fulfilling prophecy by embracing the clash of civilizations theory.[401] What I like about Wright's article is that it contains real evidence that this is coming true. For example, the infamous Muslim Travel Ban is now referred to as "the blessed ban" by extremist groups like ISIS and Al-Shabaab in Somalia, and they have even used video footage of Donald Trump as recruitment propaganda.[402] Trump's words of hate are now being used as a tool to make new terrorists. It is absurd, but it is clearly true.

Islamophobia not only helps our enemies, but it also threatens our own democratic freedoms as well. Following Trump's election, the Southern Poverty Law Center reported on a surge in bias-motivated hate crimes in the seven days following the election. Further, membership in anti-Muslim hate groups saw a quick spike, increasing by at least 300 percent.[403] A mosque in Ypsilanti, Michigan was burned to the ground. Another—in Tucson, Arizona—was broken into and its copies of the Quran ripped apart. In Bloomington, Minnesota, a homemade bomb exploded at an Islamic center during morning prayers.

In the time since Trump's election, we have only seen more of this devastating hate and those who would use violence feel emboldened and unchained.

As I mentioned near the start of this book, in May 2017, a deranged thirty-five-year-old neo-Nazi named Jeremy Christian brutally murdered two men on a Portland, Oregon bus (and injured a third person) when they tried to stop the white supremacist from yelling anti-Muslim slurs at two young women. After the double murder, the *New York Times* reported that the known white supremacist regularly expressed anti-Muslim sentiment on social media, and had advocated for the idea of a "whites-only area" around Portland and the greater Pacific Northwest.[404]

Multiply small incidents like this by the number of many Muslim communities across the country, and you will begin to see the true scale of what is going on today. Of what Muslims across the West face, yes, but also what defenders of decency and law—such as those brave bus passengers who intervened—also face on a daily basis for standing up to hate.

According to an April 2017 report from the Government Accountability Office (GAO), out of the eighty-five violent extremist incidents that resulted in deaths since September 12, 2001, it was white supremacist & right-wing militia groups who were responsible for sixty-two out of the eighty-five (or 73 percent of total terrorist incidents). Though Muslims have certainly been responsible for some high-profile terrorist attacks, the vast majority of attacks in the United States by sheer number are done by right-wing white supremacists, not by people who look like me (or pray towards Mecca five times a day).[405]

***

The forty-ninth victim of the 2019 New Zealand mosque massacre was a seventeen-year-old boy named Muhammad Haziq Mohd-Tarmizi. The Malaysian teenager was attending Friday prayers with his mother, father, and younger brother—who all survived—when he was fatally shot in the back. "Muhammad was a great young man who had the respect of his friends and teachers," his school principal fondly remembered. "Conscientious, self-motivated and [he] just wanted to do well. Teachers have noted that he has grown in confidence in the short time he has been here. He was ready, as one teacher said, to flourish."[406]

Potential is just another thing that is destroyed by murderous attacks of hate-filled terror. What would have occurred . . . but for the horrible act of violence? Sadly, we will never know.

**

As I have noted earlier in this book, we Americans saw the return of high-profile white supremacist violence with the "Unite the Right" protest rally in Charlottesville, Virginia in August 2017. Although their stated goal was to oppose the removal of a statue of Confederate leader Robert E. Lee from Emancipation Park in Charlottesville, these protesters included a motley crew of white supremacists, white nationalists, neo-Confederates, Klansmen, neo-Nazis, and various other right-wing militias.

These white supremacists chanted racist and anti-Semitic slogans, carried semi-automatic rifles, swastikas, Confederate battle flags, anti-Muslim banners, and "Trump/Pence 2020" political signs. For anyone who still doesn't believe that a white Christian double-standard still exists today, you need to ask yourself: *What if the white supremacist neo-Nazi protestors in Charlottesville (or during the January 2021 violent insurrection at the US Capitol) had been black Muslims instead?*

Seriously. How long would that have been tolerated?

Unlike his unwillingness to condemn white supremacists, Trump has not found it so difficult to condemn acts of murderousness when committed by non-whites in the past. The *Washington Post* reported that Donald Trump tweeted about the terrorist attacks in Paris in November 2015 only three hours after they occurred. The following month, he tweeted about the mass shooting in San Bernardino, California only ninety minutes after the violence *began*.[407] And when terrorists drove a van into a crowd on London Bridge in August 2017, Trump wasted no time in tweeting about the need to be "smart, vigilant and tough" even before authorities had identified terrorism as the motive behind the attack.

In the same article, the *Post* noted that it took Trump several days to praise the two Good Samaritans who were fatally stabbed trying to defend women from Islamophobic threats in Portland, Oregon.

It would be remiss of me to fail to point out that Trump's awkwardness and inappropriate behavior are not limited to prevarication on acts of terror by certain groups. He emanates awkwardness and malapropism whenever he is dealing with minority groups. For example, who can forget how Trump famously said that he has "a great relationship with the blacks" . . . which is totally something that a non-racist would say.[408]

In May 2017, Trump delivered a speech taking aim at the Black Lives Matter (BLM) movement, publicly slamming "hostility and violence against police" without ever acknowledging America's long history of systemic racism and police brutality against generations of African Americans. [409]

Those who spoke for Trump were not much better. His first attorney general Jeff Sessions was once rejected as a federal judge over allegations that he had once called a black attorney "boy" and had also suggested that a white lawyer working for black clients should be considered a "race traitor."

Sessions also once joked that the only issue he had with the Ku Klux Klan (KKK) was their marijuana usage, and he even referred to black civil rights groups as "un-American" organizations trying to "force civil rights down the throats of people who were trying to put problems behind them."[410]

Trump himself once famously said that "anyone who cannot name our enemy is not fit to lead this country."[411] By continuing to promote the clash of civilizations theory by dividing our nation on racial, ethnic, and religious lines, Trump has only proved himself unfit to lead since he only condemns dark-skinned folks while failing to publicly condemn neo-Nazi white supremacists who helped to elect him into office.[412]

***

The fiftieth victim of the 2019 New Zealand mosque massacre was a fourteen-year-old boy named Sayyad Milne. "I've lost my little boy; he's just turned fourteen!" his father told the *New Zealand Herald* through his tears. "A brave little soldier. It's so hard to see him just gunned down by someone who didn't care about anyone or anything."[413]

The fourteen-year-old boy was buried on the same day that New Zealand's prime minister, Jacinda Ardern, announced a national ban on all military-style semi-automatic weapons and assault rifles; the kinds of guns used in the Christchurch massacre. One day later, Prime Minister Ardern joined a large crowd of fellow New Zealanders to listen to the Muslim call to prayer in a park vigil, showing solidarity with nearly 2 billion Muslims worldwide.

"New Zealand mourns with you, we are one!" said Prime Minister Ardern to Muslims around the world after the deadliest act of Islamophobic terrorism in modern history.

***

We are one.

Those words still resonate with me today. They do so, because I can think of no more powerful sentiment for dispelling the needless hate and violence that plagues the human race today.

We are one. But there is another secret. *We have always been one.*

This separation . . . This intolerance . . . The secret is that it has *not* always been this way.

And I believe that if we can simply remember who we are— that we are all the same inside—then it will once again be possible for us to live in harmony and accomplish wondrous things as a single human race of nearly eight billion individual human beings.

Although ideological extremists want you to believe that the West and Muslims are fundamentally incompatible with each other, we should remember that history also teaches us that many of the most important advancements in human history can be traced directly to Muslim innovation and Muslim interaction with other cultures.

A person that I truly admire in the world of academe is Professor Glen Cooper, a BYU- and Columbia-trained expert on discoveries and inventions arising from Islamic civilizations. According to his well-documented research,[414] it was Islamic civilizations which gave the West its blueprint for university education today. In eighth century Baghdad, Muslim intellectuals first translated Greek and Indian science and philosophy into Arabic texts that, when later translated into Latin, catalyzed the European renaissance that we all praise today. It was also these same Islamic scientific texts which transformed Western science and ushered in a period of European dominance which many believe ultimately led to the Industrial Revolution.

Many people might be further surprised to learn that it was Muslim scholars who invented decimal fractions and trigonometry adapted for modern astronomy and cartography today. It was these mathematical models of the heavens that came from Islamic observatories, which fueled Copernicus's discoveries. And Avicenna's tenth-century *Canon of Medicine* became the central basis of Western medical study for the next seven hundred years.

It was the astrolabe—an analog computational device used in astronomy in the Islamic world—that shaped the future of navigation, allowing sailors around the world to determine their latitude until the end of time.

And the list goes on and on.

"We need to get past the 'West is Best' thinking," Professor Cooper said during a September 2017 magazine interview on Muslim contributions to the world.[415] "The contributions of Islamic science and education are immense. Without diminishing the accomplishments of the West, we need to acknowledge the great debt that our civilization owes to the people we look down on today."

The French philosopher Albert Camus once said that "peace is the only battle worth waging." We are currently living at a critical juncture in human history when ideological extremists like Donald Trump and ISIS share a similar destructive worldview. They have much in common, these two. They are seeking to divide our world along racial, religious, and/or ethnic lines. And we cannot let them win.

Instead, we must collectively summon our better angels to teach our children—and future generations—about the shared historical roots of our single human race to ensure the protection of this one beloved planet which belongs to all eight billion of us together.

**

The fifty-first, final, and youngest victim of the 2019 New Zealand mosque massacre was a three-year-old Black Muslim child named Mucad Ibrahim. Born in New Zealand to parents who had fled Somalia's civil war twenty years earlier, the youngest member of the Ibrahim family often looked forward to weekly Friday prayers at their Christchurch mosque, if only because he enjoyed being in the company of his father and older brother.

According to the *Washington Post*, when the white supremacist stormed into the mosque and started shooting indiscriminately that fateful day, the young toddler's father immediately threw his body atop both of his sons, telling them to play dead. However, in the chaotic mayhem that followed, the three-year-old toddler instead jumped up and started to run *toward* the white supremacist gunman. In the estimation of the survivors who witnessed it, the child may have thought what was happening was a video game.

"In front of me was a Somali kid—maybe three years old," a witness later recalled.[416] "[The gunman] shot him three or four times."

This cute little baby was dead simply because of the irrational fear of a Muslim planet. He was a three-year-old child. What threat did he pose to anyone?

I have chosen to close my argument, and my book, with three-year-old Mucad Ibrahim because he makes starkly clear the mindset of those who choose hate and fear. Of those whose corrupt beliefs are so strong that they would murder a tiny child simply because of their religious identity.

It is, in the end, all for the same non-specific, impersonal fear of a Muslim planet. The Christchurch shooter was worried that Muslims were taking over. But what were they taking over? What would things look like if they did? These pluralistic, integrating Muslims who were airline pilots and college professors and homemakers and literal small children—what did they want to do that was so sinister? Was it to be slightly different? To wear religious garb that was different, and pray in a different house of worship (to, I hasten to add, the same monotheistic Abrahamic God as that of Christians and Jews)?

I would not deign to interview him if given the opportunity, but I suspect that if compelled to explain himself, the Christchurch shooter would affirm the same things that practitioners of hate have always affirmed. That he did not particularly hate airplane pilots and college professors and so on. It was not personal. But he hated the spread of Islam. Why? It was going to do something sinister. What was that sinister thing? I suspect that he would not be able to give me a good answer.

In the end, it is up to all of us to combat fear with hope, and hatred with love. Yet, we must understand that we are up against foes that are driven by a fear so deep that it bites at the very core of their being. And at the same time, though it might seem absurd, we must acknowledge that this fear is of nothing specific. Of nothing personal. It is simply the old song of hatred that has been drunkenly sung off-tune for thousands of years, and regrettably there will always be those people who find that they like that sinister racist tune.

The greatest fear is the fear of the unknown. As we have seen throughout this book, one of the things that people around the world with negative attitudes toward Muslims have in common is that they claim they have never met one in their everyday lives. Misconceptions are rife, and they are scary. I think one of the cures for the darkness of hate is the light of knowledge. In this connection, I will close with the idea that education is the key. We must, all of us—Muslim and non-Muslim alike—seek to combat hatred with love, and also stereotypes with truth. We must help our neighbors understand Islam beyond the stereotypical ideas that they might find in Hollywood movies and right-wing media outlets. Assuredly, we will have foes in this fight. Great conglomerates exist with moneyed interests in keeping people afraid, and in stoking misconceptions and stereotypes, no matter how hurtful. There are also politicians who will try to retain their power by promoting the idea that Muslims are inherently dangerous and invading, so we all ought to stockpile guns and get ready to defend our families from the nonspecific threat they present.

But we can do it.

Thomas Jefferson once said, "I like the dreams of the future better than the history of the past." (And this from a man who kept a copy of the Quran in his personal library.)

There are now three Muslim members of the US Congress. Soon there will be more.

Progress is being made.

We must fight fear with love, and with the truth.

We owe this truth of our common humanity to everyone—such as the aforementioned fifty-one innocent victims of the 2019 Christchurch, New Zealand mosque massacre—who tragically lost their lives senselessly to weaponized hatred in their house of worship. But we also owe it to the hundreds and thousands of people around the world who may be murdered in the future if we do not take strong decisive action against racist haters everywhere.

As a proud Muslim, I believe we can succeed together.

Now it requires only the courage.

I hope you will join me in trying to find it.

Endnotes

Introduction

1   "Muslims and Islam: Key findings in the U.S. and around the world," Pew Research Center, August 9, 2017, available at https://www.pewresearch.org/fact-tank/2017/08/09/muslims-and-islam-key-findings-in-the-u-s-and-around-the-world/ (Accessed February 6, 2020).

2   "Most American voters support limited travel ban: poll," Reuters, July 5, 2017, available at https://www.reuters.com/article/us-usa-immigration-poll/most-american-voters-support-limited-travel-ban-poll-idUSKBN19Q2FW (Accessed December 10, 2020).

3   "FBI: Spike in US hate crimes for third year in a row," BBC World News, November 13, 2018, available at https://www.bbc.com/news/world-us-canada-46189391 (Accessed February 6, 2020).

4   Andrew Gumbel, "'The violence is always there': life as a Sikh in Trump's America," *The Guardian* (UK), September 19, 2018, available https://www.theguardian.com/world/2018/sep/19/sikh-in-america-hate-crime-surge-trump-religion (Accessed December 10, 2020).

Chapter 1

5   Charlie Mitchell, "'Welcome, brother': a community that stressed peace is undone by violence," *Sydney Morning Herald*, March 8, 2019, available at https://www.smh.com.au/world/oceania/welcome-brother-a-community-that-stressed-peace-is-undone-by-violence-20190318-p5152x.html (Accessed August 17, 2019).

6   Scott Shane, "Killings in Norway Spotlight Anti-Muslim Thought in
       U.S." *The New York Times*, March 8, 2011, available at https://www.
       nytimes.com/2011/07/25/us/25debate.html (Accessed August 17,
       2019).

7   Asher Moses, "From fantasy to lethal reality: Breivik trained on Modern
       Warfare game," *Brisbane Times*, July 24, 2011, available at https://
       www.brisbanetimes.com.au/technology/from-fantasy-to-lethal-
       reality-breivik-trained-on-modern-warfare-game-20110725-1hw41.
       html#ixzz1T7mI8lhn (Accessed August 17, 2019).

8   Anna Fifield & Kate Evans, "New Zealand mosque shootings: Voices
       of the victims," *The Washington Post*, March 18, 2019, available at
       https://www.washingtonpost.com/world/new-zealand-mosque-shoot-
       ings-voices-of-the-victims/2019/03/17/ce62df2a-4913-11e9-b871-
       978e5c757325_story.html (Accessed August 17, 2019).

9   Amanda Coletta, "Quebec City mosque shooter scoured Twitter for
       Trump, right-wing figures before attack," *The Washington Post*, April 8,
       2018, available at https://www.washingtonpost.com/news/worldviews/
       wp/2018/04/18/quebec-city-mosque-shooter-scoured-twitter-for-
       trump-right-wing-figures-before-attack/ (Accessed August 17, 2019).

10   Lois Beckett, "Pittsburgh shooting: suspect railed against Jews and
       Muslims on site used by 'alt-right'," *The Guardian Newspaper*, October
       27, 2018, available at https://www.theguardian.com/us-news/2018/
       oct/27/pittsburgh-shooting-suspect-antisemitism (Accessed August
       17, 2019).

11   Amy Taxin, Christopher Weber and Michael Balsamo, "'He is now
       part of the history of evil,' say parents of accused California synagogue
       shooter," Associated Press, April 29, 2019, available at https://www.
       chicagotribune.com/nation-world/ct-california-synagogue-shooter-
       history-of-evil-20190429-story.html (Accessed December 7, 2020).

12   Matthew Haagjacey Fortin, "Two Killed in Portland While Trying to
       Stop Anti-Muslim Rant, Police Say," *The New York Times*, May 27,
       2017, available at https://www.nytimes.com/2017/05/27/us/portland-
       train-attack-muslim-rant.html (Accessed August 17, 2019).

13   Samantha Grasso, "Hours after Donald Trump signs Muslim ban, a
       Texas mosque burned to the ground," *The Daily Dot*, January 28, 2017,
       available   at   https://www.dailydot.com/irl/victoria-texas-mosque-
       islamic-center-burned-muslim-ban/ (Accessed August 17, 2019).

14   Ted Genoways, "The Only Good Muslim Is a Dead Muslim," *The New Republic*, May 15, 2017, available at https://newrepublic.com/article/142346/kansas-meatpacking-somali-muslim-refugee-murder-plot-trump-supporters (Accessed August 17, 2019).

15   Lizzie Dearden, "Man threatens to blow up Islamic bookshop and 'kill the Muslims' in London," *The Independent Newspaper*, August 3, 2017, available at https://www.independent.co.uk/news/uk/crime/islamic-book-shop-bomb-plot-david-moffatt-catholic-kill-all-muslims-london-cricklewood-broadway-a7874506.html?amp (Accessed August 17, 2019).

16   Harriet Sherwood, Damien Gayle and Alice Ross, "Hero imam praises group that saved Finsbury Park suspect from angry crowd," *The Guardian Newspaper*, June 19, 2017, available at https://www.theguardian.com/uk-news/2017/jun/19/imam-praised-for-protecting-finsbury-park-suspect-from-crowd (Accessed August 17, 2019).

17   Arsalan Iftikhar, "My Take: Sikh temple shooting is act of terrorism," CNN Belief Blog, August 6, 2012, available at http://religion.blogs.cnn.com/2012/08/06/my-take-sikh-temple-shooting-is-act-of-terrorism/ (Accessed August 17, 2019).

18   Joshua Berlinger, "Frazier Glenn Cross found guilty of murder in Jewish center shootings," CNN, August 31, 2015, available at https://www.cnn.com/2015/08/31/us/kansas-jewish-center-gunman-guilty/index.html (Accessed December 7, 2020).

19   Arsalan Iftikhar, "Freedom of Religion Requires Freedom From Fear," *The Atlantic*, October 9, 2015, available at https://www.theatlantic.com/politics/archive/2015/10/protesting-american-mosques-at-gunpoint/409987/ (Accessed August 17, 2019).

20   "Dead, injured and missing: Christchurch shooting victims," *Sydney Morning Herald* (Australia), March 17, 2019, available at https://www.smh.com.au/world/oceania/dead-injured-and-missing-christchurch-shooting-victims-20190317-p514w8.html (Accessed December 7, 2020).

21   Tim Arango, Nicholas Bogel-Burroughs and Katie Benner, "Minutes Before El Paso Killing, Hate-Filled Manifesto Appears Online," *The New York Times*, August 3, 2019, available at https://www.nytimes.com/2019/08/03/us/patrick-crusius-el-paso-shooter-manifesto.html (Accessed August 17, 2019).

22   Norimitsu Onishi, "The Man Behind a Toxic Slogan Promoting White Supremacy" *New York Times*, September 20, 2019, available at https://www.nytimes.com/2019/09/20/world/europe/renaud-camus-great-replacement.html (Accessed October 31, 2020).

23   Sarah Wildman, "'You will not replace us': a French philosopher explains the Charlottesville chant" VOX.com, August 15, 2017, available at https://www.vox.com/world/2017/8/15/16141456/renaud-camus-the-great-replacement-you-will-not-replace-us-charlottesville-white (Accessed October 31, 2020).

24   James McAuley, "How Gay Icon Renaud Camus Became the Ideologue of White Supremacy," *The Nation Magazine*, June 17, 2019, available at https://www.thenation.com/article/archive/renaud-camus-great-replacement-brenton-tarrant/ (Accessed October 31, 2020).

25   Report, "'The Great Replacement': The Violent Consequences of Mainstreamed Extremism," Institute for Strategic Dialogue, July 2019, available at https://www.isdglobal.org/wp-content/uploads/2019/07/The-Great-Replacement-The-Violent-Consequences-of-Mainstreamed-Extremism-by-ISD.pdf (Accessed February 10, 2021).

26   Convention on the Prevention and Punishment of the Crime of Genocide, Dec. 9 1948, S. Exec. Doc. O, 81-1 (1949), 78 U.N.T.S. 277 available at https://treaties.un.org/doc/publication/unts/volume%2078/volume-78-i-1021-english.pdf (Accessed January 15, 2021).

27   Richard Skretteberg, "Trapped in the world's largest refugee camp," Norwegian Refugee Council, August 25, 2019, available at https://www.nrc.no/perspectives/2019/trapped-in-the-worlds-largest-refugee-camp/ (Accessed December 7, 2020).

28   "Myanmar fugitive monk Wirathu hands himself in to face sedition charges," Reuters, November 2, 2020, available at https://www.deccan-herald.com/international/myanmar-fugitive-monk-wirathu-hands-himself-in-to-face-sedition-charges-910379.html (Accessed December 7, 2020).

29   "Portrait of Myanmar's 'Buddhist Bin Laden' Wirathu chills Cannes," *The Straits Times* (Singapore), May 24, 2017, available at https://www.straitstimes.com/asia/se-asia/portrait-of-myanmars-buddhist-bin-laden-wirathu-chills-cannes (Accessed December 7, 2020).

30   Muhammad Lila, "Dalai Lama Pleads for Myanmar Monks to End Violence Amid Damning Rights Report," ABC News, April 22, 2013, available at https://abcnews.go.com/International/dalai-lama-pleads-

myanmar-monks-end-violence-amid/story?id=19013148   (Accessed December 7, 2020).

31   Arsalan Iftikhar, "Islamophobic Genocide of Myanmar's Rohingya Muslims," Georgetown University Bridge Initiative, September 5, 2017, available at https://bridge.georgetown.edu/research/islamopho-bic-genocide-of-myanmars-rohingya-muslims/ (Accessed August 17, 2019).

32   Human Rights Watch, "International Court of Justice Orders Burmese Authorities to Protect Rohingya Muslims from Genocide," January 27, 2020, available at https://www.hrw.org/news/2020/01/27/interna-tional-court-justice-orders-burmese-authorities-protect-rohingya-muslims# (Accessed December 7, 2020).

33   George Soros, "Soros: As a Jew in Budapest, I Too Was a Rohingya," *Newsweek*, May 31, 2015, available at https://www.newsweek.com/soros-jew-budapest-i-too-was-rohingya-337443 (Accessed August 17, 2019).

34   Laignee Barron, "The Holocaust Museum Says There Is 'Mounting Evidence' of Genocide in Myanmar," TIME, November 15, 2017, available at https://time.com/5024975/myanmar-rohingya-genocide-holocaust-museum/ (Accessed August 17, 2019).

35   Mia Swart, "ICJ orders Myanmar to protect Rohingya," Al-Jazeera News, January 23, 2020, available at https://www.aljazeera.com/news/2020/1/23/icj-orders-myanmar-to-protect-rohingya (Accessed December 10, 2020).

36   Report, ""Eradicating Ideological Viruses: China's Campaign of Repression Against Xinjiang's Muslims," Human Rights Watch, September 9, 2018, available at https://www.hrw.org/report/2018/09/09/eradicating-ideological-viruses/chinas-campaign-repression-against-xinjiangs (Accessed December 7, 2020).

37   Cristina Maza, "Saudi Arabia's Mohammed bin Salman Defends China's Use of Concentration Camps for Muslims During Visit to Beijing," *Newsweek*, February 22, 2019, available at https://www.news-week.com/saudi-arabia-mohammad-bin-salman-defends-china-con-centration-camps-muslims-1340592 (Accessed December 7, 2020).

38   "PM 'doesn't know much' about condition of Uighurs in China," *The Express Tribune* (Pakistan), January 8, 2019, available at https://tribune.com.pk/story/1883992/1-pm-doesnt-know-much-condition-uighurs-china (Accessed December 7, 2020).

39   Arsalan Iftikhar, "Pakistan & Saudi Arabia Throw China's Muslims Under the Bus," Georgetown University Bridge Initiative, March 4, 2019, available at https://bridge.georgetown.edu/research/pakistan-saudi-arabia-throw-chinas-muslims-under-the-bus/ (Accessed August 17, 2019).

40   Azeem Ibrahim, "Muslim Leaders Are Betraying the Uighurs," *Foreign Policy*, July 8, 2019, available at https://foreignpolicy.com/2019/07/08/muslim-leaders-are-betraying-the-uighurs/ (Accessed August 17, 2019).

41   Conrad Hackett, "By 2050, India to have world's largest populations of Hindus and Muslims," Pew Research Center, April 21, 2015, available at https://www.pewresearch.org/fact-tank/2015/04/21/by-2050-india-to-have-worlds-largest-populations-of-hindus-and-muslims/ (Accessed December 21, 2020).

42   William Dalrymple, "Narendra Modi: man of the masses," *New Statesman* (UK), May 12, 2014, available at https://www.newstatesman.com/politics/2014/05/narendra-modi-man-masses (Accessed December 21, 2020).

43   Mick Krever, "Will Modi be India's Putin?" CNN, May 19, 2014, available at https://amanpour.blogs.cnn.com/2014/05/19/will-modi-be-indias-putin/ (Accessed December 21, 2020).

44   Pankaj Mishra, "Narendra Modi and the new face of India," *The Guardian* (UK), May 16, 2014, available at https://www.theguardian.com/books/2014/may/16/what-next-india-pankaj-mishra (Accessed December 21, 2020).

45   Gardiner Harris, "For India's Persecuted Muslim Minority, Caution Follows Hindu Party's Victory," *New York Times*, May 16, 2014, available at https://www.nytimes.com/2014/05/17/world/asia/india-muslims-modi.html (Accessed December 21, 2020).

46   Shashank Bengali, "Indian Muslims wary of man poised to take reins," *Los Angeles Times*, May 15, 2014, available at https://www.latimes.com/world/asia/la-fg-india-elections-20140514-story.html (Accessed December 21, 2020).

47   Ratnadir Choudhury, "India's 1st Illegal Immigrant Detention Camp Size Of 7 Football Fields," NDTV (India), September 12, 2019, available at https://www.ndtv.com/india-news/assam-detention-centre-inside-indias-1st-detention-centre-for-illegal-immigrants-after-nrc-school-ho-2099626 (Accessed December 21, 2020).

48   Rana Ayyub, "In India, Trump validates Modi's divisive agenda," *Washington Post*, February 24, 2020, available at https://www.

washingtonpost.com/opinions/2020/02/24/india-trump-validates-modis-divisive-agenda/#click=https://t.co/4LJNO1EE8o (Accessed December 21, 2020).

49 Tony Birtley, "India death toll rises after worst violence in decades," *Al-Jazeera News*, March 2, 2020, available at https://www.aljazeera.com/videos/2020/3/2/india-death-toll-rises-after-worst-violence-in-decades (Accessed December 21, 2020).

50 Associated Press, "WATCH: Trump defends India's Modi over controversial citizenship law," *PBS NewsHour*, February 25, 2020, available at https://www.pbs.org/newshour/world/trump-defends-indias-modi-over-controversial-citizenship-law (Accessed December 21, 2020).

51 "When Donald Trump called PM Modi father of India," *India Today*, September 24, 2019, available at https://www.indiatoday.in/india/story/when-donald-trump-called-pm-modi-father-of-india-1602819-2019-09-24 (Accessed December 21, 2020).

52 Hannah Ellis-Petersen & Azizur Rahman, "Coronavirus conspiracy theories targeting Muslims spread in India," *The Guardian* (UK), April 13, 2020, available at https://www.theguardian.com/world/2020/apr/13/coronavirus-conspiracy-theories-targeting-muslims-spread-in-india (Accessed December 21, 2020).

53 Jeffrey Gettleman, Kai Schultz and Suhasini Raj, "In India, Coronavirus Fans Religious Hatred," *New York Times*, April 12, 2020, available at https://www.nytimes.com/2020/04/12/world/asia/india-coronavirus-muslims-bigotry.html (Accessed December 21, 2020).

54 Barack Obama, Twitter post, August 5, 2019, 3:01 p.m., https://twitter.com/BarackObama/status/1158453079035002881 (Accessed August 17, 2019).

55 Kelly Weill, "More Than 500 Attacks on Muslims in America This Year," *The Daily Beast*, May 21, 2019, *The Guardian*, August 4, 2019 available at https://www.thedailybeast.com/more-than-500-attacks-on-muslims-in-america-this-year?ref=scroll (Accessed August 17, 2019).

56 Jeff Sparrow, "What induces men to imitate the Christchurch massacre?" *The Guardian*, August 4, 2019, available at https://www.theguardian.com/commentisfree/2019/aug/05/what-induces-men-to-imitate-the-christchurch-massacre (Accessed August 17, 2019).

57 Report, "ADL Report: White Supremacist Murders More Than Doubled in 2017," Anti-Defamation League, January 17, 2018, available at https://

www.adl.org/news/press-releases/adl-report-white-supremacist-murders-more-than-doubled-in-2017 (Accessed December 7, 2020).

58   "Researcher: Disparities Exist in News Coverage of Terror Attacks," University of Alabama, February 19, 2019, available at https://news. ua.edu/2019/02/researcher-disparities-exist-in-news-coverage-of-terror-attacks/ (Accessed December 7, 2020).

59   Benjamin Kentish, "Terror attacks receive five times more media coverage if perpetrator is Muslim, study finds," *The Independent* (UK), July 3, 2017, available at https://www.independent.co.uk/news/world/americas/terror-attacks-media-coverage-muslim-islamist-white-racism-islamophobia-study-georgia-state-university-a7820726.html (Accessed December 7, 2020).

60   Mona Chalabi, "Terror attacks by Muslims receive 357% more press attention, study finds," *The Guardian Newspaper*, July 20, 2018, available at https://amp.theguardian.com/us-news/2018/jul/20/muslim-terror-attacks-press-coverage-study (Accessed August 17, 2019).

61   Mallory Simon & Sara Sidner, "Tackle white supremacy as terrorism, experts say," CNN.com, May 15, 2019, available at https://www.cnn.com/2019/05/14/us/white-supremacy-terrorism-soh/index.html (Accessed August 17, 2019).

62   Mark Potok, "The Trump Effect," Southern Poverty Law Center, February 15, 2017, available at https://www.splcenter.org/fighting-hate/intelligence-report/2017/trump-effect (Accessed December 7, 2020).

Chapter 2

63   Theodore Schleifer, "Donald Trump: 'I think Islam hates us'," CNN.com, March 10, 2016, available at http://www.cnn.com/2016/03/09/politics/donald-trump-islam-hates-us/index.html (Accessed August 19, 2019).

64   Charlie Mitchell, "The extraordinary life of Abdus Samad, a scientist who came from poverty," Stuff.co (New Zealand), March 27, 2019, available at https://www.stuff.co.nz/national/christchurch-shooting/111559905/the-extraordinary-life-of-abdus-samad-a-scientist-who-came-from-poverty (Accessed December 7, 2020).

65   "Donald Trump 'Proud' to be a Birther," The Laura Ingraham Show, March 30, 2011, available at https://www.youtube.com/watch?v=WqaS9OCoTZs (Accessed August 19, 2019).

66   Chris Megerian, "What Donald Trump has said through the years about where President Obama was born," *Los Angeles Times*, September 16,

2016, available at http://www.latimes.com/politics/la-na-pol-trump-birther-timeline-20160916-snap-htmlstory.html (Accessed August 19, 2019).

67 Transcript, *Meet the Press*, NBC News, November 22, 2015, available at http://www.nbcnews.com/meet-the-press/meet-press-november-22-2015-n467821 (Accessed August 19, 2019).

68 Dan Pfeiffer, "President Obama's Long-Form Birth Certificate," The White House, April 27, 2011, available at https://obamawhitehouse.archives.gov/blog/2011/04/27/president-obamas-long-form-birth-certificate (Accessed August 19, 2019).

69 CNN Political Unit, "Blitzer and Trump go at it over Trump's 'birther' claims," CNN.com, May 29, 2012, available at http://politicalticker.blogs.cnn.com/2012/05/29/firing-off-trump-stands-by-birther-comments/ (August 19, 2019).

70 Meghan Keneally, "President Obama's Long History of Insulting Donald Trump," ABC News, November 10, 2016, available at http://abcnews.go.com/Politics/president-obamas-long-history-insulting-donald-trump/story?id=43442367 (Accessed August 19, 2019).

71 Chris Moody & Kristen Holmes, "Donald Trump's history of suggesting Obama is a Muslim," CNN.com, September 18, 2015, available at http://www.cnn.com/2015/09/18/politics/trump-obama-muslim-birther/ (Accessed August 19, 2019).

72 Isra'a Emhail, "Christchurch mosque attack victim Maheboob Khokhar was on first visit to New Zealand," Radio New Zealand, April 9, 2019, available at https://www.rnz.co.nz/news/national/386676/christchurch-mosque-attack-victim-maheboob-khokhar-was-on-first-visit-to-new-zealand (Accessed December 7, 2020).

73 "GOP Quickly Unifies Around Trump; Clinton Still Has Modest Lead," Public Policy Polling, May 10, 2016, Diamond, "Trump doubles down on calls for mosque, available at http://www.publicpolicypolling.com/main/2016/05/gop-quickly-unifies-around-trump-clinton-still-has-modest-lead.html (Accessed August 19, 2019).

74 David Mark & Jeremy Diamond, "Trump: 'I want surveillance of certain mosques'" CNN.com, November 21, 2015 available at http://www.cnn.com/2015/11/21/politics/trump-muslims-surveillance/ (Accessed August 19, 2019).

75 Jeremy Diamond, "Trump doubles down on calls for mosque surveillance" CNN.com, June 15, 2016, available at http://www.cnn

.com/2016/06/15/politics/donald-trump-muslims-mosque-surveillance (Accessed August 19, 2019).

76   Vaughn Hillyard, "Trump's plan for a Muslim database draws comparison to Nazi Germany," MSNBC.com, November 20, 2015, available at http://www.msnbc.com/msnbc/trump-would-certainly-implement-muslim-database (Accessed August 19, 2019).

77   Jeremy Diamond, "Trump would 'certainly implement' national database for U.S. Muslims," CNN.com, November 20, 2015, available at http://www.cnn.com/2015/11/19/politics/donald-trump-barack-obama-threat-to-country/ (Accessed August 19, 2019).

78   https://twitter.com/HillaryClinton/status/667703375035789312 (Accessed August 19, 2019).

79   Report, "A New Era in American Politics: The Trump Administration and Mainstream Islamophobia," The Bridge Initiative (Georgetown University), June 23, 2017, available at https://bridge.georgetown.edu/wp-content/uploads/2017/06/final-trump-admin-report.pdf (Accessed August 19, 2019).

80   "Republicans Prefer Blunt Talk About Islamic Extremism, Democrats Favor Caution," Pew Research Center, February 3, 2016, available at http://www.pewforum.org/2016/02/03/republicans-prefer-blunt-talk-about-islamic-extremism-democrats-favor-caution/ (Accessed August 19, 2019).

81   Report, "U.S. Muslims Concerned About Their Place in Society, but Continue to Believe in the American Dream," Pew Research Center, July 26, 2017, available at http://assets.pewresearch.org/wp-content/uploads/sites/11/2017/07/25171611/U.S.-MUSLIMS-FULL-REPORT.pdf (Accessed August 19, 2019).

82   Arsalan Iftikhar, "Pew Study: U.S. Muslims Feel Unwelcome, Yet Hopeful," The Bridge Initiative (Georgetown University), July 27, 2017 available at http://bridge.georgetown.edu/pew-study-u-s-muslims-feel-unwelcome-yet-hopeful/ (Accessed August 19, 2019).

83   Matea Gold, "Bannon film outline warned U.S. could turn into 'Islamic States of America'," Washington Post, February 3, 2017, available at https://www.washingtonpost.com/politics/bannon-film-outline-warned-us-could-turn-into-islamic-states-of-america/2017/02/03/f73832f4-e8be-11e6-b82f-687d6e6a3e7c_story.html?utm_term=.c7c733b0c797 (Accessed August 19, 2019).

84 Rebecca Savransky, "Bannon in 2010: 'Islam is not a religion of peace'," *The Hill Newspaper*, February 1, 2017, available at http://thehill.com/homenews/administration/317280-bannon-in-2010-islam-is-not-a-religion-of-peace (Accessed August 19, 2019).

85 Benjamin Haas, "Steve Bannon: 'We're going to war in the South China Sea . . . no doubt'" *The Guardian* (UK), February 1, 2017 available at https://www.theguardian.com/us-news/2017/feb/02/steve-bannon-donald-trump-war-south-china-sea-no-doubt (Accessed December 7, 2020).

86 Ben Mathis-Lilley, "How Trump Has Cultivated the White Supremacist Alt-Right for Years," Slate.com, August 14, 2017, available at http://www.slate.com/blogs/the_slatest/2017/08/14/donald_trump_s_ties_to_alt_right_white_supremacists_are_extensive.html (Accessed August 19, 2019).

87 Steve Reilly & Brad Heath, "Steve Bannon's own words show sharp break on security issues," *USA Today*, January 31, 2017, available at https://www.usatoday.com/story/news/2017/01/31/bannon-odds-islam-china-decades-us-foreign-policy-doctrine/97292068/ (Accessed August 19, 2019).

88 Josh Harkinson, "The Dark History of the White House Aides Who Crafted Trump's 'Muslim Ban'," *Mother Jones Magazine*, January 30, 2017, available at http://www.motherjones.com/politics/2017/01/stephen-bannon-miller-trump-refugee-ban-islamophobia-white-nationalist/ (Accessed August 19, 2019).

89 Fact Sheet, "Pamela Geller," Southern Poverty Law Center, available at https://www.splcenter.org/fighting-hate/extremist-files/individual/pamela-geller (August 19, 2019).

90 Connie Bruck, "How Hollywood Remembers Steve Bannon," *The New Yorker*, May 1, 2017, available at http://www.newyorker.com/magazine/2017/05/01/how-hollywood-remembers-steve-bannon (Accessed August 19, 2019).

91 Reena Flores, "Trump campaign fires back after Jewish group blasts anti-Semitic imagery in Trump ad," CBS News, November 6, 2016, available at https://www.cbsnews.com/news/trump-campaign-fires-back-adl-blasts-anti-semitic-imagery-trump-ad/ (Accessed August 19, 2019).

92 Jack Moore, "Here Is a Horrifying Anecdote About Steve Bannon's Views on Black Voters," *GQ Magazine*, November 28, 2016, available

at https://www.gq.com/story/steve-bannon-black-voters (Accessed August 19, 2019).

93　Andrew Kaczynski & Nathaniel Meyersohn, "Trump Campaign CEO Once Blasted 'Bunch Of Dykes' From The 'Seven Sisters Schools'," BuzzFeed, August 29, 2016, available at https://www.buzzfeednews.com/article/andrewkaczynski/trump-campaign-ceo-once-blasted-bunch-of-dykes-from-the-seve (Accessed August 19, 2019).

94　Andrew Kaczynski & Chris Massie, "White nationalists see advocate in Steve Bannon who will hold Trump to his campaign promises" CNN.com, November 15, 2016, available at http://www.cnn.com/2016/11/14/politics/white-nationalists-on-bannon (Accessed August 19, 2019).

95　Oliver Darcy, "Steve Bannon returns to Breitbart after ouster from White House," CNN.com, August 8, 2017, available at http://money.cnn.com/2017/08/18/media/steve-bannon-returns-breitbart/index.html (Accessed August 19, 2019).

96　Alexander Smith & Vladimir Banic, "Sebastian Gorka Made Nazi-Linked Vitezi Rend 'Proud' by Wearing Its Medal," NBC News, April 8, 2017, available at https://www.nbcnews.com/news/world/sebastian-gorka-made-nazi-linked-vitezi-rend-proud-wearing-its-n742851 (Accessed August 19, 2019).

97　Allegra Kirkland, "Did Gorka Really Wear A Medal Linked To Nazi Ally To Trump Inaugural Ball?" Talking Points Memo, February 13, 2017, available at http://talkingpointsmemo.com/dc/sebastian-gorka-inauguration-medal-order-vitez-horthy (Accessed August 19, 2019).

98　Lili Bayer, "EXCLUSIVE: Controversial Trump Aide Sebastian Gorka Backed Violent Anti-Semitic Militia," The Forward Newspaper, April 3, 2017, available at http://forward.com/news/national/367937/exclusive-controversial-trump-aide-sebastian-gorka-backed-violent-anti-semi (Accessed August 19, 2019).

99　Maggie Haberman, "Sebastian Gorka Likely to Be Out of White House Role, Officials Say," The New York Times, April 30, 2017, available at https://www.nytimes.com/2017/04/30/us/politics/sebastian-gorka-white-house.html (Accessed August 19, 2019).

100　Bob Dreyfuss, "Sebastian Gorka, the West Wing's Phony Foreign-Policy Guru," Rolling Stone, August 10, 2017, available at http://www.rollingstone.com/politics/features/sebastian-gorka-the-west-wings-phony-foreign-policy-guru-w496912 (Accessed August 19, 2019).

101 Greg Jaffe, "For a Trump adviser, an odyssey from the fringes of Washington to the center of power," February 20, 2017, available at https://www.washingtonpost.com/world/national-security/for-a-trump-adviser-an-odyssey-from-the-fringes-of-washington-to-the-center-of-power/2017/02/20/0a326260-f2cb-11e6-b9c9-e83fce42fb61_story.html?utm_term=.dba6d0f5993c (Accessed August 19, 2019).

102 Steven Simon & Daniel Benjamin, "The Islamophobic Huckster in the White House," *The New York Times*, February 24, 2017, available at https://www.nytimes.com/2017/02/24/opinion/the-islamophobic-huckster-in-the-white-house.html (Accessed August 19, 2019).

103 Zaid Jilani & Alex Emmons, "Former Donald Trump Adviser Calls Racial Profiling 'Common Sense'," *The Intercept*, June 30, 2016, available at https://theintercept.com/2016/06/30/former-donald-trump-adviser-calls-racial-profiling-common-sense/ (Accessed August 19, 2019).

104 Laura Stampler, "Trump's Deputy Assistant, Sebastian Gorka, Has Frequently Denounced Islam," *Teen Vogue*, February 22, 2017, available at http://www.teenvogue.com/story/trumps-deputy-assistant-sebastian-gorka-has-frequently-denounced-islam (Accessed August 19, 2019).

105 Spencer Ackerman, "FBI Fired Sebastian Gorka for Anti-Muslim Diatribes," *The Daily Beast*, June 21, 2017, available at http://www.thedailybeast.com/fbi-fired-sebastian-gorka-for-anti-muslim-diatribes (Accessed August 19, 2019).

106 Shane Harris, "Conservative Pundit Sebastian Gorka Brings 'Global Jihadist Movement' Theory Into White House," *The Wall Street Journal*, February 21, 2017, available at https://www.wsj.com/articles/conservative-pundit-sebastian-gorka-brings-global-jihadist-move-ment-theory-into-white-house-1487650120?tesla=y&mg=prod/accounts-wsj (Accessed August 19, 2019).

107 Ibid.

108 Aqela Susu, "He was a 'loving and caring' man," *The Fiji Times*, March 18, 2019, available at https://www.fijitimes.com.fj/he-was-a-loving-and-caring-man/ (Accessed December 7, 2020).

109 Fact Sheet, "Frank Gaffney Jr.," Southern Poverty Law Center, available at https://www.splcenter.org/fighting-hate/extremist-files/individual/frank-gaffney-jr (August 19, 2019).

110 Report, "A Journalist's Manual: Field Guide to Anti-Muslim Extremists," Southern Poverty Law Center, October 25, 2016, available

at https://www.splcenter.org/20161025/journalists-manual-field-guide
-anti-muslim-extremists (Accessed August 19, 2019).

111 Report, "A New Era in American Politics: The Trump Administration
and Mainstream Islamophobia," Georgetown University Bridge
Initiative, June 2017, available at https://bridge.georgetown.edu/wp
-content/uploads/2017/06/final-trump-admin-report.pdf   (Accessed
December 7, 2020).

112 Rosie Gray, "Frank Gaffney Strikes Back," *BuzzFeed News*, December
14, 2015, available at https://www.buzzfeednews.com/article/rosiegray
/frank-gaffney-strikes-back (Accessed August 19, 2019).

113 Peter Beinart, "The Demonization of American Muslims," *The Atlantic*,
March 19, 2017, available at https://www.theatlantic.com/politics/
archive/2017/03/frank-gaffney-donald-trump-and-the-denationalization
-of-american-muslims/519954/ (Accessed August 19, 2019).

114 Josh Harkinson, "Trump Campaign CEO Was a Big Promoter of Anti-
Muslim Extremists," *Mother Jones Magazine*, September 15, 2016,
available at http://www.motherjones.com/politics/2016/09/stephen
-bannon-donald-trump-muslims-fear-loathing/ (Accessed August 19,
2019).

115 Ibid.

116 Frank Gaffney, "America's First Muslim President?" *The Washington
Times*, June 9, 2009, available at http://www.washingtontimes.com
/news/2009/jun/9/americas-first-muslim-president/ (Accessed August
19, 2019).

117 Tina Nguyen, "Trump Transition Team Turns to Anti-Muslim
Conspiracy Theorist," *Vanity Fair*, November 16, 2016, available at
https://www.vanityfair.com/news/2016/11/donald-trump-frank-
gaffney-transition (Accessed August 19, 2019).

118 Philip Bump, "Meet Frank Gaffney, the anti-Muslim gadfly reportedly
advising Trump's transition team," *Chicago Tribune*, November 15,
2016, available at http://www.chicagotribune.com/news/nationworld
/politics/ct-anti-muslim-frank-gaffney-trump-transition-team-20161115
-story.html (Accessed August 19, 2019).

119 Scott Shane, Matthew Rosenberg & Eric Lipton, "Trump Pushes Dark
View of Islam to Center of U.S. Policy-Making," *The New York Times*,
February 1, 2017, available at https://www.nytimes.com/2017/02/01
/us/politics/donald-trump-islam.html?mcubz=1 (Accessed August 19,
2019).

120 National Public Radio, "'Less Than Human': The Psychology of Cruelty," NPR Talk of the Nation, March 29, 2011, available at http://www.npr.org/2011/03/29/134956180/criminals-see-their-victims-as-less-than-human (Accessed August 19, 2019).

121 Aaron Blake, "Trump's full inauguration speech transcript, annotated," *Washington Post*, January 20, 2017, available at https://www.washingtonpost.com/news/the-fix/wp/2017/01/20/donald-trumps-full-inauguration-speech-transcript-annotated/?utm_term=.71cda3cdcf1a (Accessed August 19, 2019).

122 "Stephen Miller: 5 Fast Facts You Need to Know," Heavy.com, February 13, 2017, available at http://heavy.com/news/2016/12/stephen-miller-donald-trump-speechwriter-inauguration-day-speech-who-is-jeff-sessions-aide-duke (Accessed August 19, 2019).

123 Tim Mak, "The Troublemaker Behind Donald Trump's Words," *The Daily Beast*, January 19, 2017, available at http://www.thedailybeast.com/articles/2017/01/19/the-troublemaker-behind-donald-trump-s-words (Accessed August 19, 2019).

124 Graeme Wood, "His Kampf" *The Atlantic*, June 2017 issue available at https://www.theatlantic.com/magazine/archive/2017/06/his-kampf/524505/ (Accessed August 19, 2019).

125 Kayleigh Roberts, "Who Is Stephen Miller? 12 Things You Need to Know About Trump's Senior Policy Adviser" *Cosmopolitan Magazine*, August 3, 2017 available at http://www.cosmopolitan.com/politics/a8778142/stephen-miller-trump-senior-policy-advisor-facts/ (Accessed August 19, 2019).

126 Josh Harkinson, Meet the White Nationalist Trying To Ride The Trump Train to Lasting Power" *Mother Jones Magazine*, October 27, 2016 available at http://www.motherjones.com/politics/2016/10/richard-spencer-trump-alt-right-white-nationalist/ (Accessed August 19, 2019).

127 Mehdi Hasan, "Donald Trump's 'brain' Stephen Miller is also obsessed with Muslims and Mexicans," *The New Statesman* (UK), August 11, 2017 available at http://www.newstatesman.com/culture/observations/2017/08/donald-trumps-brain-stephen-miller-also-obsessed-muslims-and-mexicans (Accessed August 19, 2019).

128 William Cohan, "How Stephen Miller Rode White Rage From Duke's Campus to Trump's West Wing," *Vanity Fair Magazine*, May 2017, available at https://www.vanityfair.com/news/2017/05/stephen-miller-duke-donald-trump (Accessed August 19, 2019).

129 Lisa Mascaro, "McCain: 'Sinister' attacks on Clinton aide Huma Abedin must stop," *Los Angeles Times*, July 18, 2012, available at http://articles.latimes.com/2012/jul/18/news/la-pn-mccain-sinister-attacks-on-clinton-aide-huma-abedin-must-stop-20120718 (Accessed August 19, 2019).

130 Ed Kilgore, "Stephen Miller Is Writing the Big Speech on Islam That Trump Is Delivering in Saudi Arabia," *New York Magazine*, May 17, 2017, available at https://nymag.com/intelligencer/2017/05/stephen-miller-writing-big-trump-speech-on-islam-yikes.html (Accessed December 7, 2020).

131 Aaron Blake, "Stephen Miller's authoritarian declaration: Trump's national security actions 'will not be questioned'," *Washington Post*, February 13, 2017, available at https://www.washingtonpost.com/news/the-fix/wp/2017/02/13/stephen-millers-audacious-controversial-declaration-trumps-national-security-actions-will-not-be-questioned/?utm_term=.bd21767f589f (Accessed August 19, 2019).

132 Saiqa Chaudhari, "Musa Vali Suleman Patel who has family in Bolton was killed in the devastating attack," *The Bolton News* (UK), March 25, 2019, available at https://www.theboltonnews.co.uk/news/17523976.musa-vali-suleman-patel-family-bolton-killed-devastating-attack (Accessed December 7, 2020).

133 Press Release, "EXECUTIVE ORDER: PROTECTING THE NATION FROM FOREIGN TERRORIST ENTRY INTO THE UNITED STATES," The White House, January 27, 2017, available at https://www.whitehouse.gov/the-press-office/2017/01/27/executive-order-protecting-nation-foreign-terrorist-entry-united-states (Accessed August 19, 2019).

134 Michael Shear & Helene Cooper, "Trump Bars Refugees and Citizens of 7 Muslim Countries," *The New York Times*, January 27, 2017, available at https://www.nytimes.com/2017/01/27/us/politics/trump-syrian-refugees.html (Accessed August 19, 2019).

135 American Civil Liberties Union (ACLU), "INTERNATIONAL REFUGEE ASSISTANCE PROJECT V. TRUMP - AMENDED COMPLAINT," March 10, 2017, available at https://www.aclu.org/legal-document/international-refugee-assistance-project-v-trump-amended-complaint (Accessed August 19, 2019).

136 Cecilia Wang, "Trump Begins His Unconstitutional Program of Anti-Muslim Discrimination," American Civil Liberties Union (ACLU) Blog, January 28, 2017, available at https://www.aclu.org/blog/national-security/discriminatory-profiling/trump-begins-his-unconstitutional-program-

anti?redirect=blog/speak-freely/trump-begins-his-unconstitutional
-program-anti-muslim-discrimination (Accessed August 19, 2019).

137   Ariane de Vogue & Eli Watkins, "Judges temporarily block part of
Trump's immigration order, WH stands by it," CNN.com, January 28,
2017, available at http://www.cnn.com/2017/01/28/politics/2-iraqis-
file-lawsuit-after-being-detained-in-ny-due-to-travel-ban/index.html
(Accessed August 19, 2019).

138   Ben Jacobs, "US travel ban hits major setback as judges uphold temporary restraining order," *The Guardian* (UK) Newspaper, February 9,
2017, available at https://www.theguardian.com/us-news/2017/feb/09
/judges-deny-trump-travel-ban-enforcement-uphold-order (Accessed
August 19, 2019).

139   Rebecca Savransky, "Giuliani: Trump asked me how to do a Muslim
ban 'legally'," *The Hill Newspaper*, January 29, 2017, available at
http://thehill.com/homenews/administration/316726-giuliani
-trump-asked-me-how-to-do-a-muslim-ban-legally (Accessed August
19, 2019).

140   Jenna Johnson, "Trump calls for 'total and complete shutdown of
Muslims entering the United States'," *Washington Post*, December
7, 2015, available at https://www.washingtonpost.com/news/post
-politics/wp/2015/12/07/donald-trump-calls-for-total-and-complete-
shutdown-of-muslims-entering-the-united-states/?utm_term=
.a266732ff576 (Accessed August 19, 2019).

141   Press Release, "Executive Order Protecting The Nation From
Foreign Terrorist Entry Into The United States," The White House,
March 6, 2017, available at https://www.whitehouse.gov/the-press
-office/2017/03/06/executive-order-protecting-nation-foreign
-terrorist-entry-united-states (Accessed August 19, 2019).

142   "Summary of Second Trump Executive Order on Visa Issuance/Screen-
ing and Refugees," American Immigration Lawyers Association (AILA),
March 6, 2017, available at http://www.aila.org/infonet/summary
-second-trump-exec-order-visa-issuance (Accessed August 19, 2019).

143   "Timeline of the Muslim Ban," American Civil Liberties Union (ACLU)
of Washington, available at https://www.aclu-wa.org/pages/timeline-
muslim-ban (Accessed August 19, 2019).

144   Video, "Arsalan Iftikhar Discusses Muslim Ban 2.0," Al-Jazeera English,
March 7, 2017, available at https://youtu.be/MZSEj39riy8 (Accessed
August 19, 2019).

145   Meridith McGraw, Adam Kelsey & Meghan Keneally, "A timeline of Trump's immigration executive order and legal challenges," ABC News, June 29, 2017, available at http://abcnews.go.com/Politics/timeline -president-trumps-immigration-executive-order-legal-challenges /story?id=45332741 (Accessed August 19, 2019).
146   Veronica Stracqualursi & Meghan Keneally, "Supreme Court allows parts of Trump travel ban to take effect," ABC News, June 26, 2017, available at http://abcnews.go.com/Politics/supreme-court-agrees -review-trump-travel-ban-case/story?id=48279061 (Accessed August 18, 2019).
147   "Trump travel ban: Who counts as a 'bona fide' relative?" BBC News, July 14, 2017, available at http://www.bbc.com/news/world-us-canada -40455303 (Accessed August 19, 2019).

Chapter 3

148   Angelina Jolie, "Beauty doesn't fade . . ." AZ quotes, http://www .azquotes.com/quote/885347 (Accessed August 20, 2019).
149   Charlie Mitchell, "Shooting survivor relived Christchurch massacre to find out if his brother survived," Stuff.co (New Zealand), March 19, 2019, available at https://www.stuff.co.nz/national/christchurch-shooting /111387666/shooting-survivor-relived-christchurch-massacre-to-find -out-if-his-brother-survived (Accessed December 7, 2020).
150   Video, "Antifa, Women & Doomsday," Australian Broadcasting Corporation (ABC), September 4, 2017, available at http://www.abc .net.au/tv/qanda/txt/s4708044.htm (Accessed December 10, 2020).
151   Jon Henley, "Bus seats mistaken for burqas by members of anti-immi-grant group," The Guardian (UK), August 2, 2017, available at https:// www.theguardian.com/world/2017/aug/02/bus-seats-mistaken-burqas -anti-immigrant-group-norwegian (Accessed December 7, 2020).
152   Reuters Staff, "Norway proposes ban on full-face veils in schools," Reuters, June 12, 2017, available at https://www.reuters.com/article /us-religion-burqa-norway/norway-proposes-ban-on-full-face-veils -in-schools-idUSKBN1930WY (Accessed December 10, 2020).
153   Philip Oltermann, "Angela Merkel endorses party's call for partial ban on burqa and niqab," The Guardian (UK), December 6, 2016, available at https://www.theguardian.com/world/2016/dec/06/angela-merkel -cdu-partial-ban-burqa-niqab-german (Accessed August 20, 2019).
154   Report, "Living in Insecurity: Germany is Failing Victims of Racist Violence," Amnesty International, June 9, 2016, available at https://www

.amnesty.org/en/documents/eur23/4112/2016/en/ (Accessed August 20, 2019).

155 Kate Connolly and Jack Shenker, "The headscarf martyr: murder in German court sparks Egyptian fury," *The Guardian* (UK), July 7, 2009, available at https://www.theguardian.com/world/2009/jul/07/german-trial-hijab-murder-egypt (Accessed August 20, 2019).

156 Waseem Abbassi, "Hijab becomes symbol of resistance, feminism in the age of Trump," *USA Today*, March 15, 2017, available at https://www.usatoday.com/story/news/nation-now/2017/03/15/hijab-becomes-symbol-resistance-feminism-age-trump/98475212/ (Accessed August 20, 2019).

157 Helena Andrews, "Muslim Women Don't See Themselves as Oppressed, Survey Finds," *New York Times*, June 8, 2006, available at http://www.nytimes.com/2006/06/08/world/middleeast/08women.html?module=ArrowsNav&contentCollection=Middle%20East&action=keypress&region=FixedLeft&pgtype=article (Accessed August 20, 2019).

158 Sam Sherwood, "Father only held daughter once before he was killed at Masjid Al Noor," Stuff.co (New Zealand), March 26, 2019, available at https://www.stuff.co.nz/national/christchurch-shooting/111567060/father-only-held-daughter-once-before-he-was-killed-at-al-noor-mosque (Accessed December 7, 2020).

159 Elaine Sciolino, "Chirac Wants Religious Attire Banned in Public Schools," *The New York Times*, December 17, 2003, available at http://www.nytimes.com/2003/12/17/international/europe/chirac-wants-religious-attire-banned-in-public-schools.html?mcubz=0 (Accessed August 20, 2019).

160 "Cannes bans burkinis over suspected link to radical Islamism," BBC News, August 12, 2016, available at http://www.bbc.com/news/world-europe-37056742 (Accessed August 20, 2019).

161 Sirin Kale, "Mayor Bans Burkinis From Public Beaches as 'Symbol of Islamic Extremism'," *Broadly* (VICE), August 12, 2016, available at https://broadly.vice.com/en_us/article/3dxx33/france-cannes-mayor-bans-burkinis-beach-symbol-islamic-extremism (Accessed August 20, 2019).

162 Richard Lough, "French PM defends burkini ban but some in cabinet wary," Reuters, August 25, 2016, available at https://www.reuters.com/article/us-religion-burqa-france/french-pm-defends-burkini-ban-but-some-in-cabinet-wary-idUSKCN1101K1 (Accessed August 20, 2019).

163   "France's highest administrative court suspends ban on burkinis," *Deutsche Welle* (Germany), August 25, 2016, available at http://www.dw.com/en/frances-highest-administrative-court-suspends-ban-on-burkinis/a-19503814 (Accessed December 10, 2020).

164   Video, "Arsalan Iftikhar on French Burkini Ban," Al-Jazeera English, August 20, 2016, available at https://www.youtube.com/watch?v=luT5Ly138zs (Accessed August 20, 2019).

165   Transcript, "Senator Hanson's Speech on Full Face Covering in Public," August 17, 2017, available at https://www.facebook.com/notes/pauline-hansons-please-explain/senator-hansons-speech-on-full-face-covering-in-public/657980254406290/ (Accessed August 20, 2019).

166   Katharine Murphy, "Pauline Hanson wears burqa in Australian Senate while calling for ban," *The Guardian* (UK), August 17, 2017, available at https://www.theguardian.com/australia-news/2017/aug/17/pauline-hanson-wears-burqa-in-australian-senate-while-calling-for-ban (Accessed August 20, 2019).

167   Mel Buttigieg, "Hanson: 'We have to take a strong stance against Muslims'," Yahoo News Australia, June 15, 2016, available at https://au.news.yahoo.com/a/31842693/we-have-to-take-a-strong-stance-against-muslims-pauline-hanson-compares-refugees-to-pitbulls (Accessed December 10, 2020).

168   "Pauline Hanson asks PM for Trump-style ban on Muslim travel," *The Weekend Australian*, June 6, 2017, available at http://www.theaustralian.com.au/national-affairs/pauline-hanson-asks-pm-for-trumpstyle-ban-on-muslim-travel/news-story/beef4a6efa03d69bf4df b7a67614f5a3 (Accessed August 20, 2019).

169   Susan Carland, "The most troubling thing about Pauline Hanson's view of Muslims? The facts no longer matter," *The Guardian* (UK), July 19, 2016, available at https://www.theguardian.com/commentisfree/2016/jul/19/the-most-depressing-thing-about-pauline-hansons-view-of-muslims-the-facts-no-longer-matter (Accessed August 20, 2019).

170   Charlotte Cook & Katie Scotcher, "Christchurch mosque attack victim Lilik Abdul Hamid was 'very sincere, very giving, very selfless'," Radio New Zealand, March 19, 2019, available at https://www.rnz.co.nz/news/national/384977/christchurch-mosque-attack-victim-lilik-abdul-hamid-was-very-sincere-very-giving-very-selfless (Accessed December 7, 2020).

171 Mimi Thi Nguyen, "The Biopower of Beauty: Humanitarian Imperialisms and Global Feminisms in an Age of Terror," *Signs: Journal of Women in Culture and Society* 36, no. 2 (Winter 2011): 359-383. See also http://www.journals.uchicago.edu/doi/full/10.1086/655914 (Accessed August 20, 2019).

172 Lila Abu-Lughod, "The Muslim Woman," EuroZine, September 1, 2006, available at http://www.eurozine.com/the-muslim-woman/ (Accessed December 7, 2020).

173 Ibid.

174 Eugene Volokh, "Evangelical Christian college suspends professor for posting that Christians and Muslims 'worship the same God'," *Washington Post*, December 16, 2015, available at https://www .washingtonpost.com/news/volokh-conspiracy/wp/2015/12/16/ evangelical-christian-college-suspends-professor-for-posting-that-chris-tians-and-muslims-worship-the-same-god/?utm_term=.0c19b0ea1746 (Accessed December 10, 2020).

175 Sarah Pulliam Bailey, "How a Facebook comment turned into a night-mare for 'the evangelical Harvard'," *The Washington Post*, January 22, 2016, available at https://www.washingtonpost.com/news/acts -of-faith/wp/2016/01/22/can-wheaton-college-survive-its-never -ending-controversy-over-muslim-and-christian-worship/?utm_ term=.8d4f5023b753 (Accessed August 20, 2019).

176 Manya Brachear Pashman, "Wheaton College could face long-term fallout over professor controversy," *Chicago Tribune*, February 22, 2016, available at http://www.chicagotribune.com/news/ct-wheaton-college -professor-fallout-met-20160222-story.html (Accessed August 21, 2019).

177 "Christchurch mosque victim's widow: 'He was the perfect man'," Radio New Zealand, March 18, 2019, available at https://www.rnz .co.nz/national/programmes/checkpoint/audio/2018687135/christ-church-mosque-victim-s-widow-he-was-the-perfect-man (Accessed December 7, 2020).

178 Report, "Forgotten Women: The Impact of Islamophobia on Muslim Women," European Network Against Racism (ENAR), May 26, 2016, available at https://www.enar-eu.org/Forgotten-Women-the-impact -of-Islamophobia-on-Muslim-women (Accessed December 10, 2020).

179 Joel Rogers de Waal, "The majority of voters doubt that Islam is compatible with British values," YouGov (UK), March 30, 2015, available at https://yougov.co.uk/topics/politics/articles-reports/2015/03/30/majority-voters-doubt-islam-compatible-british-val (Accessed December 7, 2020).

180 Report, "Forgotten Women: The Impact of Islamophobia on Muslim Women," European Network Against Racism (ENAR), May 26, 2016, available at https://www.enar-eu.org/Forgotten-Women-the-impact-of-Islamophobia-on-Muslim-women (Accessed December 10, 2020).

181 Ibid.

182 Thomas Walkom, "Quebec's anti-niqab law brings Trumpism to Canada: Walkom," *Toronto Star*, October 23, 2017 available at https://www.thestar.com/opinion/commentary/2017/10/23/quebecs-anti-niqab-law-brings-trumpism-to-canada-walkom.html (Accessed August 20, 2019).

183 Hathifa Fayyad, "Quebec to vote on controversial face veil ban," Al-Jazeera, October 17, 2017, available at http://www.aljazeera.com/news/2017/10/quebec-vote-controversial-face-veil-ban-171017194038893.html (Accessed August 21, 2019).

184 Catherine Porter, "Behind Quebec's Ban on Face Coverings, a Debate Over Identity" *New York Times*, October 25, 2017 available at https://www.nytimes.com/2017/10/25/world/canada/quebec-ban-face-coverings.html (Accessed August 21, 2019).

185 Hathifa Fayyad, "Quebec to vote on controversial face veil ban," Al-Jazeera, October 17, 2017 available at http://www.aljazeera.com/news/2017/10/quebec-vote-controversial-face-veil-ban-171017194038893.html (Accessed December 8, 2020).

186 Davide Mastracci, "Stop Talking About the Niqab," *Ryerson Review of Journalism*, October 15, 2015, available at http://rrj.ca/stop-talking-about-the-niqab/ (Accessed August 20, 2019).

187 Report, "Faith and Religion in Public Life: Canadians deeply divided over the role of faith in the public square," Angus Reid Institute (Canada), November 16, 2017, available at http://angusreid.org/faith-public-square/ (Accessed December 8, 2020).

188 Amira Elghawaby, "Reflections on Quebec's Bill 62: This is not our song," *THIS Magazine* (Canada), October 20, 2017, available at https://this.org/2017/10/20/reflections-on-quebecs-bill-62-this-is-not-our-song (Accessed August 21, 2019).

189 "Quebec court suspends part of contentious face veil ban," Al-Jazeera News, December 2, 2017, available at https://www.aljazeera.com/amp /news/2017/12/quebec-court-suspends-part-contentious-face-veil -ban-171202145842965.html (Accessed August 21, 2019).

190 "Canada court lets women wear veil for citizenship oath," Agence France-Presse (AFP), September 16, 2015, available at https://tribune .com.pk/story/957659/canada-court-lets-women-wear-veil-for-citizenship -oath (Accessed December 10, 2020).

191 Alia Al-Saji, "The racialization of Muslim veils: A philosophical analysis," Philosophy and Social Criticism 36(8) 875–902, available at http:// web.mit.edu/~sgrp/2013/no1/Al-Saji2010.pdf (Accessed August 21, 2019).

192 Megan Specia, "The New Zealand Shooting Victims Spanned Generations and Nationalities," The New York Times, March 19, 2019, available at https://www.nytimes.com/2019/03/19/world/asia/new -zealand-shooting-victims-names.html (Accessed December 7, 2020).

193 Jana Kasperkevic, "Top US court rules for Muslim woman denied Abercrombie job over hijab," June 1, 2015, available at https://www .theguardian.com/law/2015/jun/01/supreme-court-rules-favor-muslim -woman-hijab-abercrombie-fitch (Accessed August 21, 2019).

194 Report, "Civil Rights Report 2017: Workplace Discrimination," Council on American-Islamic Relations (CAIR), October 25, 2017, available at http://www.islamophobia.org/reports/202-civil-rights -report-2017-workplace-discrimination.html (Accessed September 2, 2019).

195 Press Release, "Abercrombie Resolves Religious Discrimination Case Following Supreme Court Ruling in Favor of EEOC," U.S. Equal Employment Opportunity Commission (EEOC), July 28, 2015, available at https://www.eeoc.gov/eeoc/newsroom/release/7-28-15.cfm (Accessed September 2, 2019).

196 Lane Sainty & Hannah Ryan, "A Man Whose Uncle Was Killed In Christchurch Says His Family Is 'Helpless'" As They Wait For The Body," March 17, 2019, available at https://www.buzzfeed.com/lane-sainty/uncle-killed-al-noor-mosque-christchurch (Accessed December 7, 2020).

197 Molly Petrilla, "The next big untapped fashion market: Muslim women," Fortune, July 15, 2015, available at http://fortune.com/2015/07/15/ muslim-women-fashion/ (Accessed September 2, 2019).

198   Ibid.

199   Jess Cartner-Morley, "The great cover up: why we're all dressing mod-
estly now," *The Guardian* (UK), September 13, 2017, available at https://
www.theguardian.com/fashion/2017/sep/13/the-great-cover-up-why-
were-all-dressing-modestly-now (Accessed September 2, 2019).

200   Sarah Young, "Hijab-wearing model Halima Aden makes history as Allure magazine cover girl," *The Independent* (UK), June 21,
2017, available at https://www.independent.co.uk/life-style/fashion/
halima-aden-hijab-muslim-model-allure-magazine-cover-girl-fash-
ion-beauty-a7800501.html (Accessed September 2, 2019).

201   Abdi Latif Dahir, "The journey of a Muslim woman from refugee to
state legislator tells you America can still be great," *Quartz*, November
15, 2016, available at https://qz.com/835900/the-journey-of-a-muslim-
woman-from-refugee-to-state-legislator-tells-you-america-can-still-
be-great/ (Accessed September 2, 2019).

202   "The Legislator: Ilhan Omar," *TIME Magazine*, November 2016, available at http://time.com/collection/firsts/4898550/ilhan-omar-firsts/
(Accessed September 2, 2019).

203   Jennifer Rankin & Philip Oltermann, "Europe's right hails EU court's
workplace headscarf ban ruling," *The Guardian* (UK), March 14, 2017,
available at https://www.theguardian.com/law/2017/mar/14/employ-
ers-can-ban-staff-from-wearing-headscarves-european-court-rules
(Accessed September 2, 2019).

Chapter 4

204   Ian Traynor, "'I don't hate Muslims. I hate Islam,' says Holland's rising political star," *The Guardian* (UK), February 16, 2008, available at
http://www.theguardian.com/world/2008/feb/17/netherlands.islam
(Accessed December 10, 2020).

205   Jeffrey Goldberg, "Is It Time for the Jews to Leave Europe?" *The
Atlantic*, April 2015, available at http://www.theatlantic.com/maga-
zine/archive/2015/04/is-it-time-for-the-jews-to-leave-europe/386279/
(Accessed September 7, 2019).

206   Murtaza Hussain, "Islamic State's Goal: 'Eliminating The Grayzone' of
Coexistence Between Muslims and the West," *The Intercept*, November
17, 2015, available at https://theintercept.com/2015/11/17/islamic-
states-goal-eliminating-the-grayzone-of-coexistence-between-mus-
lims-and-the-west/ (Accessed September 16, 2019).

207   Hannah Roberts, "EXCLUSIVE The pot-smoking Paris suicide bomber: Ex-wife reveals 'blood brother' terrorist was a jobless lay-about who spent his time taking drugs and sleeping . . . and never went to the mosque," *The Daily Mail* (UK), November 17, 2015, available at http://www.dailymail.co.uk/news/article-3322385/Ex-wife-Comptoir-Voltaire-caf-bomber-reveals-jobless-layabout-spent-day-bed-smoking-pot-French-say-blew-mistake-fiddling-suicide-vest.html (Accessed September 7, 2019).

208   Adam Shatz, "Magical Thinking About ISIS," *London Review of Books*, Vol. 37 No. 23, December 3 2015, available at http://www.lrb.co.uk/v37/n23/adam-shatz/magical-thinking-about-isis (Accessed December 8, 2020).

209   Imran Khan, Twitter post, March 17, 2019, 12:59 a.m., https://twitter.com/ImranKhanPTI/status/1107144298565431301 (Accessed December 8, 2020).

210   Imran Khan, Twitter post, March 15, 2019, 2:48 a.m., https://twitter.com/ImranKhanPTI/status/1106446970414157824 (Accessed December 8, 2020).

211   "World reacts with sadness, anger to New Zealand mosque shootings," Reuters, March 15, 2019, available at https://www.reuters.com/article/us-newzealand-shootout-reaction/world-reacts-with-sadness-anger-to-new-zealand-mosque-shootings-idUSKCN1QW0PA (Accessed December 8, 2020).

212   Adam Shatz, "Magical Thinking About ISIS," *London Review of Books*, Vol. 37 No. 23, December 3 2015, available at http://www.lrb.co.uk/v37/n23/adam-shatz/magical-thinking-about-isis (Accessed December 8, 2020).

213   "LIBE Committee hearing on antisemitism, Islamophobia and hate speech in Europe," European Union Agency for Fundamental Rights (FRA), June 30, 2015, available at http://fra.europa.eu/en/speech/2015/libe-committee-hearing-antisemitism-islamophobia-and-hate-speech-europe (Accessed September 7, 2019).

214   Tanya Basu, "What Does 'Islamophobia' Actually Mean?" *The Atlantic*, October 15, 2014, available at https://www.theatlantic.com/international/archive/2014/10/is-islamophobia-real-maher-harris-aslan/381411/ (Accessed September 7, 2019).

215   Julian Petlet and Robin Richardson, *Pointing the Finger: Islam and Muslims in the British Media* (London: OneWorld, 2011), available

at https://books.google.ca/books?id=FQnrAQAAQBAJ&pg=PT16&
lpg=PT16&dq=islamophobia+in+french+1916&source=bl&ots=S4
wSG6_eFh&sig=Z1iuGrAkV-coXeC0M2OITSO7QYg&hl=en&sa=X
&ved=0CEYQ6AEwBmoVChMIza_Sga76xwIVi3uSCh0q4Qcm#v=on
epage&q=islamophobia%20in%20french%201916&f=false (Accessed
September 14, 2019).

216 Adar Primor, "Le Pen Will Fight anti-Semitism, Says His Jewish
Running Mate," *Ha'aretz* (Israel), March 18, 2004, available at http://
www.haaretz.com/print-edition/news/le-pen-will-fight-anti-semi-
tism-says-his-jewish-running-mate-1.117310 (Accessed December 10,
2020).

217 Andre Gingrich, "Anthropological Analyses of Islamophobia and
Anti-Semitism in Europe," *American Ethnologist*, Vol. 32, No.
4 (Nov., 2005), pp. 513-515, available at http://www.jstor.org/
stable/3805340?seq=1#page_scan_tab_contents (Accessed September
7, 2019).

218 Michelle Hale Williams, "A new era for French far right politics?
Comparing the FN under two Le Pens," *Análise Social*, Vol. 46, No.
201, As Direitas no Sul da Europa (2011), pp. 679-695, available at
http://www.jstor.org/stable/41494868?seq=1#page_scan_tab_contents
(Accessed September 7, 2019).

219 Ibid.

220 Helene Fouquet, "Anti-Euro Party's Le Pen Gains Supporters, French
Poll Shows," Bloomberg News, February 12, 2014, available at http://
www.bloomberg.com/news/articles/2014-02-12/anti-euro-party-s-
le-pen-gains-supporters-french-poll-shows (Accessed September 7,
2019).

221 "Why the French are so strict about Islamic head coverings," *The
Economist*, July 6, 2014, available at http://www.economist.com/
blogs/economist-explains/2014/07/economist-explains-2 (Accessed
September 14, 2019).

222 Daniel Philpott, "Part One: Framing the West's Cultural War with
Islam," Georgetown University Berkley Center, January 22, 2015,
available at https://berkleycenter.georgetown.edu/essays/part-one-
framing-the-west-s-cultural-war-with-islam (Accessed January 15,
2021).

223 Peter Allen, "Woman is thrown out of Paris opera after cast refused
to perform unless she removed Muslim veil," *The Daily Mail* (UK),

October 20, 2014, available at http://www.dailymail.co.uk/news/article-2799981/woman-thrown-paris-opera-cast-refused-perform-unless-removed-muslim-veil.html (Accessed September 14, 2019).

224 Jeffrey Goldberg, "Is It Time for the Jews to Leave Europe?" *The Atlantic*, April 2015, available at http://www.theatlantic.com/magazine/archive/2015/04/is-it-time-for-the-jews-to-leave-europe/386279/ (Accessed December 8, 2020).

225 Arsalan Iftikhar, "French Ambassador on Muslims, Riots and Progress," *DiversityInc Magazine*, March 20, 2008, available at http://www.themuslimguy.com/column-french-ambassador-on-muslims-riots-progress/ (Accessed September 14, 2019).

226 Ibid.

227 Jason Burke & Lorenzo Tondo, "Suspect in Nice terror attack phoned his family hours before rampage," *The Guardian* (UK), October 30, 2020, available at https://www.theguardian.com/world/2020/oct/30/nice-terror-suspect-phoned-family-hours-before-church-attack-brahim-aouissaoui (Accessed December 8, 2020).

228 Pankaj Mishra, "Macron's Clash of Civilizations Is Misguided," Bloomberg Opinion, October 28, 2020, available at https://www.bloomberg.com/opinion/articles/2020-10-28/macron-s-clash-of-civilizations-with-islam-is-misguided (Accessed December 8, 2020).

229 Full text of legislation available at http://www.assemblee-nationale.fr/dyn/15/textes/l15b3560_proposition-loi (Accessed December 9, 2020).

230 "French Parliament considers 'internment camps' for Muslims," *TRT World* (Turkey), December 9, 2020, available at https://www.trtworld.com/magazine/french-parliament-considers-internment-camps-for-muslims-42202 (Accessed December 9, 2020).

231 "How Marine Le Pen made a party co-founded by Nazi collaborators mainstream," Canadian Broadcasting Corporation (CBC) Radio, May 5, 2017, available at https://www.cbc.ca/radio/day6/episode-336-sidney-crosby-s-concussion-awesome-mix-vol-2-marine-le-pen-captain-canuck-and-more-1.4099052/how-marine-le-pen-made-a-party-co-founded-by-nazi-collaborators-mainstream-1.4099073 (Accessed November 7, 2020).

232 Dominic Harris, "Curry, cricket and community—the pillars of a life lost in Christchurch terrorist attack," Stuff.co (New Zealand), March 22, 2019, available at https://www.stuff.co.nz/national/christchurch-shooting/111463646/curry-cricket-and-community--the-pillars-of-

a-life-lost-in-christchurch-terrorist-attack (Accessed December 8, 2020).

233   Gerard Wiegers, *The Middle East and Europe: Encounters and Exchanges*, G. J. H. van Gelder, Ed de Moor Rodopi, 1992, https://books.google.com/books?id=YTUavFMto28C&pg=PA94&lpg=PA94&dq=Ahmad+ibn+Qasim+Al-Hajari&source=bl&ots=rZTv9j2zy4&sig=BRqBf8PwLPUGzjOmuwhKQu25wUY&hl=en&sa=X&ved=0CCgQ6AEwAWoVChMItc21qaTMyAIVQVY-Ch3RcAb6#v=onepage&q=Ahmad%20ibn%20Qasim%20Al-Hajari&f=false (Accessed September 14, 2019).

234   Gary K. Waite, "Reimagining Religious Identity: The Moor in Dutch and English Pamphlets, 1550–1620," *Renaissance Quarterly*, Vol. 66, No. 4 (Winter 2013), pp. 1250-129, available at http://www.jstor.org/stable/10.1086/675092?seq=1#page_scan_tab_contents   (Accessed September 14, 2019).

235   Cynthia Schneider, "Geert Wilders: Rise of an anti-Islam opportunist," CNN.com, May 8, 2015, available at http://www.cnn.com/2015/05/08/opinions/schneider-geert-wilders/ (Accessed September 14, 2019).

236   Ibid.

237   Winston Ross, "Geert Wilders: The 'Prophet' Who Hates Muhammad," *Newsweek*, January 19, 2015, available at http://www.newsweek.com/2015/01/30/geert-wilders-prophet-who-hates-muhammad-300266.html (Accessed September 14, 2019).

238   Ibid.

239   Winston Ross, "Geert Wilders: The 'Prophet' Who Hates Muhammad," *Newsweek*, January 19, 2015, available at http://www.newsweek.com/2015/01/30/geert-wilders-prophet-who-hates-muhammad-300266.html (Accessed December 10, 2020).

240   Ibid.

241   Winston Ross, "Geert Wilders" *Newsweek*, January 19, 2015.

242   Ibid.

243   "Dutch far-right firebrand Geert Wilders fails to draw large crowd at Pegida rally," *The Guardian* (UK), April 13, 2015, available at http://www.theguardian.com/world/2015/apr/13/geert-wilders-pegida-germany-dutch-far-right (Accessed September 14, 2019).

244   Christopher Dickey, "Geert Wilders Says There's No Such Thing as Moderate Islam," *Newsweek*, January 16, 2012, available at http://www

.newsweek.com/geert-wilders-says-theres-no-such-thing-moderate-islam-64171 (Accessed September 16, 2019).

245   Nancy Foner and Patrick Simon, eds. *Fear, Anxiety, & National Identity: Immigration and Belonging in North America and Western Europe*, (New York: Russell Sage Foundation, 2015), 173.

246   Ibid at 173-74.

247   Zack Adesina and Oana Marocico, "Islamophobic crime in London 'up by 70%'," British Broadcasting Corporation (BBC), September 7, 2015, available at http://www.bbc.com/news/uk-england-london-34138127 (Accessed September 16, 2019).

248   Andrew Woodcock, "Hate crimes aime *[sic]* at Muslims to get own category, bringing Islamophobia in line with anti-Semitism," *The Independent* (UK), October 13, 2015, available at http://www.indepen-dent.co.uk/news/uk/crime/anti-muslim-hate-crimes-to-get-own-cat-egory-bringing-islamophobia-in-line-with-anti-semitism-a6691811. html (Accessed September 16, 2019).

249   "Anti-Semitic and Islamophobic hate crime attacks surge in London," Agence France-Presse (AFP), September 7, 2015, available at http://www.rawstory.com/2015/09/anti-semitic-and-islamophobic-hate-crime-attacks-surge-in-london/ (Accessed September 16, 2019).

250   Nicole Bosch & Delia Wiest, "Transatlantic Discourse on Integration: The Migration-Security Nexus in the Light of the German EU-Presidency: A Conference Report," European Forum for Migration Studies, May 2007, available at http://www.efms.uni-bamberg.de/pdf/tagungsbericht_gmf11.pdf (Accessed September 16, 2019).

251   Juan Moreno, "Welcoming the Refugees: Has Germany Really Changed?" *Der Spiegel*, September 11, 2005, available at http://www.spiegel.de/international/germany/refugees-are-welcome-in-germany-but-for-how-long-a-1052070.html (Accessed September 16, 2019).

252   Conrad Hackett, "5 facts about the Muslim population in Europe," Pew Research Center, January 15, 2015, available at http://www.pewre-search.org/fact-tank/2015/01/15/5-facts-about-the-muslim-popula-tion-in-europe/ (Accessed September 16, 2019).

253   Ibid.

254   Richard Wike, "Ratings of Muslims rise in France after Charlie Hebdo, just as in U.S. after 9/11," Pew Research Center, June 3, 2015, available at http://www.pewresearch.org/fact-tank/2015/06/03/ratings-of-mus-lims-in-france-and-us/ (Accessed September 16, 2019).

255 "Daily Chart: Islam in Europe," *The Economist*, January 7, 2015, available at http://www.economist.com/blogs/graphicdetail/2015/01/daily-chart-2 (Accessed September 16, 2019).

256 Sam Sherwood, "Christchurch terror attack: Son was on the phone to his mum when he was shot and killed," Stuff.co, March 17, 2019, available at https://www.stuff.co.nz/national/crime/111348557/christ-church-terror-attack-son-was-on-the-phone-to-his-mum-when-he-was-shot-and-killed (Accessed December 8, 2020).

257 Matthew Taylor, "Racist and anti-immigration views held by children revealed in schools study," *The Guardian* (UK), May 19, 2015 available at https://www.theguardian.com/education/2015/may/19/most-children-think-immigrants-are-stealing-jobs-schools-study-shows (Accessed September 16, 2019).

258 Ibid.

259 "Protesters demand end to Sweden mosque attacks," Agence France-Presse (AFP), January 2, 2015, available at http://www.theguardian.com/world/2015/jan/02/sweden-mosque-attacks-fires-protests-gothenburg-malmo-stockholm (Accessed September 16, 2019).

260 Ibid.

261 Chris Solomon, "Growing Islamophobia heightens political risk for Europe," *Global Risk Insights*, February 2, 2015, available at http://globalriskinsights.com/2015/02/growing-islamophobia-heightens-political-risk-europe/ (Accessed September 16, 2019).

262 Ibid.

263 "Religion and ritual slaughter—Much ado about not much," *The Economist*, February 18, 2014, available at http://www.economist.com/blogs/erasmus/2014/02/religion-and-ritual-slaughter (Accessed September 16, 2019).

264 Nick Cumming-Bruce and Steven Erlanger, "Swiss Ban Building of Minarets on Mosques," *The New York Times*, November 29, 2009, available at http://www.nytimes.com/2009/11/30/world/europe/30swiss.html?_r=0 (Accessed September 16, 2019).

265 Mathieu von Rohr, "Swiss Minaret Ban Reflects Fear of Islam, Not Real Problems," *Der Spiegel* (Germany), November 30, 2009, available at http://www.spiegel.de/international/europe/opinion-swiss-minaret-ban-reflects-fear-of-islam-not-real-problems-a-664176.html (Accessed September 16, 2019).

266 Ibid.

267   Mathieu von Rohr, "Swiss Minaret Ban Reflects Fear of Islam, Not Real Problems," *Der Spiegel* (Germany), November 30, 2009, available at https://www.spiegel.de/international/europe/opinion-swiss-minaret-ban-reflects-fear-of-islam-not-real-problems-a-664176.html (Accessed December 10, 2020).

268   "Europe's Growing Muslim Population," Pew Research Center, November 29, 2017, available at http://www.pewforum.org/2017/11/29/europes-growing-muslim-population/ (Accessed September 16, 2019).

269   "The One Percent Problem: Muslims in the West and the Rise of the New Populists," The Brookings Institution, July 24, 2019, available at https://www.brookings.edu/product/muslims-in-the-west/ (Accessed September 17, 2019).

Chapter 5

270   Bobby Ghosh, "Islamophobia: Does America Have a Muslim Problem?" *TIME Magazine*, August 30, 2010, available at http://content.time.com/time/magazine/article/0,9171,2011936,00.html (Accessed December 8, 2020).

271   Arsalan Iftikhar, *Islamic Pacifism: Global Muslims in the Post-Osama Era* (Charleston: CreateSpace, 2011) p. 52.

272   Arsalan Iftikhar, "Freedom of Religion Requires Freedom From Fear" *The Atlantic*, October 9, 2015, available at http://www.theatlantic.com/politics/archive/2015/10/protesting-american-mosques-at-gunpoint/409987/ (Accessed September 9, 2019).

273   Matthe Theunissen, "Family of man killed in Christchurch terror attacks accept his doctorate," Radio New Zealand, May 3, 2019, available at https://www.rnz.co.nz/news/national/388401/family-of-man-killed-in-christchurch-terror-attacks-accept-his-doctorate (Accessed December 8, 2020).

274   Laurie Goodstein, "Across Nation, Mosque Projects Meet Opposition" *The New York Times*, August 7, 2010, available at http://www.nytimes.com/2010/08/08/us/08mosque.html?pagewanted=all&_r=0 (Accessed September 19, 2019).

275   Fareed Zakaria, "Build the Ground Zero Mosque," *Newsweek*, August 6, 2010, available at http://www.newsweek.com/fareed-zakaria-build-ground-zero-mosque-71589 (Accessed September 19, 2019).

276   Jeffrey Goldberg, "A Task for George W. Bush," *The Atlantic*, August 9, 2010, available at https://www.theatlantic.com/politics/archive/2010/08/a-task-for-george-w-bush/61133/ (Accessed December 8, 2020).

277   John L. Esposito, *Unholy War: Terror in the Name of Islam*, Oxford University Press, 2003, https://books.google.com/books?id=fK4Xuy OJvccC&pg=PT2&lpg=PT2&dq=esposito+%22most+influential+Isl amic+scholar%22+%22international+herald+tribune%22&source=bl &ots=BtOgWRGrrJ&sig=ACfU3U3j-Qu7Ug0P8FQB2XB7tWeEez6IJ g&hl=en&sa=X&ved=2ahUKEwiJmI7Qx7_tAhVsu1kKHTVcC_IQ6 AEwA3oECAcQAg#v=onepage&q=esposito%20%22most%20influ-ential%20Islamic%20scholar%22%20%22international%20herald%20 tribune%22&f=false (Accessed December 8, 2020).

278   Arsalan Iftikhar, "Why is Islamophobia Acceptable in the U.S.?" *Esquire Magazine* (Middle East Edition), January 2011, available at https://www.scribd.com/doc/280507941/Arsalan-Esquire-Magazine-Islamophobia-America-January-2011 (Accessed September 19, 2019).

279   Huma Munir, "Munir: Sydney siege, media pervert image of Islam," *The Austin (TX) Statesman*, December 17, 2014, available at https://www.statesman.com/article/20141217/NEWS/312179578   (Accessed December 9, 2020).

280   Arsalan Iftikhar, "Report: Muslims Most Negatively Portrayed Minority in US Media," Georgetown University Bridge Initiative, September 18, 2019, available at https://bridge.georgetown.edu/research/report-muslims-most-negatively-portrayed-minority-in-us-media/ (Accessed September 19, 2019).

281   Liat Clark, "US media helped anti-Muslim bodies gain influence, dis-tort Islam," *Wired Magazine* (UK), November 30, 2012, available at http://www.wired.co.uk/news/archive/2012-11/30/anti-muslim-influ-ence-on-us-media (Accessed September 19, 2019).

282   Mariam Nabbout, "Jordanian mother dies day after funeral of son killed in New Zealand attack," *Stepfeed*, March 25, 2019, available at https://stepfeed.com/jordanian-mother-dies-day-after-funeral-of-son-killed-in-new-zealand-attack-5812 (Accessed December 8, 2020).

283   Marc Ambinder, "Oklahoma's Preemptive Strike Against Sharia Law," *The Atlantic*, October 25, 2010, available at https://www.theatlantic.com/politics/archive/2010/10/oklahomas-preemptive-strike-against-sharia-law/65081/ (Accessed September 19, 2019).

284   Andy Barr, "Oklahoma bans Sharia law," *Politico*, November 3, 2010, available at https://www.politico.com/story/2010/11/oklahoma-bans-sharia-law-044630 (Accessed December 8, 2020).

285 Scott Shane, "In Islamic Law, Gingrich Sees a Mortal Threat to U.S.," *The New York Times*, December 22, 2011, available at https://www.nytimes.com/2011/12/22/us/politics/in-shariah-gingrich-sees-mortal-threat-to-us.html (Accessed December 9, 2020).

286 Marc Ambinder, "Oklahoma's Preemptive Strike Against Sharia Law," *The Atlantic*, October 25, 2010, available at https://www.theatlantic.com/politics/archive/2010/10/oklahomas-preemptive-strike-against-sharia-law/65081/ (Accessed September 19, 2019)

287 Ibid.

288 Daniel Cox & Robert P. Jones, "Most Support Congressional Hearings on Alleged Extremism in U.S. Muslims Communities," Public Religion Research Institute (PRRI), February 6, 2011, available at https://www.prri.org/research/majority-say-congressional-hearings-on-alleged-extremism-in-american-muslim-community-%e2%80%98good-idea%e2%80%99/ (Accessed December 9, 2020).

289 Eliyahu Stern, "Don't Fear Islamic Law in America," *The New York Times*, September 3, 2011, available at https://www.nytimes.com/2011/09/03/opinion/dont-fear-islamic-law-in-america.html (Accessed September 19, 2019).

290 Ibid.

291 Noah Feldman, "Why Shariah?" *The New York Times Magazine*, March 16, 2008, available at http://www.nytimes.com/2008/03/16/magazine/16Shariah-t.html?pagewanted=1&_r=3&sq=sharia&st=cse&scp=2 (Accessed September 19, 2019).

292 Arsalan Iftikhar, *Scapegoats: How Islamophobia Helps Our Enemies & Threatens Our Freedoms* (New York: Skyhorse Publishing, 2015), 46.

293 Arsalan Iftikhar, "The Fear of a Sharia Planet," Pacific Standard Magazine, October 6, 2011, available at https://psmag.com/news/the-fear-of-a-sharia-planet-36734 (Accessed September 21, 2019).

294 Charlie Mitchell, "Shockwave sent through Palestinian community after six die in Christchurch terror attack," Stuff.co (New Zealand), March 20, 2019, available at https://www.stuff.co.nz/national/christchurch-shooting/111361340/shockwave-sent-through-palestinian-community-after-six-die-in-christchurch-terror-attack (Accessed December 9, 2020).

295 Report, "Fear, Inc.:The Roots of the Islamophobia Network in America," Center for American Progress, August 26, 2011, available at https://cdn.americanprogress.org/wp-content/uploads/issues/2011/08/

pdf/islamophobia.pdf?_ga=2.119447498.2118020364.1607542527-
2083755371.1607542527 (Accessed December 9, 2020).

296 Fact Sheet, "David Yerushalmi," Anti-Defamation League (ADL),
available at https://www.adl.org/resources/profiles/david-yerushalmi
(Accessed December 9, 2020).

297 Fact Sheet, "David Yerushalmi," Southern Poverty Law Center, available at https://www.splcenter.org/fighting-hate/extremist-files/indi-
vidual/david-yerushalmi (Accessed December 9, 2020).

298 Dylan Baddour "Who is Pamela Geller?" *The Albany Times Union*
(NY), May 4, 2015, available at https://www.timesunion.com/news/
slideshow/Who-is-Pamela-Geller-108986.php (Accessed December 9,
2020).

299 Report, "Stop Islamization of America (SIOA)," Ant-Defamation
League, March 2011, available at https://www.scribd.com/docu-
ment/487538691/Stop-Islamization-of-America-SIOA-ADL-
March-2011 (Accessed December 9, 2020).

300 Fact Sheet, "Pamela Geller," Southern Poverty Law Center, available
at https://www.splcenter.org/fighting-hate/extremist-files/individual/
pamela-geller (Accessed September 21, 2019).

301 Laurie Goodstein, "Drawing U.S. Crowds with Anti-Islam Message,"
The New York Times, March 7, 2011, available at http://www.nytimes.
com/2011/03/08/us/08gabriel.html?pagewanted=all&_r=0 (Accessed
September 21, 2019).

302 "Anti-Sharia Law Bills in the United States," Southern Poverty Law
Center, August 8, 2017, available at https://www.splcenter.org/hate-
watch/2017/08/08/anti-sharia-law-bills-united-states (Accessed
September 21, 2019).

303 Patrick Strickland, "US: Are 'anti-Sharia' bills legalising
Islamophobia?" Al-Jazeera, October 1, 2017, available at http://www.
aljazeera.com/news/2017/09/anti-sharia-bills-legalising-islamopho-
bia-170928150835240.html (Accessed September 21, 2019).

304 http://publicpolicyalliance.org/legislation/american-laws-for
-american-courts/ (Accessed September 21, 2019).

305 Dan Kopf & Annalisa Merelli, "The legalization of Islamophobia is
underway in the United States," *Quartz*, September 14, 2017, available
at https://qz.com/1074415/anti-sharia-bills-exploit-islamophobia-in-
the-us-like-anti-catholic-politics-used-to/ (Accessed September 21,
2019).

306 Elsadig Elsheikh, Basima Sisemore and Natalia Ramirez Lee, "Legalizing Othering: The United States of Islamophobia," Haas Institute for a Fair & Inclusive Society, September 2017, available at http://haasin-stitute.berkeley.edu/sites/default/files/haas_institute_legalizing_other-ing_the_united_states_of_islamophobia.pdf (Accessed December 10, 2020).

307 Press Release, "Federal Court Strikes Down Oklahoma Sharia and International Law Ban" August 15, 2013, available at https://www.aclu.org/news/federal-court-strikes-down-oklahoma-sharia-and-interna-tional-law-ban (Accessed September 21, 2019).

308 Elsadig Elsheikh, Basima Sisemore and Natalia Ramirez Lee, "Legalizing Othering: The United States of Islamophobia," Haas Institute for a Fair & Inclusive Society, September 2017, available at http://haasin-stitute.berkeley.edu/sites/default/files/haas_institute_legalizing_other-ing_the_united_states_of_islamophobia.pdf (Accessed December 10, 2020).

309 Ibid.

310 https://www.splcenter.org/hatewatch/2018/02/05/anti-sharia-law-bills-united-states (Accessed September 21, 2019).

311 Justin Juozapavicius, "Oklahoma lawmaker asks Muslims: 'Do you beat your wife?'" Associated Press, March 4, 2017, available at https://apnews.com/article/581f82ec9d994c7088cd6e6594334881 (Accessed December 10, 2020).

312 Dylan Goforth, "Oklahoma lawmaker John Bennett doubles down on anti-Muslim vitriol at tea party event," October 3, 2014, available at http://www.tulsaworld.com/news/government/oklahoma-lawmaker-john-bennett-doubles-down-on-anti-muslim-vitriol/article_13fdbb7c-eef9-5368-b4aa-12d56ea139d7.html (Accessed September 21, 2019).

313 "Shooting victim's twin: 'We must bury my brother as soon as pos-sible'," Radio New Zealand, March 18, 2019, available at https://www.rnz.co.nz/national/programmes/checkpoint/audio/2018687126/shooting-victim-s-twin-we-must-bury-my-brother-as-soon-as-pos-sible (Accessed December 9, 2020).

314 Ibid.

315 http://www.cruz.senate.gov/files/documents/Bills/20170110_Muslim BrotherhoodTerroristDesignationAct.pdf? (Accessed September 21, 2019).

316   Julie Hirschfeld Davis, David E. Sanger and Maggie Haberman, "Trump to Order Mexican Border Wall and Curtail Immigration," *New York Times*, January 24, 2017, available at https://www.nytimes.com/2017/01/24/us/politics/wall-border-trump.html?_r=0 (Accessed December 10, 2020).

317   Abigail Hauslohner, "How an obscure U.S. policy effort could hurt American Muslims," *Washington Post*, January 11, 2017, available at https://www.washingtonpost.com/national/how-an-obscure-policy-effort-could-hurt-american-muslims/2017/01/11/8ce93184-d76e-11e6-b8b2-cb5164beba6b_story.html?utm_term=.ac725dc4f224 (Accessed September 21, 2019).

318   Ibid.

319   Editorial, "All of Islam Isn't The Enemy," *New York Times*, February 9, 2017, available at https://www.nytimes.com/2017/02/09/opinion/all-of-islam-isnt-the-enemy.html (Accessed September 21, 2019).

320   Steve Coll, "IRA Announces End to 25-Year Violent Campaign," *Washington Post*, September 1, 1994, available at https://www.washingtonpost.com/archive/politics/1994/09/01/ira-announces-end-to-25-year-violent-campaign/84c692f3-7ec2-402c-855f-f132f6770951/?utm_term=.afc70169ed17 (Accessed December 10, 2020).

321   Arsalan Iftikhar, "Protocols of the Elders of Mecca," *The Islamic Monthly*, December 18, 2017, available at https://www.theislamic-monthly.com/protocols-elders-mecca/ (Accessed December 9, 2020).

322   Lauren Ferri &Daniel Piotrowski, "The little girl who'll never meet her dad: Christchurch victim's baby is born five months after her father was shot dead in mosque massacre—and is given the most fitting name possible," *The Daily Mail* (UK), August 31, 2019, available at https://www.dailymail.co.uk/news/article-7415257/Christchurch-victims-little-girl-born-five-months-shot-dead-named-him.html (Accessed December 9, 2020).

323   Steven Piggott, "Politicians, Anti-Muslim Leaders Urge Trump To Designate Muslim Brotherhood as Terrorist Organization," Southern Poverty Law Center (SPLC), February 13, 2017, available at https://www.splcenter.org/hatewatch/2017/02/13/politicians-anti-muslim-leaders-urge-trump-designate-muslim-brotherhood-terrorist (Accessed December 10, 2020).

324   David Noriega, "How One Policy Change Could Wipe Out Muslim Civil Liberties," *BuzzFeed*, November 16, 2016, available at https://

162

www.buzzfeed.com/davidnoriega/the-muslim-brotherhood-and-muslim-civil-rights-groups?utm_term=.rplOVVaj3#.nw3nXXpMq (Accessed September 21, 2019).

325 Arsalan Iftikhar, "Calling the Muslim Brotherhood a terrorist group would make all Muslims scapegoats," *Washington Post*, May 6, 2019, available at https://www.washingtonpost.com/posteverything/wp/2017/02/08/calling-the-muslim-brotherhood-a-terrorist-group-would-hurt-all-american-muslims/?utm_term=.0c94818d8c74 (Accessed December 10, 2020).

326 David Shipler, "Pamela Geller and the Anti-Islam Movement," *The New Yorker*, May 12, 2015, available at https://www.newyorker.com/news/news-desk/pamela-geller-and-the-anti-islam-movement (Accessed September 21, 2019).

327 Bridge Initiative Team, "'Civilization Jihad': Debunking The Conspiracy Theory" Georgetown University, February 2, 2016, available at http://bridge.georgetown.edu/civilization-jihad-debunking-the-conspiracy-theory/ (Accessed December 9, 2020).

328 Sue Surkes, "Top employee at EU-, UN-funded Gaza hospital quotes 'Protocols of Zion'," *The Times of Israel*, February 14, 2017, available at http://www.timesofisrael.com/top-employee-at-eu-un-funded-gaza-hospital-quotes-protocols-of-zion/?utm_source=dlvr.it&utm_medium=twitter (Accessed December 9, 2020).

329 Arsalan Iftikhar, "Protocols of the Elders of Mecca," *The Islamic Monthly*, December 18, 2017, available at https://www.theislamic-monthly.com/protocols-elders-mecca/ (Accessed December 9, 2020).

330 Kurt Bayer, "Christchurch terror attack: Heartbreak for Suhail Shahid's family left to pick up the pieces," *New Zealand Herald*, March 27, 2019, available at https://www.nzherald.co.nz/nz/christchurch-terror-attack-heartbreak-for-suhail-shahids-family-left-to-pick-up-the-pieces/BMPFVP5X6ZJBU7CJ6WU5IC5SZM/ (Accessed December 9, 2020).

331 Kurt Bayer, "Brother of mosque terror victim moves family to Christchurch to support bereft family," *New Zealand Herald*, April 17, 2019, available at https://www.nzherald.co.nz/nz/brother-of-mosque-terror-victim-moves-family-to-christchurch-to-support-bereft-family/JJB6HWQVNL2733M6U7G4G4TXNA/ (Accessed December 9, 2020).

332 Blake Hounshell & Nahal Toosi, "CIA Memo: Designating Muslim Brotherhood Could 'Fuel Extremism'," *POLITICO Magazine*, February

8, 2017, available at https://www.politico.com/magazine/story/2017/02/cia-memo-designating-muslim-brotherhood-could-fuel-extremism-214757 (Accessed December 9, 2020).

333 Ibid.

334 Wendy Grossman Kantor, "Hero Died While Tackling New Zealand Mass Shooter: 'He Makes Me Proud,' Says Sister," *PEOPLE Magazine*, March 19, 2019, available at https://people.com/crime/hero-died-tackling-new-zealand-mass-shooter-he-makes-me-proud-says-sister/ (Accessed December 9, 2020).

335 "US: Don't Target Muslim Brotherhood," Human Rights Watch, February 8, 2017, available at https://www.hrw.org/news/2017/02/08/us-dont-target-muslim-brotherhood (Accessed September 21, 2019).

336 Arsalan Iftikhar, "Protocols of the Elders of Mecca," *The Islamic Monthly*, December 18, 2017, available at https://www.theislamic-monthly.com/protocols-elders-mecca/ (Accessed December 9, 2020).

337 "Christchurch mosque shootings: Faces of the dead, missing and injured," *New Zealand Herald*, March 16, 2019, available at https://www.nzherald.co.nz/nz/christchurch-mosque-shootings-faces-of-the-dead-missing-and-injured/6XQFDX7GO5D442MIUH3YRYWNYE/ (Accessed December 9, 2020).

338 Theodore Schleifer, "I think Islam hates us," CNN, March 10, 2016, available at https://www.cnn.com/2016/03/09/politics/donald-trump-islam-hates-us/index.html (Accessed December 9, 2020).

339 Arsalan Iftikhar, "Calling the Muslim Brotherhood a terrorist group would make all Muslims scapegoats," *The Washington Post*, May 6, 2019, available at https://www.washingtonpost.com/outlook/2019/05/06/calling-muslim-brotherhood-terrorist-group-would-make-all-muslims-scapegoats/ (Accessed December 10, 2020).

Chapter 6

340 "New Zealand futsal international Atta Elayyan killed in Christchurch terror attack," ESPN.com, March 17, 2019, available at https://www.espn.com/soccer/new-zealand/story/3802517/new-zealand-futsal-international-atta-elayyan-killed-in-christchurch-terror-attack (Accessed December 9, 2020).

341 Amina Chaudary, "Samuel Huntington, Misunderstood," *PostGlobal* (*The Washington Post/Newsweek*), March 9, 2009, available at http://newsweek.washingtonpost.com/postglobal/needtoknow/2009/03/

samuel_huntington_misunderstoo.html (Accessed September 24, 2019).

342 Ibid.

343 "Samuel Huntington, Political Scientist, Dies at 81," Associated Press, December 27, 2008, available at http://www.nytimes.com/2008/12/28/us/28huntington.html (Accessed September 24, 2019).

344 Amartya Sen, *Identity and Violence: The Illusion of Destiny*, (New York: W.W. Norton and Company, 2007).

345 Ibid.

346 Amina Chaudary, "Samuel Huntington, Misunderstood," *PostGlobal* (*The Washington Post/Newsweek*), March 9, 2009, available at http://newsweek.washingtonpost.com/postglobal/needtoknow/2009/03/samuel_huntington_misunderstoo.html (Accessed September 24, 2019)..

347 Megan Specia, "The New Zealand Shooting Victims Spanned Generations and Nationalities," *The New York Times*, March 19, 2019, available at https://www.nytimes.com/2019/03/19/world/asia/new-zealand-shooting-victims-names.html (Accessed December 9, 2020).

348 Emily Bazelon, "Department of Justification," *New York Times Magazine*, February 28, 2017, available at https://www.nytimes.com/2017/02/28/magazine/jeff-sessions-stephen-bannon-justice-department.html (Accessed September 24, 2019).

349 Gideon Rachman, "Trump in the China Shop," *The New York Review of Books*, March 7, 2017, available at http://www.nybooks.com/daily/2017/03/07/trump-in-the-china-shop/ (Accessed September 24, 2019).

350 Franklin Foer, "It's Putin's World," *The Atlantic*, March 2017, available at https://www.theatlantic.com/magazine/archive/2017/03/its-putins-world/513848/ (Accessed September 24, 2019).

351 M. Arsalan Suleiman, "Return of the Clash: Operationalizing a Tainted Worldview," The Elliott School of International Affairs, The Washington Quarterly, 40.4 (2017): 49–70, available at https://doi.org/10.1080/0163660X.2017.1406707 (Accessed September 24, 2019).

352 "Christchurch shootings: The people killed as they prayed," BBC News, August 21, 2019, available at https://www.bbc.com/news/world-asia-47593693 (Accessed December 9, 2020).

353 Kishore Mahbubani & Lawrence Summers. "The Fusion of Civilizations," *Foreign Affairs*, May/June 2016, available at https://www.

foreignaffairs.com/articles/2016-04-18/fusion-civilizations (Accessed September 24, 2019)

354 Robert Wright, "Highbrow Tribalism," *Slate*, November 2, 1996, available at http://www.slate.com/articles/news_and_politics/the_earthling/1996/11/highbrow_tribalism.html (Accessed December 9, 2020).

355 Ibid.

356 Arsalan Iftikhar, "Mr. President: Next Stop Jakarta," CNN.com, April 7, 2009, available at http://www.cnn.com/2009/POLITICS/04/07/iftikhar.obama.speech/index.html (Accessed September 24, 2019).

357 Edward Said, "Islam Through Western Eyes," *The Nation*, April 26, 1980, available at https://www.thenation.com/article/islam-through-western-eyes/ (Accessed September 24, 2019).

358 Kimberly Yam, "Bill Clinton's Remarks To Muslims Prompted Hasan Minhaj To Create 'Patriot Act'," *Huffington Post*, November 8, 2018, available at https://www.huffpost.com/entry/bill-clinton-hasan-minhaj_n_5be4a123e4b0dbe871a8cd01 (Accessed September 24, 2019).

359 Ewen MacAskill, "Clinton aides claim Obama photo wasn't intended as a smear," *The Guardian* (UK), February 25, 2008, available at https://www.theguardian.com/world/2008/feb/25/barackobama.hillaryclinton (Accessed September 24, 2019).

360 Mike Allen, " Obama Campaign Slams Clinton Over Photo," *Politico*, February 25, 2008, available at https://www.cbsnews.com/news/obama-campaign-slams-clinton-over-photo/ (Accessed December 9, 2020).

361 Ismat Sarah Mangla, "Hillary Clinton has an unfortunate way of talking about American Muslims," Quartz.com, October 20, 2016, available at https://qz.com/814438/presidential-debate-hillary-clinton-contributes-to-anti-muslim-bias-in-the-way-she-talks-about-american-muslims/ (Accessed September 24, 2019).

362 Alex Kane, "Author Deepa Kumar on the imperial roots of anti-Muslim sentiment," *Mondoweiss*, July 2, 2012, available at https://mondoweiss.net/2012/07/author-deepa-kumar-on-the-imperial-roots-of-anti-muslim-sentiment/ (Accessed September 24, 2019).

363 Benjamin Millar, "Christchurch victims from all walks of life and corners of globe," *Sydney Morning Herald* (Australia), March 17, 2019, available at https://www.smh.com.au/world/oceania/

christchurch-victims-from-all-walks-of-life-and-corners-of-globe-
20190317-p514yo.html (Accessed December 9, 2020).

364   Arsalan Iftikhar, "The first 100 days- for the Muslim World," CNN.com,
       April 29, 2009, available at http://ac360.blogs.cnn.com/2009/04/29/
       the-first-100-days-for-the-muslim-world/ (Accessed September 24,
       2019).

365   Rahul Mahajan, "'We Think the Price Is Worth It'," *Fairness & Accuracy
       in Reporting* (FAIR), November 1, 2001, available at https://fair.org/
       extra/we-think-the-price-is-worth-it/ (Accessed December 9, 2020).

366   Arsalan Iftikhar, "Madeleine Albright on the future of human rights,"
       DiversityInc Magazine, April 2008, available at http://www.themus-
       limguy.com/column-madeleine-albright-on-future-of-human-rights/
       (Accessed September 24, 2019).

367   "'I have forgiven him': A look at some of the victims of the New Zealand
       mosque attacks," France24 News, March 18, 2019, available at https://
       www.france24.com/en/20190318-new-zealand-victims-christchurch-
       mosque-attacks (Accessed December 9, 2020).

368   Convention Relating to the Status of Refugees (adopted 28 July 1951,
       entered into force 22 April 1954) 189 UNTS 137 (Refugee Convention)
       art 33, available at http://www.unhcr.org/3b66c2aa10.html (Accessed
       December 9, 2020).

369   Press Release, "This is a primarily refugee crisis, not only a migra-
       tion phenomenon," UN High Commissioner for Refugees (UNHCR),
       September 4, 2015, available at https://data2.unhcr.org/en/news/12789
       (Accessed December 9, 2020).

370   Convention Relating to the Status of Refugees (adopted 28 July 1951,
       entered into force 22 April 1954) 189 UNTS 137 (Refugee Convention)
       art 33, available at http://www.unhcr.org/3b66c2aa10.html (Accessed
       December 9, 2020).

371   Isabela Cocoli, "HRW: Migrant Crisis Political Because of
       Islamophobia," Voice of America, September 11, 2015, available at
       https://www.voanews.com/a/human-rights-watch-migrant-crisis-
       islamophobia/2960306.html (Accessed January 2, 2018).

372   "Indian newlyweds came to Christchurch with a dream. On Friday,
       that dream died," CNN, March 18, 2019, available at https://lite.cnn.
       com/en/article/h_c615401e31147615691e753111c203f2   (Accessed
       December 9, 2020).

373   Hilary Whiteman, "Indian newlyweds came to Christchurch with a dream. On Friday, that dream died," CNN.com, March 18, 2019, available at https://www.cnn.com/2019/03/18/asia/new-zealand-massacre-india-victim-repatriation-intl/index.html (Accessed January 15, 2021).

374   Michael Scherer, "Exclusive: Donald Trump Says He Might Have Supported Japanese Internment," December 8, 2015, available at http://time.com/4140050/donald-trump-muslims-japanese-internment/ (Accessed September 26, 2019).

375   Geoffrey Nunberg, *Going Nucular: Language, Politics, and Culture in Confrontational Times*, New York: PublicAffairs, 2005 at 291, available at https://books.google.com/books?id=erFvBAAAQBAJ&pg=PA291&lpg=PA291&dq=propaganda+%E2%80%98name+of+the+Vatican+committee+charged+with+propagating+the+faith%E2%80%99&source=bl&ots=lNSiGXfGbo&sig=ACfU3U12wApJ-0cRzNNVqPHswCLyRMoExQ&hl=en&sa=X&ved=2ahUKEwiNu77Wi-_kAhUOyFkKHZs4DYsQ6AEwC3oECAgQAQ#v=onepage&q=propaganda%20%E2%80%98name%20of%20the%20Vatican%20committee%20charged%20with%20propagating%20the%20faith%E2%80%99&f=false (Accessed September 26, 2019).

376   John Hanc, "Rallying the Public: A look back at government efforts to 'spin' a war," *New York Newsday*, December 5, 2001, at B3 available at https://www.newsday.com/lifestyle/rallying-the-public-a-look-back-at-government-efforts-to-spin-a-war-1.755576 (Accessed September 26, 2019).

377   Ibid.

378   Dictionary.com, "nativism," http://dictionary.reference.com/search?q=nativism (Accessed September 26, 2019).

379   "Three Centuries of Germans in America," Dr. Frederick Luebcke, American Studies Newsletter No. 1 (September 1983), available at https://usa.usembassy.de/etexts/ga-asn0983Luebke.htm (Accessed September 26, 2019).

380   Takao Ozawa v. U.S., 260 U.S. 178 (1922) available at https://www.loc.gov/item/usrep260178/ (Accessed January 15, 2021).

381   Immigration Act of 1924, SIXTY EIGHTH CONGRESS. SESS.I. Ch. 185, 190. 1924, available at https://www.legisworks.org/congress/68/publaw-139.pdf (Accessed September 26, 2019).

382   Hannah Miller, "Anniversary prompts bleak memories," *UCLA Daily Bruin*, February 18, 1997, available at http://dailybruin.com/1997/02/18/anniversary-prompts-bleak-memo/ (Accessed September 26, 2019).

383   Final Recommendation of the Commanding General, Western Defense
      Command and Fourth Army, to the Secretary of War (Feb. 14, 1942),
      (quoted in, Hohri v. United States, 782 F.2d 227, 231 (D.C. Cir. 1986),
      vacated, 482 U.S. 64 (1987)).

384   "Mass Incarceration Fact Sheet for America's Concentration Camps:
      Remembering The Japanese American Experience," Japanese American
      National Museum, available at http://www.janm.org/nrc/resources/
      accmass (Accessed January 15, 2021).

385   Arsalan Iftikhar, "Demonizing the Other," *Islamica Magazine*, Issue
      17 (2006), available at https://www.scribd.com/document/34402238/
      Islamica-Demonizing-the-Other (Accessed September 26, 2019).

386   Kat Chow, "As Chinese Exclusion Act Turns 135, Experts Point To
      Parallels Today," National Public Radio (NPR), May 5, 2017, available at
      https://www.npr.org/sections/codeswitch/2017/05/05/527091890/the-
      135-year-bridge-between-the-chinese-exclusion-act-and-a-proposed-
      travel-ban (Accessed December 9, 2020).

387   Ibid.

388   Ibid.

389   "New Zealand mosque attack: Who were the victims?" Al-Jazeera
      News, March 22, 2019, available at https://www.aljazeera.com/
      news/2019/3/22/new-zealand-mosque-attack-who-were-the-victims
      (Accessed December 10, 2020).

390   Arsalan Iftikhar, "What the President Should Say in Cairo," CNN
      Anderson Cooper 360 Blog, June 3, 2009, available at http://ac360.blogs.
      cnn.com/2009/06/03/obama-in-the-middle-east-draft/ (September 26,
      2019).

391   Ibid.

392   Ibid.

393   Report, "The Super Survey: Two Decades of Americans' Views on
      Islam & Muslims," The Bridge Initiative (Georgetown University),
      November 19, 2015, available at http://bridge.georgetown.edu/the-
      super-survey-two-decades-of-americans-views-on-islam-muslims/
      (Accessed September 26, 2019).

394   Ibid.

395   "Muslims Widely Seen As Facing Discrimination," Pew Research
      Center, September 9, 2009, available at https://www.pewresearch.org/
      politics/2009/09/09/muslims-widely-seen-as-facing-discrimination/
      (Accessed December 10, 2020).

396 Kim Zetter, "Caught Spying on Student, FBI Demands GPS Tracker Back," *WIRED*, October 7, 2010, available at https://www.wired.com/2010/10/fbi-tracking-device/ (Accessed September 26, 2019).

397 Report, "The Super Survey: Two Decades of Americans' Views on Islam & Muslims," The Bridge Initiative (Georgetown University), November 19, 2015, available at http://bridge.georgetown.edu/the-super-survey-two-decades-of-americans-views-on-islam-muslims/ (Accessed September 26, 2019).

398 Ibid at 122.

399 Sam Sherwood, "Christchurch shooting victim Tariq Omar remembered as a 'gentle, generous' man," Stuff.co (New Zealand), April 8, 2019, available at https://www.stuff.co.nz/national/christchurch-shooting/111873820/christchurch-shooting-victim-tariq-omar-remembered-as-a-gentle-generous-man (Accessed December 10, 2020).

400 "A Roundtable Of Reactions: The Lingering Horror Of The Paris Killings," National Public Radio (NPR), November 14, 2015, available at https://www.npr.org/2015/11/14/456045276/a-roundtable-of-reactions-the-lingering-horror-of-the-paris-killings (Accessed September 26, 2019).

401 Robert Wright, "The Clash of Civilizations That Isn't," *The New Yorker*, February 25, 2015, available at https://www.newyorker.com/news/news-desk/clash-civilizations-isnt (Accessed September 26, 2019).

402 Liam Stack, "Qaeda Affiliate Uses Video of Donald Trump for Recruiting," *New York Times*, January 1, 2016, available at https://www.nytimes.com/2016/01/02/world/africa/al-qaeda-uses-video-of-trump-for-recruiting.html (Accessed September 26, 2019).

403 "Hate Groups Increase for Second Consecutive Year as Trump Electrifies Radical Right," Southern Poverty Law Center, February 15, 2017, available at https://www.splcenter.org/news/2017/02/15/hate-groups-increase-second-consecutive-year-trump-electrifies-radical-right (Accessed September 26, 2019).

404 Matthew Haag & Jacey Fortin, "Two Killed in Portland While Trying to Stop Anti-Muslim Rant, Police Say," *New York Times*, May 27, 2017, available at https://www.nytimes.com/2017/05/27/us/portland-train-attack-muslim-rant.html (Accessed September 26, 2019).

405 United States Government Accountability Office, Countering Violent Extremism: Actions Needed to Define Strategy and Assess Progress of Federal Efforts (GAO-17-300) (Washington, DC: U.S. Government

Accountability Office, 2017) available at http://www.gao.gov/assets/690/683984.pdf (Accessed September 26, 2019).

406 Michael Wright, "Missing Malaysian teenager Muhammad Haziq Mohd-Tarmizi confirmed killed in Christchurch terror attack," Stuff. co (New Zealand), March 21, 2019, available at https://www.stuff.co.nz/national/christchurch-shooting/111444991/missing-malaysian-teenager-muhammed-haziq-tarmizi-confirmed-killed-in-christchurch-terror-attack (Accessed December 10, 2020).

407 Amy Wang, "Trump breaks silence on Charlottesville: 'No place for this kind of violence in America'," *Washington Post*, August 12, 2017, available at https://www.washingtonpost.com/news/the-fix/wp/2017/08/12/trump-responds-to-charlottesville-protests/?utm_term=.35789e58d676 (Accessed September 26, 2019).

408 Lydia O'Connor and Daniel Marans, "Here Are 16 Examples Of Donald Trump Being Racist," December 13, 2016, available at https://www.huffingtonpost.com/entry/president-donald-trump-racist-examples_us_584f2ccae4b0bd9c3dfe5566 (Accessed September 26, 2019).

409 Dave Boyer, "Trump takes aim at Black Lives Matter, slams 'hostility and violence' against police," *Washington Times*, May 15, 2017, available at https://www.washingtontimes.com/news/2017/may/15/donald-trump-police-need-better-protection/ (Accessed December 10, 2020).

410 Ryan Reilly, "Jeff Sessions Was Deemed Too Racist To Be A Federal Judge. He'll Now Be Trump's Attorney General," *Huffington Post*, November 17, 2016, available at https://www.huffingtonpost.com/entry/trump-attorney-general-jeff-sessions-racist-remarks_us_582cd73ae4b099512f80c0c2?cn5id4ygk5rf9lik9 (Accessed September 26, 2019).

411 Jose DelReal, "Trump blames Clinton's 'weakness' for attacks," *Washington Post*, September 19, 2016, available at https://www.washingtonpost.com/news/post-politics/wp/2016/09/19/trump-blames-clintons-weakness-for-attacks/ (Accessed September 26, 2019).

412 Arsalan Iftikhar, "What If Charlottesville Protesters Were Black Muslims?" The Bridge Initiative (Georgetown University), August 13, 2017, available at http://bridge.georgetown.edu/what-if-charlottesville-protesters-were-black-muslims/ (Accessed September 26, 2019).

413 Juliet Williams, "Students look to love at New Zealand school hit by tragedy," Associated Press (AP), March 17, 2019, available at https://

apnews.com/article/f04e9d2af97f4c3a9725305211474f62 (Accessed December 10, 2020).

414 Andrew Bay, "Islamic Renaissance Man," *BYU Magazine*, Summer 2017, available at https://magazine.byu.edu/article/islamic-renaissance-man/ (Accessed December 10, 2020).

415 Ibid.

416 Andrew Prentice, "Christchurch shooter's one mistake that saved dozens of lives: How the accused terrorist stormed the Linwood mosque from the wrong side—giving worshippers time to escape or hide," *The Daily Mail* (UK), March 18, 2019, available at https://www.dailymail.co.uk/news/article-6822233/Accused-Australian-terrorist-said-stormed-Linwood-mosque-wrong-side.html (Accessed December 10, 2020).

Index

Huffington Post, 179
Human Rights Watch, 25, 29, 168, 186
Hungary, 62, 128, 137-138, 186
Huntington, Samuel, 65, 171-174, 177
Hussain, Ghulam, 47
Hussain, Karam Bibi, 47
Hussain, Zeeshan Raza, 47
Hussein, Saddam, 67
Hyderabad (India), 176

I
Ice Cube, viii
Ibrahim, Mucad, 205-206
Illinois, 90
Iman (Fashion Model), ix
immigration 2, 4-5, 7-8, 14, 20, 67,
    73-75, 117-118, 121, 126-127, 135,
    137, 175, 190-192,
Immigration Act of 1924, 190
India, xi, 29, 34-40, 84, 176, 187, 192
Indian Scientists' Response to
    COVID-19 (ISRC), 38
Indonesia, 88, 177
Infowars, 7
Ingraham, Laura, 7, 49
Institute for Strategic Dialogue
    (ISD), 20
Insurrection (January 2021 US
    Capitol), 44
International Court of Justice (see
    also Hague), 27
internment camps, 28-33, 37, 114, 123
Investigative Project, 155
Iowa, 51
Ipsos-Mori, 133
Iran, 16, 73, 75, 175
Iraq, 73, 75-76, 82, 110, 186
Irish Republican Army (IRA), 163
ISIS, x, 91, 111-113, 163, 168, 177,
    198, 204-205
Islamica Magazine/Islamic
    Monthly, 172

Islamophobie, 115
Islam, Yusuf (see also Cat Stevens), 104
Islamic Center of Wheaton (IL), 91
Ismail, Junaid, 161
Israel, 109-110
Italy, 21, 93, 102, 133, 137

J
Jackson, Rev. Jesse, 91
Jacksonville Jaguars, ix
Japanese people, 170, 188, 190-191
Jefferson, Thomas, 207
Jesuits, 188
Jewish Law, 151-152
Jewish people, xi, 8, 19, 27, 35, 39,
    54, 59-60, 84-85 109-110, 120,
    125, 131-132, 135, 138, 142-143,
    148, 151-152, 169, 195, 205
JFK Assassination, 52
"Jihad Watch", 155
Jim Crow America, 170
Jinping, Xi, 32
Joint Terrorism Task Force
    (JTTF), 64
Jolie, Angelina, 79
Jones, Alex, 7
Jordan, 149
Justice Quarterly, 147

K
Kabul Beauty School, 88-90
Kadir, Ozair, 192
Kagan, Elena, 150
Kansas, 10
Kansas City (Missouri), 14
Kant, Immanuel, 151
Karachi (Pakistan), 47, 184
Karas, Adel, 13
Kashmir, 36
Kennedy, John F., 52
Kenya, 103, 180
Khan, Imran, 32-33, 113, 123